ecpr PRESS

Integrating Indifference

A Comparative, Qualitative and Quantitative Approach to the Legitimacy of European Integration

Virginie Van Ingelgom

Translated by Katharine Throssell

ecpr PRESS

© Virginie Van Ingelgom 2014

First published by the ECPR Press in 2014

The ECPR Press is the publishing imprint of the European Consortium for Political Research (ECPR), a scholarly association, which supports and encourages the training, research and cross-national co-operation of political scientists in institutions throughout Europe and beyond.

ECPR Press
University of Essex
Wivenhoe Park
Colchester
CO4 3SQ
UK

Typeset by ECPR Press

Printed and bound by Lightning Source

British Library Cataloguing in Publication Data

A catalogue record for this book is available from the British Library

ISBN: 978-1-907-301-48-3
PDF ISBN: 978-1907-301-82-7
EPUB ISBN: 978-1910-259-21-4
KINDLE ISBN: 978-1910-259-22-1

www.ecpr.eu/ecprpress

ECPR – Monographs

Series Editors:
Dario Castiglione (University of Exeter)
Peter Kennealy (European University Institute)
Alexandra Segerberg (Stockholm University)
Peter Triantafillou (Roskilde University)

Other books available in this series

Agents or Bosses? (ISBN: 9781907301261) Ozge Kemahlioglu

Causes of War: The Struggle for Recognition (ISBN: 9781907301018)
Thomas Lindemann

Citizenship: The History of an Idea (ISBN: 9780954796655) Paul Magnette

Civil Society in Communist Eastern Europe (ISBN: 9781907301278) Matt
Killingsworth

*Coercing, Constraining and Signalling: Explaining UN and EU Sanctions After
the Cold War* (ISBN: 9781907301209) Francesco Giumelli

Constraints On Party Policy Change (ISBN: 9781907301490) Thomas M.
Meyer

Contesting Europe. Exploring Euroscepticism in Online Media Coverage (ISBN:
9781907301513) Pieter De Wilde, Asimina Michailidou and Hans-Jörg Trenz

*Deliberation Behind Closed Doors: Transparency and Lobbying in the European
Union* (ISBN: 9780955248849) Daniel Naurin

Democratic Institutions and Authoritarian Rule in Southeast Europe
(ISBN: 9781907301438) Danijela Dolenec

*Economic Knowledge in Regulation: The Use of Expertise by Independent
Agencies* (ISBN: 9781907301452) Lorna S. Schrefler

*European Integration and its Limits: Intergovernmental Conflicts and their
Domestic Origins* (ISBN: 9780955820373) Daniel Finke

Functional Representation and Democracy in the EU (ISBN: 9781907301650)
Corinna Wolff

Gender and Vote in Britain: Beyond the Gender Gap? (ISBN: 9780954796693)
Rosie Campbell

Globalisation: An Overview (ISBN: 9780955248825) Danilo Zolo

Greece in the Euro: Economic Delinquency or System Failure?
(ISBN: 9781907301537) Eleni Panagiotarea

*Joining Political Organisations: Institutions, Mobilisation and Participation in
Western Democracies* (ISBN: 9780955248894) Laura Morales

Organising the European Parliament (ISBN: 9781907301391) Nikoleta
Yordanova

Paying for Democracy: Political Finance and State Funding for Parties
(ISBN: 9780954796631) Kevin Casas-Zamora

*Policy Making In Multilevel Systems: Federalism, Decentralisation, and
Performance in the OECD Countries* (ISBN: 9781907301339) Jan Biela, Annika
Hennl and Andre Kaiser

Political Conflict and Political Preferences: Communicative Interaction Between Facts, Norms and Interests (ISBN: 9780955820304) Claudia Landwehr

Political Parties and Interest Groups in Norway (ISBN: 9780955820366) Elin Haugsgjerd Allern

Regulation in Practice: The de facto Independence of Regulatory Agencies (ISBN: 9781907301285) Martino Maggetti

Representing Women?: Female Legislators in West European Parliaments (ISBN: 9780954796648) Mercedes Mateo Diaz

Schools of Democracy (ISBN: 9781907301186) Julien Talpin

The Nordic Voter: Myths of Exceptionalism (ISBN: 9781907301506) Åsa Bengtsson, Kasper M. Hansen, Ólafur Þ. Harðarson, Hanne Marthe Narud and Henrik Oscarsson

The Personalisation of Politics: A Study of Parliamentary Democracies (ISBN: 9781907301032) Lauri Karvonen

The Politics of Income Taxation: A Comparative Analysis (ISBN: 9780954796686) Steffen Ganghof

The Return of the State of War: A Theoretical Analysis of Operation Iraqi Freedom (ISBN: 9780955248856) Dario Battistella

Transnational Policy Innovation: The role of the OECD in the Diffusion of Regulatory Impact Analysis (ISBN:9781907301254) Fabrizio De Francesco

Urban Foreign Policy and Domestic Dilemmas: Insights from Swiss and EU City-regions (ISBN: 9781907301070) Nico van der Heiden

Why Aren't They There? The Political Representation of Women, Ethnic Groups and Issue Positions In Legislatures (ISBN: 9780955820397) Didier Ruedin

Widen the Market, Narrow the Competition: Banker Interests and the Making of a European Capital Market (ISBN: 9781907301087) Daniel Mügge

Please visit www.ecpr.eu/ecprpress for information about new publications.

Contents

List of Figures and Tables   vii

Acknowledgements   xi

Introduction   1

Chapter One: Contextual Analysis of Successive Approaches to European Legitimacy and to Citizens' Attitudes   17

Chapter Two: Revising the 'End' of the Permissive Consensus   45

Chapter Three: Focus Groups as a Microscope   81

Chapter Four: Revisiting 'Framing Europe'   107

Chapter Five: Neither Eurosceptic nor Europhile: The Median European   151

Chapter Six: Conclusion: Integrating Uncertainties   175

Appendices   189

Bibliography   217

Index   231

List of Figures and Tables

Figures

Figure 2.1: Evolution of support for EU membership, net support and
the support index (1973–2002, EU8)   51

Figure 2.2: Evolution of (national) means of the index of support for
European integration (1973–2002, EU8)   53

Figure 2.3: Illustration of measures of variance and kurtosis (index)   60

Figure 2.4: Evolution of the variances of the index of support for
European integration (1973–2002, EU8)   62

Figure 2.5: Evolution of kurtosis of the index of support for European
integration (1973–2002, EU8)   65

Figure 2.6: Public support for European integration
(1973–2011, EU8 and EU)   77

Figure 3.1: Evolution of indifferent and undecided positions between
1990 and 2002 and the 'neither-nor' category between 1990 and 2011
(France, Belgium and United Kingdom)   91

Figure 3.2: Multiple Correspondence Analysis – active modalities and
classes constructed   95

Figure 3.3: Diagram of Room Layout (Brussels)   103

Figure 3.4: Example of board with cards for question: 'Who profits from
Europe?'   105

Tables

Table 1.1: Transformations in modes of legitimatisation, theoretical
models and studies of citizens' attitudes towards the integration process   19

Table 2.1: Construction of the index of support for European integration   49

Table 2.2: Analysis of means of the index of support for European
integration (1973–2002, EU8)   55

Table 2.3: Analysis of the means of the index of support for European
integration (1973–2002, EU8)   57

Table 2.4: Analysis of the variances of the index of support for European
integration (1973–2002, EU8)   63

Table 2.5: Evolution and analysis of kurtosis for the index of support for European integration (1973–2002, EU8) 66

Table 2.6: Indifferent and undecided attitudes towards European integration by country (1973–2002, EU8) 69

Table 2.7: Indifferent and undecided attitudes towards European integration by country (1991–2002, EU8) 70

Table 2.8: Occupations and indifferent and undecided attitudes (1991–2002, EU8) 70

Table 2.9: Effects of individual-level variables on index of support towards the EU: multinomial logistic regression 74

Table 2.10: Pearson's correlations between the membership and regret questions 78

Table 3.1: EU member countries consensus-majoritarianism dimension score 90

Table 3.2: Indicator of support for one's country belonging to the EU (EU-15) in 2006 and 2011 90

Table 3.3: Auto positioning on left–right scale: (respondents to the ad) and selected participants 101

Table 3.4: Vote or hypothetical vote in European Constitutional Treaty referendum and country membership (respondents to ad) and selected participants 101

Table 3.5: Discussion scenario 104

Table 4.1: Coding protocol for the group interviews 114

Table 4.2: Themes mobilised in justifying or rejecting the European integration process, by group (N=917) 116

Table 4.3: Distribution of European themes coded within the collective interviews 119

Table 4.4: Distribution of the occurrences of the words 'Euro', 'Europe', and 'European', per total words spoken 119

Table 4.5 Themes to do with the single market, by country 141

Table 4.6: Themes linked to the view that states have become too small, by country 145

Table 4.7: Themes to do with the eradication of borders, by country 145

Table 4.8: Themes to do with governance and the democratic deficit, by country 147

Table 4.9: Specific themes, by country 147

Table 5.1: Participants evaluating their country's membership of the EU as 'neither good nor bad' (N = 33/133) 153

Table 5.2: Distribution of occurrences of the words 'Euro-', 'Europe' and 'European' plus related codes, as a percentage of total words spoken 155

Table 5.3: Distribution of explicit references to Europe, its policies, history, institutions (N = 133) 155

Table 5.4: Distribution of favourable and unfavourable evaluations in participants' contributions (N = 133) 157

Table 5.5: Distribution of the occurrences of the argument 'benefit for future generations' (N = 133) 161

Table 5.6: Distribution of occurrences of arguments related to distance (N = 133) 165

Table 5.7: Distribution of occurrences of arguments related to British otherness and alienation (N = 133) 167

Table 5.8: Distribution of the occurrences of arguments related to fatalism (N = 133) 169

Table A1.1: Index of support towards European integration (1973–2002, EU8) 189

Table A1.2: Index of support, percentages by year (EU8, 1973–2002) 190

Table A1.3: Values of mean (1973–2002, EU8) 190

Table A1.4: Values of variances (1973–2002, EU8) 191

Table A1.5: Values of kurtosis (1973–2002, EU8) 191

Acknowledgements

Arriving at this stage of writing acknowledgements for my first book – furthermore, in English – was not an inevitable outcome of my thesis nor an unconfessed wish when I began it in 2006. This book has taken longer to write than I had hoped, but now I understand how each day was important. So was each meeting and discussion. Although I have had many great moments during its development, I have faced rough times too. And in my way, I made it through. But this journey, both intellectual and personal, was only possible because of the help and the presence of important people – colleagues, friends and family (these categories being not exclusive to one other). During these years, I have amassed a great amount of personal and professional debts. I hope that finishing this book will now give me the time and energy to return the support of those who have supported me tirelessly – whatever their own projects may be.

My first thankful words go to my thesis co-supervisors Sophie Duchesne and André-Paul Frognier, without whom nothing would have been possible. It is no exaggeration to say that this book owes as much to their friendly collaboration as did their first chapter written together in *Beliefs in Government*. I know all I owe to Sophie and to her constant support and trust in me from the very beginning. She was there at each step of my intellectual and personal journey and I want to tell her – in writing – how grateful I am for what she did for me as a colleague (because she has always treated me as such) and as a friend, when offering levity or comfort over this long journey. I would also like to thank André-Paul for his always-wise advice. Thank you so much for trusting me even when I did not trust myself, and for offering me enough freedom to let my work evolve, methodologically and theoretically. His open mind was as precious as his broad knowledge and long experience. I only wish every doctoral student could receive from their supervisor half as much as I did from both of them.

I am also deeply indebted to my other colleagues from the Citizens Talking About Europe Project: Elizabeth Frazer, Florence Haegel and Guillaume Garcia. Our collective adventure was as essential to this book as it was to my personal journey and nascent career. The 24 focus groups conducted in Brussels, Paris and Oxford are only the visible part of what I owe them. The submerged part of the iceberg is enormous and comprises, among others, long hours of discussion, a number of papers given together, common publications, deep methodological reflections, friendly dinners and high tables in New College, and a beautiful first book, *Overlooking Europe*.

At an institutional level, my gratitude goes to the FRS – FNRS and the Institut de Sciences Politiques Louvain-Europe. They granted me the funding that made this research possible and offered me a comfortable three-year postdoctoral position that gave me time to digest and rewrite my doctoral thesis. Some other institutions have provided me with valuable resources and, more importantly, a great intellectual environment at different stages of my work: the Sciences Po

European Studies Center (CEE), the Department of Politics and International Relations, University of Oxford, and the European Union Center of Excellence and Department of Political Science, Université de Montréal. I would also like to thank the Sciences Po European Studies Center (CEE), the Maison Française d'Oxford and the 'Research in Paris' Programme of the City of Paris, for complementary financial support over the course of this research.

As this book relies in part on data gathered in the framework of the Citizens Talking About Europe project, I am deeply grateful to all 411 citizens who applied to take part in these focus groups, and in particular to the 133 who participated in group sessions. I would like to thank again a number of people who assisted the CITAE research team, at the group organisation and data-handling stages, who worked through more than 72 hours of discussion and 3,000 pages of transcript: Patty Chang, Paul Honey, Adam Humphreys, Gemma Hersh, Géraldine Thiry, Anouk Lloren, Sophie Langohr, Vanessa Hick and Vincent Guilluy. This project was supported by the administrative staff at CEVIPOF, Sciences Po Paris, the Department of Politics and International Relations, University of Oxford and the Institut de Sciences Politiques Louvain-Europe, Université catholique de Louvain. I am very grateful to the UCL-Cliniques Saint-Luc in Brussels (Woluwé) who allowed us to use the welcoming Salle des Toges for the Belgian group sessions. Besides the funding of my own research, the CITAE project was funded by many institutions: the French Ministry of Research (ACI grant INT0040); Sciences Po Paris European Studies Center (CEE); the Leverhulme Foundation (grant F/01 089/1); the Nuffield College Research Fund; Programme Tournesol (grant 18123NK); the Department of Politics and International Relations, University of Oxford; and New College, Oxford.

In the editing phase I have benefited enormously from Katharine Throssell's talented pen. Her contribution to this book is much greater than a simple translation. If the mistakes and blunders in language are all mine, she helps a lot in lightening my initial text and I am very grateful to her for this. I am also grateful to Dario Castiglione and Deborah Savage, as I am to Laura Pugh, Kate Hawkins and to the staff at ECPR Press for their assistance and patience at the production stage of this book. I thank the ECPR and the Institut de Sciences Politiques Louvain-Europe for generous funding support in the translation costs.

This book also owes very much to four juries. First, I am immensely thankful to the members of my dissertation committee: Renaud Dehousse, Lieven De Winter, Juan Diez Medrano and Adrian Favell. Their sensible remarks and well-considered comments and arguments on my dissertation were valuable resources in the evolution of this book. I am also very grateful to the members of the juries that awarded my thesis the three following prizes: the Theseus Award for Promising Research on European Integration, the Best Dissertation Prize in Comparative Politics from the French Political Science Association and the Mattei Dogan Foundation, and the ECPR's Jean Blondel PhD Prize. These awards gave great visibility to my book long before its publication, granting me not only recognition, but confidence in my work. Thanks to those juries for being my first anonymous readers. In the wake of these awards, I would also like to thank all the scholars who cited my work before its publication.

From my very first paper presented at the ECPR Joint Sessions in Rennes – where I met outstanding scholars who left their mark on my ideas and on the way I address the issue in this volume – to these very last pages and the kind endorsements that accompany them, I am most grateful to those who took the time to read my papers and chapters. I had the great fortune to be able to share my thoughts with scholars from many institutions and from a variety of theoretical and methodological backgrounds. My special thanks go to Céline Belot, Damien Bol, Géraldine Bozec, Amandine Crespy, Florence Delmotte, Tom Delreux, Charlotte Dolez, Claire Dupuy, François Foret, Nuria Garcia, Cesar Garcia-Perez-de-Leon, Borbála Gönzc, Virginie Guiraudon, Marc Hooghe, Achim Hurrelmann, Sophie Jacquot, Camille Kelbel, Justine Lacroix, Jean Leca, Christopher Lord, Frédéric Mérand, Kalypso Nicolaïdis, David Paternotte, Gaëlle Pellon, Julie Pollard, Benoît Rihoux, Richard Rose, George Ross, Olivier Rozenberg, Nicolas Sauger, Sabine Saurugger, Vivien Schmidt, Steffen Schneider, Claudia Schrag, Florian Stoeckel, Ferdinand Teuber, Anja Thomas, Katharine Throssell, Vincent Tiberj, Hans-Jörg Trenz and Jonathan White. I am deeply indebted to them and all the other colleagues who, here and there, supported, discussed and criticised my work at its different stages and in diverse academic occasions.

With their unfailing presence, my family and my friends have greatly contributed to this book. Friendly thanks in particular to Cathy, Vanessa, Manu, Géraldine, Gaëlle, Ferdinand, Mus, Minet, Printen, Eric, Dimi, Céline, Kath, Johnny and Jean-Lou, for never stopping asking me how I was doing. Loving thanks to Nico, Pauline, Tom and Clémence for never asking how work was doing. A special word of thanks to Daphné and Julie who have so often provided an essential friendly refuge in Welkenraedt as Sophie, her family and the Creusois did in France, and Joan did in Barcelona. An extended thank to Claire whose path I was lucky enough to cross at CEVIPOF and who has shared so much of this experience with me from Paris, Montréal, Oxford and Louvain. This book owes her more than I can say, and certainly more than she would ever concede. She was there whenever I needed her. She has read almost every word and commented on almost every page, sometimes more than once. Our unfailing friendship was part of this journey and will continue after it.

Above all I would like to thank my brother and my mother, my load-bearing walls. Without their unswerving support, I wouldn't be who I am and I could never have been able to make the choices that were mine and do the job that I choose. I am deeply indebted to them. Thanks to Vani for being such a generous and attentive big brother. He has been by my side since the beginning, enduring my adolescent, then professional, self-doubts. He has always had a kind and funny word to make light of everything, even during the most difficult times. My last word goes to my mum, to whom I owe everything. I am thankful to her for having given us everything we needed and, more than that, all by herself. Because her presence has erased all absences, I dedicate this book to her. *Merci pour tout Suzi.*

Virginie Van Ingelgom
Welkenraedt, April 2014

Introduction

> There are few historical examples of politicians, bureaucrats, and scholars searching so frenetically for 'democracy' and 'legitimacy' that no citizen has demanded (Bartolini 2005: 407).

As is often the case, the origin of this book lies in a series of questions left unanswered by the existing literature and, in particular, by the results of European studies and more especially the analysis of citizens' attitudes towards European integration. Three surprising observations were the impetus for this book.

The first of these observations was a discrepancy I experienced personally, between my own training in European studies and my family and friends' lack of interest in European questions. For a long time there appeared to be two parallel universes, telling very different stories about European integration. On one hand, the discipline of European studies was tirelessly searching for citizens' attitudes towards the European integration process in the form of European identity or, more recently, euroscepticism. On the other, I could not help noticing the extreme lack of salience of European integration for my friends and family; for them, Europe was a non-issue.

Yet as young Belgian and European citizens my friends and I are immersed in Europe – it is all around us. Shopping trips to Maastricht and Aachen are frequent; the European institutions are close by. The weak, multi-levelled Belgian national identity seems conducive to the development of identification with Europe. As young, university-educated, former Erasmus students, middle class and living in close contact with other European countries/people, I felt that my friends and family should be among the most supportive European citizens. According to European studies they should have developed a strong sense of belonging to this Europe that surrounds them; they should condemn its democratic deficit and, more recently, regret its economic problems.

The reality was (and still is) quite different, however. My friends and family were far from demonstrating the interest in or attachment to the European project that was expected of them. They did not discuss European integration and were not really very interested in it, except when it came to my own work. This sparked the idea for this book by leading me to ask a couple of simple questions. Why is European integration not an issue for these young European elites? And, above all, how can this significant gap between the strong academic interest in Europe and the lack of salience of European integration for non-academics be explained?

The second surprising observation was directly linked to the research framework used for the Citizens Talking About Europe (CITAE) project which I was involved in.[1] The study was based on 24 focus groups conducted in Brussels, Paris and Oxford between December 2005 and June 2006. These focus groups were not only a response to a desire to study how citizens talk about European issues, they also sought to analyse how and under what conditions citizens politicise discussions of European integration. On both these levels, the eight groups conducted in Paris in winter 2006 led to a surprising observation: the French participants only evoked the Constitutional Treaty very sporadically. Yet the groups were organised less than a year after the impassioned debates that surrounded the referendum of 29 May 2005 (Schrag Sternberg 2013: 161–73). Not only was the referendum notably absent from discussions but we observed a certain indifference regarding the pursuit of integration rather than a genuine rejection (including among the defenders of the 'no' position) – and this in spite of the presence of members of both 'yes' and 'no' factions within each group (*see* Duchesne *et al.* 2013). Indicators of the eurosceptic attitudes, particularly in the working-class milieu, which are so dreaded by European institutions and European specialists, were difficult to identify in these discussions. This raised the following questions. Where was this majority of French citizens against Europe? Where and how was this euroscepticism expressed, given that only a few months after the ratification of the Treaty we could find hardly any trace of it? Finally, where was this popular opposition when the Lisbon Treaty was adopted a few months later?

The third curious observation occurred with the systematic study of the Eurobarometer survey data analyses. It seemed to me, in light of many other articles, that the decline in support for European integration was purely and simply attributed to an increase in euroscepticism. Yet the indicator of support for one's country belonging to the European Union (EU) is itself not binary! It has a median modality that reflects a composite and uncertain evaluation of the country's membership to the EU, seen as being 'neither a good, nor a bad thing'.[2] The fact that this category was rarely or ever taken into account seemed to me to be even more intriguing and problematic in light of Léon N. Lindberg and Stuart A. Scheingold's classic text *Europe's Would-Be Polity* (1970). Essential aspects of their analysis had simply disappeared from later adaptations of their model. The question of the level of support is clearly central to their work but so is that

---

1.   The CITAE project, initiated by Sophie Duchesne and Florence Haegel, was conducted in close collaboration between Sciences Po Paris, the University of Oxford and the Catholic University of Louvain. The research team, co-ordinated by Sophie Duchesne, was made up of Florence Haegel, Guillaume Garcia, Elizabeth Frazer, André-Paul Frognier and myself. As a research assistant, I was initially responsible for conducting the fieldwork in Brussels. I also helped conduct the groups that took place in Oxford. Following this, I took part in the analyses and publications produced by the research team as a whole (Duchesne, Frazer, Haegel, and Van Ingelgom 2013; Duchesne *et al.* 2010). The focus groups used in this book were conducted as part of the CITAE research project. The entirety of the data produced is accessible on the BeQuali website: http://www.bequali.fr/app/enquete/10/metadata/. I am individually responsible for the arguments and analyses presented in the current volume.

2.   'Generally speaking, do you think that (your country's) membership of the European Community (Single Market) is "A good thing", "a bad thing", "neither good nor bad"?'

of the intensity of this support, as part of a broader reflection on the salience of European integration (Lindberg and Scheingold 1970: 249–79). European studies' systematic lack of attention to indifferent and undecided citizens is clearly visible in this, even though this category was at the heart of the theory of the 'permissive consensus', along with those who supported the European integration process. The model generally evoked the tacit consent of the masses.

At the intersection of these three observations is the question of ordinary citizens' *indifference* to the European political order. The objective of this book is thus to reintroduce the notion of indifference into the study of citizens' reactions towards European integration process, as part of a reflection on the political legitimacy of the process, understood as the acceptance of a (new) political order. Starting from current debates, both scientific and political, this book thus deals with the question of political legitimacy in the particular context of the EU, focusing on western founding member-states. Overall, the originality of this book lies in the fact that it attempts to grasp the legitimacy of the EU in all its complexity, in both its active and latent aspects.

At the very moment of writing the last words of this introduction, I can only rejoice at the recent but still timid reappearance of median (Rose 2013), indifferent (Göncz, 2013 ; Rose 2013: 110–11; Van Ingelgom 2012), or ambivalent (Dakowska and Hubé 2011; de Vries 2013; Stoeckel 2013) citizens in European studies. These middle-of-the-road attitudes, marked by uncertainty – as I will argue in this book – are now held by a significant number of European citizens, more than ever previously. In May 2011, in the midst of the economic and financial crises sweeping across Europe, the category of undecided European citizens who said that European integration was 'neither a good nor a bad thing' made up 31 per cent of EU citizens, whereas those who said that it was a 'bad thing' represented only 18 per cent of them (European Commission 2011). This is a good time to study this category of citizen, who declare themselves neither eurosceptic nor europhile but whose attitude is characterised by indifference *and* ambivalence towards the European integration process. Proposing this research agenda is also and above all about drawing attention to those who are overlooked by European studies: these silent European citizens whom European integration, along with our western democracies, has not succeeded in integrating.

Studying European legitimacy: at the crossroads of normative and empirical traditions

Although legitimacy is far from being a new concept it has attracted renewed attention in European studies over the course of the last two decades. It has notably been connected to democracy and its 'crisis' at the European level (Dehousse 1995; Føllesdal and Hix 2006; Majone 1998; Moravcsik 2002, to name a few). As far as European integration is concerned, the question of its legitimacy was posed with intensity from 1992 onwards, following the debate in the wake of the negative result of the first Danish referendum to ratify the Maastricht Treaty and the close score on the positive result that followed in France. On this same occasion, the

European Communities became the European Union, shifting from the classic intergovernmental form to that of an '*unidentified political object*' – to borrow the expression of Jacques Delors (quoted in Quermonne 2001: 25). In 2005, the question of the legitimacy of the EU was again raised in the context of the failure of the French and Dutch referendums on the ratification of the Treaty Establishing a Constitution for Europe (TCE) (Schrag Sternberg 2013). These negative results were interpreted as an indication of a feeling of anxiety, or even rejection, on the part of a large portion of European public opinion, which was quickly labelled 'eurosceptic'. In the meantime, high voting abstention rates during the elections for the European Parliament continue to fuel the discourse about the 'democratic malaise' of the EU. Recently, the financial, economic and budgetary crises that have shaken the European continent have also shaken the the European project and further problematised its legitimacy. These recent events and the institutional and social transformations that are linked to them are raising their own questions regarding the legitimacy of European integration at a time when both its political project and its currency are weakened.

The question of the legitimacy of the EU has thus been widely raised, particularly in terms of absence or struggle (Schrag Sternberg 2013). Over time and using distinct normative models the diagnoses have differed as much as the remedies proposed. At the beginning of the 2000s the democratic deficit was a reality for Andreas Føllesdal and Simon Hix, whereas it was almost in the realm of myth for Andrew Moravcsik and Giandomenico Majone (Føllesdal and Hix 2006; Majone 1998; Moravcsik 2002). More recently, the debate between Simon Hix and Stefano Bartolini in the context of the think-tank *Notre Europe* has prolonged and renewed the previous debate (Hix and Bartolini 2006). Schematically speaking, Hix perceives the solution to the legitimacy crisis of the EU in its politicisation (understood as an increase in polarisation of attitudes and increased political salience), where Bartolini sees politicisation as a remedy that could be worse than the disease. This debate reveals the questions that animate European studies today, notably those touching on the possible or desirable politicisation of the European integration process (De Wilde and Zürn 2012). One can observe this in the 'constraining dissensus' model developed by Liesbet Hooghe and Gary Marks (Hooghe and Marks 2008) or the theoretical framework of politicisation recently proposed by Pieter De Wilde (De Wilde 2011). On the fringes of these normative debates, the question of the polarisation of opinions regarding European integration has also appeared within the study of citizens' attitudes (Down and Wilson 2008).

As a theoretical concept fundamental to political analysis, the notion of legitimacy has been the object of much reflection and thus is anything but a univocal concept. It is therefore important to begin by specifying the angle adopted in this book. This will enable the reader to better perceive just what this book is about. Like the study of legitimacy in the context of the nation-state, European studies has dealt with the question of legitimacy primarily from two angles, normative and empirical, by attempting to respond to two main questions. First, in light of a series of normative criteria that remain to be defined, to what extent can the European political system be considered legitimate? Second, to what extent do citizens support the process of European integration and what are the factors that influence this support?

The research agenda conducted within this domain was thus split between the search for (primarily democratic) criteria that the EU ought to fulfil and the study of public opinion, essentially using survey data. On one hand, the deficit of legitimacy is dealt with in terms of the failure of the European political order to meet certain shared criteria of 'good governance', such as democracy, efficacy and transparency, to mention only the most common (Beetham and Lord 1998; Lord and Magnette 2004). On the other hand, support for the thesis of a deficit of legitimacy is fuelled by the downward trend in support for integration recorded in the post-Maastricht era, by low and declining participation in European elections, by increasing support for eurosceptic parties and increasing participation of European citizens in protest activities (Eichenberg and Dalton 2007; Franklin, Marsch and McLaren 1994; Hooghe 2007; Imig and Tarrow 2001). The most elaborate normative theories are complemented – and sometimes opposed – by empirical studies (for a detailed presentation *see*, for example, Ehin 2008; Hurrelmann 2008). The first chapter of this book will endeavour to provide an overview of these two sections of the literature, to reveal the articulations between them, which most often remain implicit.

Conceptually, Richard Bellamy and Dario Castiglione distinguish between internal and external dimensions of legitimacy, 'relating respectively to the subjective perceptions of citizens and to more objective – and universalist – oriented criteria' (Bellamy and Castiglione 2003: 7–9). These authors underline the importance of considering the normative content of citizens' demands and beliefs when studying European legitimacy (Bellamy and Castiglione 2003: 8). This recognition of the additional need to observe the 'subjective' aspect of the legitimacy of the European political system is at the heart of my, above all, empirical approach. It thus aims to study the question of European legitimacy at the micro level, adopting an empirical perspective (Weatherford 1992: 150). In so doing, it seeks to determine what impact the integration process has had, and continues to have, on the acceptance and appropriation of the political order by the citizens. Thus, the objective is not to determine which normative criteria are appropriate in evaluating European legitimacy. This book deals with the social legitimacy of European integration defined as 'a broad societal (empirically determined) acceptance of the system' (Weiler 1991: 416).

The empirical perspective of the social scientist regarding political legitimacy is thus very different from that of the specialist of institutions, the legal scholar or the theorist of integration. Given that Max Weber's conceptualisation of legitimate domination provides the basis of more contemporary research and discussions on political legitimacy, a discussion of this literature should first briefly touch on what Weber meant by legitimacy. Breaking with the political philosophers who regarded a system as legitimate if it was established in agreement with certain rules, Weber instead conceptualised legitimacy as a social fact: legitimacy is the phenomenon by which people are willing to accept domination on normative grounds, regardless of the specific beliefs this acceptance is based on (Weber

1968: 215–16). Overall, Weber defined legitimacy in empirical terms as 'beliefs in legitimacy' and approached legitimacy as an empirical, not a normative, matter. The book focuses on social legitimacy beliefs and the understandings and constructions embedding them, building on David Beetham's notion that something is legitimate not 'because people believe in its legitimacy' but to the extent that it can be 'justified in terms of their beliefs' (Beetham 1991). From this perspective, I will therefore be studying the different beliefs that citizens mobilise in their acceptance (or not) of the European integration process, *regardless of the specific beliefs on which this acceptance is based.*

For an empirical, qualitative and quantitative approach to European legitimacy

This book aims to study the empirical, social and internal legitimacy of the European integration process. From this viewpoint, a great deal of literature has tended to focus on support for integration, in an attempt to deal with European legitimacy in empirical terms. From an Eastonian perspective, *legitimacy is defined as the interplay between specific and diffuse support* (Easton 1965, 1975). The explanation of support for integration is to be found in numerous factors that will be detailed in Chapter One of this book. Among these are political, economic, historical and cultural factors that shape support for integration (Ray 2006, among others). Here, survey data has shown itself to be a valuable tool and has thus constituted a favourite terrain for European studies. More particularly, the Eurobarometer opinion surveys, financed by the European Commission since the beginning of the 1970s, have been a precious source of data for European specialists in understanding European citizens' attitudes and thus the social legitimacy of the integration process. These studies use a series of 'trend questions' on attitudes towards European integration, which enable us to measure citizens' support for this process over time. This quantitative work has provided essential gains in knowledge, which I will come back to in Chapter One and upon which the research design of this book is based (*see* Chapter Three).

However, these analyses have also demonstrated their limits in relation to a range of questions relating to citizens and the EU. In particular, this literature operationalises legitimacy in terms of rather simply measured popular attitudes of support. Drawing on opinion polls, the bulk of this research is limited to the questions asked in the Eurobarometers. Thus it is restricted in its understanding of citizens' beliefs on legitimacy, reducing these to a few simple indicators. These are supposed to be reasonably stable, conscious and isolated from social context and intersubjective interaction (Duchesne *et al.* 2013). Thereafter, they have 'little to say about what "legitimacy" and "European integration" *mean* to survey respondents, and about how such meanings come about' (Schrag Sternberg 2013: 8).

These quantitative studies have also produced sharply contrasting results, both between themselves and compared to qualitative studies conducted on the same object. Part of the problem lies in the fact that – like the apocryphal drunk looking for lost keys under a streetlight – researchers have been drawn by the availability of a time-series of Eurobarometer studies run on the behalf of the European Commission (Ray 2006). Despite the proliferation of analyses of public support for European integration, fundamental questions remain understudied and unanswered.

More broadly, Léonard Ray rightly identifies three factors that have (de)limited the field and evolution of studies of the attitudes of European citizens:

> The evolution of research on the mass public and European integration has been driven by a number of important factors, of which the most important are political/institutional development, theoretical trends in EU studies, and the corpus of publicly available survey data (Ray 2006: 263).

In this book I hope to further understanding of citizens' attitudes by distancing my approach as much as possible from these three factors. Indeed, although this book is clearly part of this research tradition dealing with questions of how the European political order is accepted by citizens, it is set apart by a number of factors.

Firstly, a long-term analytic perspective is adopted here and survey data is re-analysed in order to gain a maximum distance from the analyses and results obtained using (normative) models of dominant legitimation marking different periods of European integration (*see* Chapter Two). It is important to put into perspective what these studies of attitudes owe to the political and institutional developments of their time – including the recent events that have led scholars to study euroscepticism and the possibility or desirability of the politicisation of European integration. Secondly, by making the connections between normative theories and empirical operationalisation of attitudes as explicit as possible, normative theories of European integration will be set aside, as far as is possible, in order to prioritise an empirical approach to the data. Finally, and this is very much a question of dealing with European legitimacy 'on the ground', I will be using both quantitative and qualitative data from a triangulation, or mixed-methods, perspective. As I will discuss in more detail in the next section, this use of combined data aims to set up a dialogue between qualitative and quantitative methods and, more importantly, between their respective results. These three approaches will provide a complementary perspective that is fundamental for understanding the processes that are underway today for ordinary citizens and for exploring '*how ordinary citizens* […] *view, experience, debate, and contest the European integration process*' (Favell and Guiraudon 2011: 19).

From this point of view, the complementary use of qualitative data provides an anchorage for this book in what has been called the 'qualitative turn in European studies'(Duchesne 2010). In the early 2000s, European studies took an important methodological turn, characterised by the multiplication of qualitative studies (Belot 2000; Bruter 2005; Diez Medrano 2003; Duchesne *et al.* 2013; Favell 2008; Gaxie, Hubé, de Lassale, and Rowell 2011; Meinhof 2004; White 2011). This qualitative research provided rich data, in the form of individual interviews, focus groups and participant observation. The results of these studies show marked differences in the questions asked, the methods used and the cases studied.[3] But they also show a remarkable convergence in their results – a convergence which, in qualitative methodology, is considered the best basis for a generalisation of results (Duchesne *et al.* 2013).

The results of qualitative studies converge, principally in emphasising the absence of salience of European issues for citizens (Duchesne 2010; Duchesne *et al.* 2013; Duchesne *et al.* 2010). By doing so, they diverge significantly from most of the so-called 'mainstream' studies that show an increase in euroscepticism or a polarisation of European citizens' opinions (De Wilde 2011; De Wilde and Zürn 2012; Eichenberg and Dalton 2007; Hooghe 2007). Although the discrepancy between the results of quantitative and qualitative work has been noted by Europeanist scholars (Duchesne 2010; Duchesne *et al.* 2013), so far there has been little effort to account for it. This book aims to build a bridge between dominant quantitative research and recent qualitative analyses. In this respect, the recently published co-authored book *Overlooking Europe* should be seen as a first step in building this bridge (Duchesne *et al.* 2013). *Overlooking Europe,* and the project on which it is based, Citizens Talking About Europe, were built on decades of careful scrutiny of European citizens' attitudes towards European integration. National and social comparisons were at the heart of the project and therefore of its results (Duchesne 2013; Haegel 2013). Although the current book was conducted at the same time and (partly) on the same data, it moves further towards building a bridge with the mainstream literature. The mixed-methods perspective helps in this, as does the re-analysis of the Eurobarometer data (*see* Chapter Two). As is often the case, the chronology of the book does not follow the research process and the second chapter is in fact the result of an interpretative analysis of qualitative data and the conclusions of *Overlooking Europe* more generally. Reconstructing the focus-group methodology as a 'second step' in the research, after the quantitative analysis, might strike the reader as a little artificial. I hope however that I am able to avoid this pitfall.

The results presented here, both quantitative and qualitative, converge with what qualitative methods show of the low salience of European integration for ordinary citizens. They also contribute to the mainstream literature both on a theoretical and empirical level. Both cumulative with previous literature and innovative in its own right, *Integrating Indifference* aims to open new perspectives on the analysis of citizens' attitudes towards European integration.

---

3.   The studies mentioned consider different cases, of which the number varies greatly from one study to the next. Céline Belot studied France and Great Britain; Adrian Favell the towns of Amsterdam, Brussels and London; Juan Diez Medrano studied the German, English and Spanish cases; Ulrike Meinhof studied Germany and Poland; Jonathan White studied Germany, Great Britain and the Czech Republic; the CITAE project studied France, Belgium and Great Britain; and the CONCORDE project studied France, Germany and Italy (with a preliminary study also conducted in Poland).

New Inspiration and Aspiration for Political Sociology

The use of complementary qualitative data situates this study firmly in the qualitative turn taken recently by European studies. This foundation also reveals the clear interest in the new sociology of European integration (Favell and Guiraudon 2009, 2011; Saurugger 2008; Saurugger and Mérand 2010).[4] Indeed, almost concomitantly with the qualitative turn in European studies, questions were raised about the place of sociology within studies of European integration (Favell and Guiraudon 2011). This parallel development was, of course, not insignificant, in that the complementary use of qualitative data is partly what characterises this new empirical sociology (Favell and Guiraudon 2011: 2).[5] We have seen an increase in the number of sociological studies on European integration, contributing to this qualitative turn in European studies. These researchers have a range of research objects and questions, their theoretical considerations are inspired by various different authors and they propose different levels of analysis. However, they all offer adaptations of important theories and concepts from classical sociology whilst using a wide range of empirical methods. This is precisely how this book aims to contribute to the study of political legitimacy: a classic concept of sociology and particularly of political sociology. Moreover, it seeks to further the scientific knowledge of citizens' relationships to politics and its legitimacy in the European context. In so doing it makes the decision to consider that the theoretical and methodological tools of empirical political sociology open new paths for research and are thus useful and necessary in tracing the contours of the political space that is emerging at the European level (Guiraudon 2006: 17). It is now obvious that it is necessary to explore the effects of the European integration project on societies as well as on political or institutional developments (Favell and Guiraudon 2009).

This book is thus inspired by this new sociology of European integration. It aspires to contribute to it through an increased understanding of the effects that European integration has on our societies and, in particular, on the acceptance of a new political order. At the heart of the concept of legitimacy is, in fact, acceptance of political power by the citizens who are subject to it. Legitimacy is a classic concern in political sociology, as the previous references to Weber's work have already made clear.

Evidently, socio-political research has never been entirely absent from European studies, still less from studies on citizens' attitudes regarding European

---

4. This interest was fed by my participation in the workshop 'Does European integration theory need sociology? Towards a research agenda' co-directed by Frédéric Mérand and Sabine Saurugger during the Joint Sessions of the ECPR in Rennes in 2008. I would like to thank again all the participants in this workshop.

5. There are, of course, exemplary works in the empirical sociology of European Union that have operationalised a variety of quantitative approaches to the subject (Favell and Guiraudon 2009: 552). To some extent, one could argue that the research inspired by David Easton's functionalist analytical framework stems from an approach that could be called sociological. This introduction doesn't aim to enter into these disciplinary debates but rather to indicate to the reader the position of the book within the literature.

integration. In the 1950s, fundamental contributions on regional integration were made by sociologists such as Karl Deutsch, who proposed a reading of increased interactions between nationals on the continent, and Ernst Haas, who studied the socialisation of elites to the European project (Deutsch 1953; Favell and Guiraudon 2011: 4; Haas 1958; Rosamond 2000: 171–75). However, it wasn't until last decade that reflection on the place of sociology within European studies went from implicit to explicit. This shift was the result of work by certain authors, chief among them Virginie Guiraudon and Adrian Favell (2009, 2011). Their reflections paved the way for a more precise understanding and definition of what one means by the new political sociology of European integration. Identifying the principal characteristics of this approach will enable me to distinguish three essential points that have guided the analysis presented in this book.

Firstly, this new sociology is particularly committed to making the evolution of European integration comprehensible, by adopting a bottom-up perspective that is complementary to the traditional top-down perspective. This approach addresses some of the frustration of certain researchers in the face of what Andy Smith described early on as an 'overly aerial' view of European studies (Smith 1999), or a 'bird's eye view', to use Virginie Guiraudon's expression (2006). In this, the sociological approach to European integration aims to shed light on a series of problems that have been primarily debated in normative or institutional terms in European studies. Close to the perspective adopted in this book, research on European citizenship conducted notably by Céline Belot and, especially, Juan Diez Medrano proposes a different approach to that of so-called 'mainstream' analysis (Belot 2000, 2002; Diez Medrano 2003). In France, pre-dating Diez Medrano's work, Belot provided a study of the sociological logics that underlie citizens' support for the European political system, rather than studying European citizenship on a normative or legal level. In analysing the different conceptions of 'Europe', she paved the way for Diez Medrano's work for francophone readers. Diez Medrano's studies are widely acclaimed today, particularly his brilliant book *Framing Europe*. The author demonstrates the contribution and specificity of a sociological approach to understanding citizens' attitudes towards European integration (Diez Medrano 2003). In studying citizens' support for European integration, the national variable remains decisive; and analysis using Eurobarometer data has not been able to explain it. In his key study, Diez Medrano puts forward a re-reading of these national differences for citizens in Germany, Spain and Great Britain. He emphasises that attitudes towards integration reflect, above all, the culturally founded cognitive perceptions that frame ordinary citizens' thoughts about the EU. Beyond their similarities, German, Spanish and British citizens have developed specific ways of seeing European integration, which stem from the specific perspectives of their national cultures and collective memories and from different shared concerns. The author uses conceptual tools from historic and ethnographic approaches to show the continuity of repertoires of national action and representation transmitted in the media. The empirical approach to the legitimacy of European integration put forward in this book is unquestionably part of this bottom-up perspective. The qualitative approach presented in the last chapters will give substance to this issue of the acceptance of the political order.

Secondly, this new sociology of European integration places socialisation at the heart of the European integration process, a move that appears almost obvious. Concerning my object of study, the acquisition of beliefs by citizens is clearly the result of socialisation, understood as the process according to which political cultures are formed, maintained and altered. Here, I argue that citizens' legitimacy beliefs towards political objects depend on the ways in which they understand and represent these objects. These representations are deeply anchored in broader representations of the social world and cannot be understood without reference to the latter. To this extent, the study of social representations of the integration process seems indispensable for my understanding of citizens' acceptance of the European political order. It is essential to take into account the effect of time here, and the 'evolving' nature of the integration process is at the heart of the research presented in the pages that follow.

Finally, although it is not alone in doing so, the new sociology of European integration brings out the permanent overlap between different levels – local, regional, national, supranational and international – which it is essential to keep in mind for any study of European integration. Seeking to estimate the precise influence of European integration on society becomes more complex if we consider that the institutions of the EU and those of the member-states do not form two distinct and independent systems but a single, multi-level, complex and cognitively integrated one. Moreover, if this has already been observed at the level of institutional actors, it seems even more the case at the level of citizens, for whom the boundary between national, European and even global political spheres is anything but clear (Duchesne *et al.* 2013). In this respect it is evident that the existing research on the attitudes of citizens towards integration, with only a few rare exceptions (Anderson 1998; Frognier 2000; Hurrelmann 2008, to name a few), has generally failed to take this imbrication of levels into account. As Fritz Scharpf argues, a large number of the studies on European legitimacy, both normative or empirical, *'have focused on the European level, rather than on the implications of the multilevel characteristics of the European Union'* (Scharpf 2007: 5). Following this author, it appears to me that the borders between the national and European spheres must be crossed in order to study European integration. Concerning the question of legitimacy, this means that European legitimacy cannot be evaluated independently of national legitimacy and *vice versa*. This also means that the European citizen does not exist independently of the national citizen. This imbrication of the national and European will remain a guiding principle for the analysis in the chapters to follow and, in particular, for the conclusions that I draw.

Structure of the book

Integrating Indifference aims to offer an original diagnosis of trends in citizens' support for European integration over the last 40 years. It quantitatively and qualitatively explores the meaning of ambivalent, uncommitted answers to survey questions related to support for European integration. Through its five analytical chapters, it offers an empirical contribution to the literature on public opinion of the EU, by exploring the logics behind indifference and ambivalence. In order to address the question of indifference and ambivalence empirically, I intertwine two levels of analysis. On the one hand, I scrutinise long-term patterns and shifts in the evolution of citizens' attitudes towards European integration, relying on classic Eurobarometer data. Here, the analysis covers eight countries: the five founding states of the European Communities (Belgium, France, Germany, Italy and the Netherlands), as well as the three member-states that joined in 1970s (Denmark, Ireland and United Kingdom). This quantitative analysis traces the evolution of Europeans' attitudes from the 1970s to the mid-2000s, in order to demonstrate that indifference and ambivalence characterise citizens' reactions over the long term. More recent data from 2011 are also produced, in order to provide perspective and demonstrate that, even as the eurozone remains in the midst of economic crisis, citizens' reactions towards European integration are still plainly characterised by uncertainty and indifference. I combine this long-term analysis, on the other hand, with in-depth case studies that use focus groups as a microscope to examine these indifferent and ambivalent reactions of ordinary citizens. Here, building on the research project Citizens Talking About Europe and its results presented in the book *Overlooking Europe*, I focus on three member-states – Belgium, France and Great Britain (Duchesne *et al.* 2013). The 24 CITAE focus groups were conducted in 2005–6, following a moment of exceptionally intense public debate on European integration: the failed EU Constitution (Schrag Sternberg 2013: 160–96). Adopting this mixed-method approach, the structure of the book is organised as follows.

Beginning with a critical review of the literature on European legitimacy, the first chapter provides a synthesis of the different theoretical models of legitimation that have been used over the course of European construction since the 1970s. The presentation of these different models provides a backdrop against which one can understand how citizens' attitudes towards European integration have been analysed in the existing literature. In particular, theoretical and empirical research on 'European legitimacy' has been one of the hallmarks of European studies since it burgeoned as an academic discipline after the difficulties in the ratification of the Maastricht Treaty in the early 1990s. The issue of the legitimacy of this entity has been placed on both the political and academic agenda because it has the quality of an emerging political system *sui generis* (Bellamy and Castiglione 2003). This first chapter carefully distinguishes between normative and empirical approaches to legitimacy and demonstrates how the citizen, from being a simple spectator, has progressively been constructed as a key actor in attempts to legitimise European integration.

The second chapter specifically questions the appropriateness of a radical distinction between a phase of *permissive consensus* and one of *constraining dissensus*. It takes issue with the argument, widely discussed in the literature, that there has been a breakdown in the permissive consensus and an increasing polarisation of ordinary citizens' opinions about the EU (De Wilde and Zürn 2012; Fligstein 2008; Hooghe and Marks 2008). Instead, it argues that existing Eurobarometer-based research on European public opinion and identity in fact overlooks the importance of rising indifference and ambivalence to the EU, its modalities and its transformation in the post-Maastricht period. Building on previous results by Ian Down and Carole J. Wilson (Down and Wilson 2008), I claim that there is in fact no evidence of a polarisation of public opinion on integration, nor is there any suggestion of a massive increase in the percentage of opponents to European integration in the eight countries under scrutiny.[6] I defend the claim that the reactions of ordinary citizens are much more complex. The evolution of attitudes in the post-Maastricht period, even in the context of the economic crisis, cannot simply be reduced to an increase in euroscepticism, particularly amongst lower socio-economic groups. This chapter concludes that it is necessary to take into account indifferent and ambivalent citizens in order to fully comprehend the question of the legitimacy of European integration. The indifference and ambivalence of citizens is indeed an overwhelming phenomenon in the post-Maastricht period and in the current context of crisis.

However, the study of this category of citizens poses substantial methodological problems. The third chapter thus deals with the issues surrounding the choice of methodology for the analysis of ordinary citizens' indecision. With the goal of contributing to the renewal of research on citizens' attitudes towards European integration, this research adopts a triangulation strategy, which is commonly considered a mixed-methods approach (Johnson, Onwuegbuzie and Turner 2007: 113). After outlining the methodological reasons for the choice of the focus groups as a research tool, I present the comparative research design in greater details. As part of the CITAE research project, we set out to gather and record discussions between citizens on the subject of Europe (Duchesne *et al.* 2013). Concretely, in 2005–6 we convened 24 focus groups, in Paris, Brussels and Oxford, each consisting of four to seven participants, a total of 133 participants.[7] Building on previous literature showing the persistence of major national and social differences regarding the level of acceptance of the European integration process (Hooghe and

---

6. Note that neither Greece nor Spain nor Portugal is part of this study. However, Table 3.2 provides data for EU15, displaying the change observed in support between 2006 and 2011.

7. For a detailed analysis of the process of recruitment and the ways in which we dealt with the difficulties inherent in our double system of comparison, see the article that I co-authored with Guillaume Garcia (Garcia and Van Ingelgom 2010). For more details regarding the research design as such, *see* Chapter Three. Suffice it to say here that we advertised for participants and that they were reimbursed (50€/£40) for their participation. They were selected on the basis of a short telephone questionnaire; those who participated then completed a longer and more detailed individual questionnaire prior to the focus group (*see* Appendices for questionnaires).

Marks 2005; Niedermayer and Sinnott 1995, to name only a few), we chose to select participants according these two levels of comparison: national (comparing citizens from Paris, Brussels and Oxford) and social (we brought together groups of executive, white-collar and working-class people, as well as activists).[8]

Using information from these 24 focus groups, the fourth chapter examines discussions about European integration in these three countries in order to capture how ordinary Europeans view, experience, debate and contest the European integration process (Favell and Guiraudon 2011: 19). By doing so, this chapter sets the stage. Analysis using Computer Aided Qualitative Coding focuses on citizens' legitimacy beliefs. It largely confirms and extends previous findings from qualitative research on citizens' reactions towards European integration (Duchesne *et al.* 2013; Duchesne *et al.* 2010). On the one hand, the focus-group participants share a common frame of reference about European integration, in which issues to do with economics, concern over the small size of European countries in a globalised world, the space for freedom of movement and questionable EU governance predominate (Diez Medrano 2003). It also reveals contrasts with previous research, concerning, for example, the participants' comparatively greater propensity to question the economic benefits of European integration: an observation which, most likely, reflects the distinct economic circumstances of the post-EMU and post-enlargement EU and which was present long before the financial crisis. On the other hand, building on the work of Juan Diez Medrano in *Framing Europe* (2003), the systematic coding of more than 50 hours of discussions led to a reaffirmation of the influence of national framing. The way citizens of Europe apprehend and evaluate European integration and, more particularly, the way they understand the functioning of Europe's political system depends directly on prior experience of their own national political community. The magnifying glass that the qualitative approach provides thus leads me to emphasise the diversity of ways in which citizens react to and/or feel a personal sense of connection to European integration, as well as the lack of autonomy between the European and national levels in the representations of citizens.

As demonstrated in earlier research, in the focus groups, we did not encounter euroscepticism but rather 'euro-indifference' (Duchesne *et al.* 2013; Duchesne *et al.* 2010). In each of the three countries qualitatively studied, one observes the same increase in the number of citizens who expressed neither explicit support nor rejection of European integration. Thus, I conclude the analysis of the 'neither/nor' category of citizens by distinguishing three logics behind this reaction: ambivalence; distance and alienation; and fatalism. These three forms correspond to different *framings* in different national contexts, however. The process of politicisation of the EU has made citizens, especially those in the lower social classes, more uncertain about the consequences of European integration. While they do not oppose integration, they are increasingly unsure about its economic consequences, find it an opaque process and, at any rate, see themselves as powerless to stop it. Indifference due to fatalism is reflected in the weakening of the belief that the European system offers any opportunity for the improvement of the

---

8. On the social and national comparisons *see Overlooking Europe* (Duchesne 2013; Haegel 2013).

conditions of its citizens. This feeling covers at least two realities: the conviction that it is impossible to have an impact on European rulers' decisions and/or the conviction that even the rulers are powerless to resolve citizens' problems, particularly in a globalised world. Indifference and ambivalence are generated by several, often intersecting, processes. There is a perception of the increasing complexity of the European Union, due to increased access to information but not matched by increased understanding, and a feeling of distance or alienation from the site of decision-making, related to the additional level of governance. There is a clear degree of fatalism as a consequence of the elite-driven integration process; and there are frequent discrepancies between norms (to be European is perceived as a normative injunction in most places) and social experiences (citizens do not experience Europe in the same ways and some of them lack any conscious experience of it at all).

In the concluding chapter, the overall results lead me to question the relevance of the theory that permissiveness, as understood in the thesis of the permissive consensus, ended with the ratification of the Maastricht Treaty. I propose an alternative interpretation, which argues that acceptance and rejection of a European political order stem from at least two rationales. On one hand, amongst the elites (understood in a broad sense as political or economic elites or even simply as those citizens interested in the political sphere) we observe a polarisation of opinion, characterised by a decline in support and a reinforcement of opposition to the processes of European integration. This tendency is emphasised and explained by the model of constraining dissensus. On the other hand, we observe the reinforcement of indifference and ambivalence amongst ordinary citizens, who are not experts in political matters, when faced with this same process. The first rationale is linked to an active form of contentment or rejection, whereas the second demonstrates a mode of tacit acceptance or rejection. This latter illustrates that the permissive consensus has not disappeared in the post-Maastricht era; rather, it has been transformed over the course of the integration process. These results suggest that we need to reconsider two commonly accepted premises: first, that the EU has become a salient issue for all citizens; and, second, that European public opinion has become polarised on the question of Europe. Although I do not challenge the contrast between the pre- and post-Maastricht period, an interpretation based purely on the dichotomy between permissive consensus and constraining dissensus appears incomplete if not erroneous.

In emphasising the complexity of the dynamics of politicisation, this book suggests that the alleged break in the permissive consensus amongst citizens needs to be put into perspective. It is therefore not clear that the popular mood regarding European integration is the mirror image of the level of dissensus amongst elites. The politicisation of European issues does not necessarily lead to the polarisation of citizens' opinions. I argue here that it is necessary to incorporate the notion and the role of indifference and ambivalence into any reflection on the legitimacy of the European integration process. Europhiles and eurosceptics, the so-called 'consenters' and 'dissenters' of James Wright (1976), have been widely studied whereas the euro-indifferents or 'assenters' have been overwhelmingly neglected. *Integrating Indifference* seeks to address that neglect.

Chapter One

Contextual Analysis of Successive Approaches to European Legitimacy and to Citizens' Attitudes

Asking research questions about EU politics does not occur in isolation from the broader social scientific context (Rosamond 2008: 601).

Given that it was initially an elite project, the fundamental question of the legitimacy of European integration – whether empirical or normative – was for many decades scarcely even posed. Instead, between the 1950s and the 1980s, the vast majority of commentators, both inter-governmentalists and (neo-) functionalists, agreed that the indirect legitimacy derived from the internal legitimacy of the member-states was sufficient. The citizen was thus largely absent from the European legitimisation process. During this period, the thesis of a permissive consensus among the citizens of European member-states was widely accepted (Lindberg and Scheingold 1970). As long as these citizens were not seen and did not see themselves as directly affected by decisions made at the European level, it was assumed that they supported European construction along with the elites of their countries. This permissive consensus allowed these national elites to pursue the integration process without any pressure from their citizens and most often in the face of general indifference. National governments considered themselves sufficiently legitimate to validate the integration process. European integration thus seemed content with a legitimacy derived from the legitimacy of the member-states and their governing elites. The question of the direct democratic legitimacy of European construction was overlooked for a long time. It really only emerged as an issue during the heated debates surrounding the ratification of the Maastricht Treaty in 1992, just as the European Union was taking on a political dimension, with its incursion into sovereign affairs and the creation of European citizenship (Quermonne 2001).[1]

The refusal to ratify the Maastricht Treaty in the referendum in Denmark and its only very tentative approval in France were considered by both academic and political observers to mark the end of the permissive consensus. It also signalled that citizens had moved from the wings to the centre-stage of affairs, providing the opportunity for the first major wave of discussions on the meaning and reach of the European project. In these debates, both academic and political commentators

---

1.   For an alternative and more nuanced analysis of the struggle for legitimacy in EU politics, moving from the 1950s to the mid-2000s and relying on discourses of leading politicians as well as the European institutions, *see* the recent book published by Claudia Schrag Sternberg (2013).

agreed that the citizen had become an essential actor in the process of legitimising the European project. The argument was that, from the moment the European Union represented a level of power distinct from the sum of the member-state governments that make it up, the question of its legitimacy and its relationship with its citizens became unavoidable. Following this, the gradual reinforcement of the supranational nature of the European project was to consolidate this interpretation and confirm the status of the European Union as a new political system in search of legitimacy (Quermonne 2001). The question of citizens' consent or of democratic legitimacy regarding the integration process thus emerged not only as an issue in the Community but also as an issue in European studies. As a result, pressing questions emerged as to the acceptance of this new political order by European citizens and their participation in decision-making.

The Maastricht Treaty led to the role of the citizen being acknowledged by Community actors as well as by experts in European studies, as part of the debates around the democratic deficit of the European Union. The years that followed also represented a pivotal period in the history of European integration and, by extension, in European studies. In particular, the vast campaigns provoked by the ratification of the Constitutional Treaty and its failures at referendum are generally referred to as 'euroscepticism'. According to Liesbeth Hooghe and Gary Marks, the need to take public opinion into account and the reinforcement of hostility to European integration on the part of an increasing proportion of citizens reflect a shift from permissive consensus to a constraining dissensus (Hooghe and Marks 2008). Post-functionalist theory thus puts forward the hypothesis that it is the politicisation, or rather the mobilisation, of public opinion regarding the policies and institutions of the European Union, mostly by national political parties, that is at the heart of this shift (Schmitter 2008: 211). The last decade has thus encouraged those who study the development of the EU to examine the possible paths of its politicisation, from the perspective that no public space can be built independently of the confrontation and crises that it provokes (Bartolini 2005). The model of constraining dissensus thus invites systematic analysis of the extent to which citizens' attitudes towards the European project have polarised in the post-Maastricht era. In other words, it pushes us to ask the following questions: can we really speak of a politicisation of the (entire) European publics? And, in the post-Maastricht period, do we observe a polarisation of the opinions and attitudes of European citizens?

Although the question of public support towards European integration appears to be fundamental to any investigation of the legitimacy of the integration process and its future, this has not always been the case. In this first chapter, I will examine the emergence of European public opinion as a legitimate research object in European studies, paralleled by a growing awareness of the place of the citizen in the European political system. The chapter will provide an overview[2]

---

2.   This overview does not aim to be exhaustive but rather to underline the mechanisms of this field of research in order to emphasise the key issues without overlooking the limitations. For a more detailed analysis of the emergence of European studies up until the end of the 1990s, *see* the work of Belot and especially her doctoral thesis (Belot 2000).

Table 1.1: Transformations in modes of legitimatisation, theoretical models and studies of citizens' attitudes towards the integration process

	Theoretical model	Mode of legitimatisation	Ideal role of citizen	Dimension of support (study of attitudes)
Period 1 (1970–1991)	Permissive consensus	Economic efficiency /indirect legitimacy	Shadow	Utilitarian support (weak level)
Period 2 (1992–2005)		Democratisation and political community /direct legitimacy	Participative	Utilitarian and affective support (strong level)
Period 3 (2005–)	Constraining dissensus	Politicisation /direct legitimacy	Politicised	euroscepticism (strong level)

of the question in order to demonstrate what current results and controversies owe to developments in this research field. This in turn will enable us to more accurately perceive the field's progress and its limits. Looking at its origins should enable us to better understand it's the mechanism at work in it. In order to do this systematically, the analysis will follow the sequence of the three historical stages outlined in Table 1.1.[3]

The chapter will begin by returning to the period that runs from the beginning of the 1970s to the beginning of the 1990s, during which the thesis of permissive consensus dominated the field and represented an indirect form of legitimacy from the perspective of the citizens. Then we will look at studies of the post-Maastricht era, a period almost universally considered to mark the end of the permissive consensus and to mark the emergence of the citizen on the European stage. Indeed, ever since the Community became the Union, it has been in search of its own direct and democratic legitimacy. Finally I will present the most recent shift in the studies of citizens' opinions and attitudes: the analysis of resistance to and challenging of the European integration process. In this context, I will particularly focus on the post-functionalist thesis of constraining dissensus developed recently by Hooghe and Marks.

---

3. It is worth noting that Céline Belot and Bruno Cautrès also propose a three-part reading of the development of Community studies dealing with the attitudes and opinions of citizens (Belot and Cautrès 2008: 154–155). However, the periods that they identify only partially reflect the structure I use here. I consider that the third period includes a major shift in studies of European citizens' attitudes, as they came to question the reasons for the rejection rather than the support of the integration process. In the book *Citizens' Attitudes to Europe Compared: Overlooking Europe* Duchesne *et al.* 2013), my co-authors and I identify a fourth period marked by the emergence of qualitative studies on these questions. In the context of this book however, I will attempt to bring together the results of both qualitative and quantitative studies as much as possible. I will thus not identify a fourth period as such, given that these qualitative studies are not seen here as part of a specific model of legitimisation.

An investigation of these different models will enable us to demonstrate how the politicised citizen, engaged on European issues, has become the central figure in European studies today, leaving behind the role of 'shadow citizen'[4] to which citizens were previously relegated. This chapter will present these models of legitimatisation, each claimed to justify furthering European integration, and show how each one is deeply anchored in the period in which it was developed. In light of this, I will show that the role accorded to the citizen in the process of the legitimisation of European integration depends on the way in which the future political order of the European Union is envisaged – a future which is today more uncertain than ever. In so doing, this chapter will provide an overview of the different existing approaches to European legitimacy as well as to the analysis of citizens' attitudes to European integration, by emphasising the often implicit links between these two fields of research.

The permissive consensus: the European citizen as a 'shadow citizen'

If studies of citizens' attitudes and opinions regarding European integration now constitute an undeniably important and distinct part of European studies, this has not always been the case (Belot 2000). Indeed, reference to the citizen has not been any more constant in European discourses than in studies dealing with attitudes towards integration (Schrag Sternberg 2013). For a long time both focused on elites rather than the weak consensus of the majority. Writing in 1958, Ernst Haas thus defended an elitist perspective, arguing that:

> The emphasis on elites in the study of integration derives its justification from the bureaucratized nature of European organizations of long standing, in which basic decisions are made by the leadership, sometimes over the opposition and usually over the indifference of the general membership (Haas 1958: 17).

During the first period (which ran up until the beginning of the 1990s), this elitist vision coupled with the permissive consensus thesis relegated the European citizen to the role of a 'shadow citizen'. Indirect legitimacy was thus considered sufficient to justify the integration process then underway.

The first theories of integration: a common denominator of elitism

During this first period, European studies were dominated by two theoretical approaches to integration, both of which illustrate the elitist character of this process and the scant attention it paid to the citizen.

---

4.   The expression 'shadow citizen' is inspired by Andy Smith's concept of the 'fantôme néces-saire', referring to the idea that although citizens were not completely absent from considerations, particularly to do with questions relating to the democratic nature of European construction, they were not considered to be key actors in this elite-driven construction (Smith 1995: 61).

The first of these, the intergovernmental approach, considers the European Communities to be like any other international institution. According to this perspective, decisions made by European institutions are legitimate because they are made by national governments that are themselves legitimate. This model considers citizens as supporting the integration process because their national governments are involved in it and because the latter are held responsible for their actions before their national parliaments. The intergovernmental approach thus denies that parliamentary democracy needs to be reinforced at the supranational level. The absence of direct legitimacy for the Communities and later the Union is not problematic for this model because it is seen to be compensated for by the recognised legitimacy of member states.

At the heart of this perspective is the notion of a 'community governed by law', developed by Walter Hallstein (Hallstein 1972: 30–55). This major and well established attempt to justify the European integration process was honed and extended by the concept of formal democratic legitimacy developed by the jurist Joseph Weiler. He argued that:

> Formal legitimacy [...] connotes that in the creation of the institution or system all requirements of the law are observed [...] we can [...] speak of formal legitimacy if we can show that the power structure was created following democratic processes and with people's consent (Weiler 1991: 415).

This is in the tradition of legal positivism but also in that of the famous Weberian notion of rational legal authority (Weber 1968). In its purest form, this perspective considers that legality is not only a necessary but also a sufficient condition of legitimacy.[5]

It has become clear that this approach, in spite of its many contributions to the study of European legitimacy from the very beginning and the reputation it has earned, cannot alone be a foundation for the legitimacy of this new political system. In keeping with this, David Beetham notes that although legal validity is a primary element of the legitimacy of a political system it can under no circumstances be considered sufficient for this legitimacy (Beetham 1991). The author argues that debates around the legitimacy of power cannot be reduced to the question of whether the person in question has a legal right to be in power; instead and above all these are debates resulting from disagreements about the justification of the law itself and whether it reflects the moral and political principles of the society in question. As Daniela Obradovic observes, the concept of legitimacy does not

---

5. This strict conception of formal legitimacy and the debates it has engendered have not exhausted the theoretical examination of the question of formal democratic legitimacy. The range of critiques and debates that followed from this theory concerning the democratic deficit of the Union also mobilise the question of formal democratic legitimacy. In so doing, they situate themselves within a framework that considers legitimacy as stemming from the application of democratic principles. I will come back to these debates in the second part of this chapter. Indeed, in spite of the charges of elitism, both the intergovernmental and neo-functionalist theories survived well beyond Maastricht and, in fact, still theoretically structure debates about the integration process today.

simply refer to the validity of given rules and those who enact them as a source of power, that is, legality. Rather, and above all, it refers to citizens' acceptance of this power, especially when it affects their daily lives (Obradovic 1996: 194).

The second theoretical model, the so-called functionalist perspective, developed alongside the intergovernmental approach. It shares with the latter the conviction that indirect legitimacy is sufficient for European integration. This perspective brought together the first theorists of regional integration, who also saw the European project as being carried on solely by elites. Based on the cascade model developed by Karl Deutsch, citizens were assumed to be favourable to the integration process and supposed to develop support in terms of shared community, a *we-feeling*, mutual support and loyalty, all as a result of increasing interactions and communication between member states (Deutsch 1953). [6] This perspective was coupled with an instrumentalist vision, based on the performance of the European system, which was eventually supposed to help create this feeling of shared community. According to functionalist theory, European citizens would eventually transfer their loyalty and their expectations to the new European institutions (Haas 1958: 16). The concept of utilitarian support is at the centre of contributions which defend the thesis according to which the Community will gain its legitimacy though the economic wellbeing that it will be able to provide (Rothschild 1977). However, just like the intergovernmental model, (neo-) functionalist theory – and in particular its elitist vision – was to be subsequently challenged because, as Justine Lacroix and Paul Magnette point out:

> Half a century of integration has provided ample evidence of the limits of these 'functionalist' beliefs, according to which mass culture, following elite culture, would ultimately adapt to the changes in scale at the economic and social level. The convergence of cultures, values and life styles is not sufficient to create shared political consciousness (Lacroix and Magnette 2008: 11).

During this first period, the legitimacy of European construction thus stemmed from the legitimacy of national elites, who were considered to be the principal actors in the decision-making process in the Communities. If citizens were taken into account, it was only to underline their consent to the actions of their national elites; and it was instead these elites whose attitudes and behaviour were meticulously studied. Demands for legitimation addressed to the system and its institutions came from member-states and the political actors that make them up and represent them officially, not from citizens. As a result, in order for the system to function and be perceived as legitimate, obedience was required only from these national political actors and not from citizens themselves. This is why these models of legitimacy are considered as indirect, from the perspective of citizens (Wallace 1993: 95–98). The birth and the initial development of the European Community were brought about by political and technical elites, who alone

---

6. *See* the recent application of this model by Theresa Kuhn (2011).

made the fundamental decisions concerning its future. These decisions were only presented to the wider public once they had formed the basis for a compromise accepted by all elites (Lindberg and Scheingold 1970: 22).

However, during the same period, the decision to elect the European Parliament via universal suffrage opened the way for a development in citizens' role within the integration process, although it did not yet make them true actors within this changing system. The debates on this question were only remotely interested in the ways in which citizens judge the institutions that were supposed to represent them, focusing instead on the problem of the distribution of power within the Community, which pitted federalists against intergovernmentalists (Belot 2000: 34; Schrag Sternberg 2013). If the citizen was considered in this, it was above all as a source of power in a political system that claimed to be democratic.

Empirical studies: an embryonic development in the shadow of the permissive consensus

In this context it is not surprising that empirical studies relating to the opinions and attitudes of citizens towards the integration process are few and far between and that those that exist are largely the result of a small number of actors rather than a structured scientific community. Some of the earliest data collection was done by Jacques Rabier, then Director of Information for the European Community. His results indicated an increase in favourable attitudes towards Europe across all member countries between 1950 and 1962. This was interpreted as a sign that citizens had a generally positive attitude about the decisions made on their behalf. Rabier's studies were precursors to the Eurobarometer surveys, which were developed in 1970 (Rabier 1966).

However, it would be erroneous to say that the citizen was completely absent from the empirical work of this period. Although few authors studied citizens' opinions at this time, Ronald Inglehart relentlessly pursued his work on citizens' attitudes to European integration – having devoted his doctoral thesis to the socialisation of Europeans (Inglehart 1967a, 1967b; Inglehart 1970a, 1970b, 1971, 1977b; Inglehart, Rabier, and Reif 1987). This author was the first to underline the existence of sociological schemas in the production of opinions and attitudes towards European integration (Belot 2000). He formulated two principal hypotheses as to the way in which socialisation determines an individual's chances of developing a belief in European legitimacy (Inglehart 1977a). The first was the 'cognitive-mobilisation hypothesis': that the ability to believe in Europe's goals and ideals depends on the cognitive abilities of the individual, which increase with their level of education. Cognitive-mobilisation theory postulates that increases in education levels lead to better understanding of and thus greater support for the European integration process, which is characterised for most citizens by its highly abstract nature (Inglehart 1970a: 46). The second hypothesis suggests that younger generations develop new priorities and values, which are compatible with the development of European integration. Indeed, for Inglehart, the 1970s were characterised by the development of what he calls the 'silent revolution', which progressively led to the development of a new hierarchy of values and a new cleavage within contemporary societies. This cleavage emerged between materialist citizens (belonging to the generations of the two world wars) and post-materialist citizens (the newer generations), the latter being also more cosmopolitan and more able to identify with and support the European Union (Inglehart 1977b).

A limited interest in citizens' attitudes is also reflected in the thesis developed by Léon N. Lindberg and Stuart A. Scheingold. As early as the 1970s, these authors proposed the term 'permissive consensus' to describe a state of legitimacy in which citizens passively approve the European integration process (Lindberg and Scheingold 1970). In their now classic work *Europe's Would-Be Polity*, they note that although opinions are generally favourable to European integration they are not very structured. Starting from the observation that only a small percentage of individuals express negative opinions towards the European Community, and emphasising the relative importance of undecided individuals, they foresee the reinforcement of the population's consensus on the European integration process (Lindberg and Scheingold 1970). They therefore affirm that citizens' support for integration will only become stronger in the long term. According to this theory it will be reinforced by the contributions of the European Communities in terms of prosperity (especially economic) to European societies. Hence the authors are clearly positioning themselves within the dominant theory of the period: functionalism.

It is worth noting that it was during this first period that foundations were laid for subsequent research, notably the salience of the notion of support as defined by David Easton, which is still used today (Belot and Cautrès 2008: 155). Indeed Lindberg and Scheingold proposed a framework for the analysis of support for integration expected of European citizens in the form of a matrix of four basic categories, which was to facilitate a more systematic and comprehensive investigation of the socio-political context of the Community (Lindberg and Scheingold 1970: 39–40). The first two categories distinguish between support based on identity, which refers to the development of links between citizens, and systemic support, which refers to the links between citizens and the political system, understood in both horizontal and vertical terms. The second dimension differentiates between utilitarian support, based on concrete interests, and affective support, which is more diffuse and more emotionally involved with a vague idea of European unity. Even though the authors don't mention it, their analytical framework is clearly inspired by the work of Easton, who distinguishes between explicit and diffuse support (Easton 1975).[7] The influence of this framework was substantial in subsequent studies on the attitudes of European citizens. As a result, the terms utilitarian support and affective support came to replace the classic Eastonian notions within the European literature.[8]

---

7. I will come back to the Eastonian notion of support in the next section because, from the 1990s onwards, it has become the (overwhelmingly) dominant paradigm for studies of citizens' attitudes towards European integration.

8. The binaries 'diffuse and explicit support' and 'affective and utilitarian support' would come to be considered synonymous by the empirical literature and subsequently used interchangeably.

To conclude, during this period nearly all observers agreed, following Lindberg and Scheingold, that the existence of a permissive consensus justified in itself the focus on elites and the lack of interest in citizens. The attitudes of the latter were considered to be, above all, the result of blind conformity to those of their elites. Acceptance of the European political order by citizens was taken for granted, to the extent that most citizens declared themselves in favour of the processes underway while the rest seemed essentially indifferent. For many years the qualified indirect legitimacy associated with the process, characterised by a symptomatic absence of the citizen in the legitimation process, was sufficient to justify the pursuit of European construction. One can thus summarise the situation of the citizen in the debate on the legitimacy of the European Community from the 1960s to the 1990s by saying that, in the eyes of the various actors involved, people apparently participated in politics as little more than 'shadow citizens', invisible but necessary, without whom our societies would have difficulty functioning (Belot 2000: 34).

Diagnosing the democratic deficit: the European citizen joins the dance

Increasing interest in the opinions and attitudes of citizens regarding the European integration process resulted from the conjunction of two major events surrounding the Maastricht Treaty at the beginning of the 1990s. Firstly, the Danish rejection of the Treaty by referendum (50.7 per cent of electors voting against the pursuit of integration) and the very close result of the French referendum that immediately followed it (only 51 per cent of French voters were in favour of integration) were interpreted as the signs of a break in the permissive consensus.[9] Secondly, the transition from the Community to the Union,[10] the adoption of qualified majority voting on the Council in a series of areas and the creation of European citizenship all led the European Union to seek its own legitimacy (Schrag Sternberg 2013: *see* Chapter Five). This legitimacy was to be direct, based on European citizens' acceptance of the validity of this new form of political and Community domination (Belot and Cautrès 2008: 157). In the academic arena, Helen Wallace, for example, declared that from the moment that

> the EC is defined as a partial polity, i.e. an entity that might develop into a form of direct governance in its own rights, the questions of what political identity, loyalty and affiliation are attached to the EC level of governance become crucial (Wallace 1993: 101).

---

9. The ruling handed down by the Constitutional Tribunal of Karlsruhe on 12 October 1993 is less well known but recognises the enduring right of all citizens to elect a real parliament. It also underlines the democratic deficit of the new Union and subsequently sparked researchers' and politicians' interest in this question (Quermonne 2001: 9–10).

10. This shift brought a number of new responsibilities into the purview of the Community. The EU was henceforth responsible for the following diverse issues: citizenship in the Union; shared visa policy; economic and monetary policy leading to the introduction of the single currency; the protection of consumers; infrastructure telecommunications and energy; co-operation and development; internal affairs and legal co-operation; as well as foreign policy and common security policy.

In the political arena, the key European actors endorsed this observation; the European Council considered that 'citizens are at the core of the European construction: the Union has the imperative to respond concretely to their needs and concerns' (Council 1996). Similarly, Jacques Delors declared that 'Europe began as an elitist project in which it was believed that all that was required was to convince the decision-makers. That phase of benign despotism is now over' (Delors 1993). Democratic themes (and defining what democracy might mean in the EU context) subsequently took an increasingly important place on the European agenda (Olsen 2003: 9; Schrag Sternberg 2013).

In the context of the EU, it was the question of the deficit of democratic legitimacy that dominated. Indeed, the democratic problems that European integration poses had been widely analysed and denounced over the course of the two previous decades. However, as Karlheinz Neunreither argued, 'while almost everyone seems to agree that a democratic deficit exists, it is far from certain that there is a general understanding of what is meant by it' (Neunreither 1994: 299). Indeed, criticisms of the democratic deficit in the EU sometimes deal with the question of the institutional deficit (the weakness of the European Parliament in the institutional balance), sometimes with the deficit of intermediary structures (weakness of media and political parties at the European level) and sometimes with the deficit in European citizens' 'taking ownership' of the political system. I am not aiming to provide an overview of this extremely extensive issue here, still less to confirm or deny the existence of these deficits, or even to make claims as to whether or not this is a heuristic debate. Instead, one can observe that, during this period, the discourse on the democratic deficit of the EU dominated not just the academic sphere (Majone 1998; Moravcsik 2002, 2004; J. H. Weiler, Haltern, and Mayer 1995): the political sphere was also under its sway. Romano Prodi, then President of the Commission, went as far as declaring that the Union suffered from a democratic 'malaise' (European Commission, 2001a and 2001b; Prodi 2001). The Union's economic accomplishments was thus no longer a sufficient source of legitimacy; the participation of citizens had become necessary. This can be illustrated by the Commission's declaration that 'it [the Union] will no longer be judged solely by its ability to remove barriers to trade or to complete an internal market; its legitimacy today depends on involvement and participation' (Commission 2001a: 11). The efficiency of the system had to be complemented by democratic procedures and leaders who were held responsible before Europe's citizens.

The deepening of European integration that emerged from the beginning of the 1990s thus led many theorists to consider indirect legitimacy obsolete or, at the very least, insufficient. Indeed, where initial approaches to integration saw indirect legitimacy as sufficient, their successors saw things differently. Instead, they considered that the non-state structure of the European political system did not mean it was exempt from the need to fulfil the classic criteria for legitimacy in liberal-democratic states. It was therefore obliged to seek direct democratic legitimacy. The citizen thus emerged on the European stage in the context of debate about the democratic deficit of European integration.

Normative theories: searching for legitimacy criteria adapted to the 'European beast'

Following the events surrounding the Treaty of Maastricht, the question of the direct legitimacy of the EU received particular attention in the literature. Within normative theories relating to European integration, this question seeks to identify the theoretical criteria of legitimacy that the EU (the nature of which is still undefined[11]) would need to establish before being considered legitimate. In western countries, the legitimacy of a given political order is intrinsically dependent on its democratic nature. The concepts of legitimacy and democracy are linked, both on a normative theoretical level and within debates about the future of the European project. Within this literature, a political system is thus considered democratic if it respects and embodies a complex combination of values and norms characteristic of a liberal democracy. According to democratic theory, the exercise of power is legitimised when it is the manifestation of collective self-determination. The functionalist perspective based on the principle of a 'government for the people' is now complemented now by the principle of 'government by the people'. It is no longer performance that legitimates decisions but rather that the latter reflects the will of the people. At the heart of these concerns lie the concepts of democracy and political community and the possibility of creating them at the European level.[12] In this context, the question of European legitimacy has found its place in normative debates and controversies among theorists of integration. These theoretical debates about the legitimacy of the European Union are articulated around one fundamental issue: should the legitimacy of the EU be evaluated according to the same criteria as at the national level (Beetham and Lord 1998)? As a result, the debate questions even the way the authors of the European project understand this emerging political system, a question that is intrinsically connected to debate on the nature of European construction. Indeed, the normative criteria of legitimacy and the place of the citizen in the legitimation process differ, depending on whether the European project is seen as a type of international organisation or as a type of political integration similar to the nation-state, or even as a new, 'post-national' kind of political integration.

These normative theoretical approaches have sought to identify the criteria of legitimacy appropriate to this new political object, necessarily linking the debate on European legitimacy to that on the 'nature of the beast' (Risse-Kappen 1996). To the extent that the EU is considered to be an 'unidentified political object', it is not surprising that it has been difficult to reach a consensus on the criteria of legitimation that this political order should develop (Ehin 2008; Horeth 1999).

---

11. For an overview and summary of the limits of an interrogation of the nature of the European construction, *see* the recent essay by Jean Leca (Leca 2009).

12. The work of David Beetham and Christopher Lord, considered one of the most successful summaries of the normative approach, divides the question of democratic legitimacy into three principal components, each representing a chapter of their book: democracy, identity and performance (Beetham and Lord 1998).

To the multitude of conceptions of the future of European integration can be added the multiplicity of normative approaches linked to theories of European integration. Indeed, during this second period, each theoretical approach generated its own normative theory of European legitimacy. It is also worth noting that these approaches are just as varied in the recommendations in terms of legitimacy that they produce. The number of theoretical publications dealing with the legitimacy of the EU has increased, making the overall presentation of this heterogeneous field of study particularly difficult. Following Justine Lacroix and Paul Magnette's mapping (and I must ask the reader, henceforth forewarned, to excuse the sometimes drastically oversimplified presentation of this field), I will also condense the current terms of the debate into four major positions (Lacroix and Magnette 2008: 6).

The first of these positions, which Lacroix and Magnette call 'civic national', emphasises that democratic principles were born in the context of the nation and thus they cannot be simply projected into the European sphere (Lacroix 2004). The main argument from this perspective is that democracy requires a community of language and shared significations, which are the fruit of a common past (Lacroix and Magnette 2008). Given that the EU cannot claim to have constructed such a community, the very idea of democracy becomes impossible. This perspective doesn't consider the EU as a political object that requires legitimising through democratic principles; instead it mobilises and actualises the intergovernmental theory mentioned above. It is represented by authors like Pierre Manent (2006) in France and David Miller (1995) in Britain.

The second position sees the European level as an open space for the development of democracy, considering the conditions for the establishment of a political democratic community (for example, shared language and values) as being historically constructed and, consequently, capable of reconstruction at the European level. As a result, this position is called the 'federalist republican position' (Lacroix and Magnette 2008: 8). An illustration of this theoretical approach, which seeks to identify the elements that are necessary for developing a European space that is favourable to European democratic practice, can be found in the most recent writings of Jürgen Habermas (2000). From this perspective, the European project takes the form of a powerful federal state, guaranteeing the cultural and linguistic diversity of its member states whilst still occupying a space of horizontal dialogue and shared political culture.

The third position can be called 'liberal post-nationalism' and is based on the publications of Joseph Weiler (1998), a legal scholar, and Richard Bellamy and Dario Castiglione (2003). This approach is akin to the 'national civic' perspective to the extent that it also considers democracy to be possible only in the context of the nation-state. Here, the EU is considered to be 'an ensemble of procedures, rights and norms, principally destined to "tame" national democracies' (Lacroix and Magnette 2008: 7). However, unlike the 'national civic' approach, here the European space provides the opportunity for the improvement of national democracies rather than their dissolution. As a result, the emphasis is put on formal democratic legitimacy, or inputs-based legitimacy, through national channels of majoritarian representation and/or electoral democracy, whereby the Union is considered a state of law rather than as a democracy of tomorrow. European integration must not be understood as a process of constructing shared civic culture but rather as a means of promoting citizens' rights. The weakening of national parliaments' control and the persistent absence of European issues in national debates are signalled as decisive factors in the democratic deficit of the EU.

Finally, a fourth position, 'republican post-nationalism', falls between the 'liberal post-nationalism' and 'republican federalism' perspectives. Inspired by Kantian cosmopolitanism, authors like Jean-Marc Ferry (2000), Kalypso Nicolaïdis (Nicolaïdis and Howse 2001) and Etienne Balibar (2001) share with the liberal variant a vision of Europe aiming to liberalise national spaces by appealing to universal principles. However, like the federal tradition, this perspective is not satisfied by the prospect of a European construction that shirks democratic principles or relegates them to the national level. Although the development of a shared civic culture is desirable for the increased connection between European nations, for these authors, it is not necessary that the European Union evolve towards a system copied from the nation-state model. Thus, instead of the federation proposed by Jürgen Habermas, they promote a 'federalism of free states', which would allow these constitutive elements to co-exist without sacrificing sovereignty.

Thus, if the shape and nature of the European project vary, the evaluation criteria differ too, as do the recommendations that they produce. For some, the democratic deficit is a reality, for others it it doesn't exist. Unanimous recognition of a democratic deficit as a diagnosis of the ills of the EU and the role of the European citizen in legitimation is undermined by contestation on the very nature of this constantly evolving political system. Indeed from the beginning of the twenty-first century, the diagnosis of a European democratic deficit was challenged by a group of academics who went as far as calling the deficit a myth. Of those advocating a revisionist interpretation, Andrew Moravcsik is undoubtedly the most well known (Magnette 2006: 115–19). When he writes '[…] if we adopt reasonable criteria for judging democratic governance, then the widespread criticism of the EU as democratically illegitimate is unsupported by the existing empirical evidence', he is condemning false analogies between national democratic systems and the new European political order (Moravcsik 2002: 605).

The ratification process for the Maastricht Treaty thus provoked a structured debate on the legitimacy of the EU. Commonly referred to as the debate on the democratic deficit, this issue was intrinsically connected to questions concerning the nature of the European construction project. This issue, along with that concerning the proper criteria of legitimacy, systematically pitted the successors of intergovernmentalism against the neo-functionalists – and both of these against the defenders of post-nationalism. Henceforth, the issue of European legitimacy was addressed in the scientific domain, both from a normative theoretical perspective and by empirical studies of citizens' attitudes to European integration. The post-Maastricht era was thus characterised by a major wave of political and academic discussion concerning the place of the citizen within the European project. To use

Fritz Scharpf's terminology (not his point of view), one may say that the outputs-based legitimacy which dominated up until this time is now complemented by inputs-based legitimacy (Scharpf 2000). The latter is structured according to two fundamental issues: the construction of a political community at the European level and the fulfilment of democracy. Performance-based criteria of legitimacy must now be complemented by the criteria of democratic legitimacy and shared identity (Beetham and Lord 1998).

The empirical studies: from utilitarian to affective support

Studies dedicated to citizens' opinions about the integration process, in the context of interrogations about the legitimacy of the EU, developed and thrived in the peculiar climate that followed the difficult ratification of the Maastricht Treaty. As the citizen became a central figure on the European political scene, the construction of a veritable community of researchers around these questions followed. Today there is a significant and well defined body of work looking at the opinions and attitudes of citizens towards integration. It is important to look at these results in order to better situate where new research is coming from.

Almost all of the studies conducted since the 1990s share a certain number of characteristics, given that they are based on similar types of data and analysis (Ray 2006). Firstly, with only a few exceptions, the studies that have developed in the last decade or two have adopted an analytical framework taken from the work of David Easton. In his book *A Systems Analysis of Political Life,* he deals with the question of legitimacy through the idea of citizens' support for the political system (Easton 1965, 1975). Without dwelling overlong on this, it is worth presenting a broad outline[13] of this concept, or more precisely, of its interpretations in the context of European studies. In spite of its limits and the criticisms that can be levelled at this paradigm, it is important to present it here because of the role it plays in the study of European attitudes. Indeed, it has become the dominant theoretical framework for studying the opinions and attitudes of citizens regarding European integration, in the context of reflections on legitimacy.[14]

---

13. A broad outline seems all the more sufficient given that most authors provide exactly this type of presentation of this analytic framework, devoting at best a few pages of their article to it and generally limiting their discussion to the classic distinction between diffuse and explicit support. It is worth noting that some authors have studied the question of the conceptualisation and operationalisation of the Eastonian framework more particularly in the context of the EU – but this hasn't made much of an impact in European studies. The discipline continues to content itself, for the most part, with brief references to David Easton's theory. For a recent example of a detailed conceptualisation and operationalisation, *see* Fuchs 2011.

14. Public opinion towards European integration provides the favourite material upon which to conduct empirical analysis of the legitimacy of the European political system. Legitimacy can also be empirically explored through the study of the practices and behaviour of citizens, such as, for example, civil disobedience and refusal to pay taxes (for a specific approach to the issue of paying taxes, *see* Frognier and Van Ingelgom 2007). However, in the case of the EU, because interactions between citizens and institutions remain rare, 'the EU does not have to face the empirical tests of political legitimacy because it is shielded against the behavioural responses of

David Easton distinguished two categories of support: explicit support, which results from citizens' satisfaction regarding the performance of the system in taking their demands into account; and diffuse support, which is expressed not in relation to performance but towards the political system in general. Following Lindberg and Scheingold, these two notions were also called instrumental (or utilitarian) support and affective support. In terms of the clarification of the concepts of legitimacy and support, Easton saw legitimacy as an interaction between diffuse and specific support. It is this interaction that explains why citizens support a political system even when they (temporarily) don't perceive any of its positive *outputs*. The key to Easton's argument is the claim that diffuse support, through a process of accumulation, constitutes a reservoir for the political system in periods of low explicit support. Inversely, when specific support is high, diffuse support also increases. Although Easton recognises that diffuse support is not independent of the results of the system in the long term, he sees specific support as varying in the short term, according to perceptions of the advantages and performance of the system.

The different aspects of support were operationalised through a series of questions in the Eurobarometer surveys. Since 1970, the European Commission has carried out biannual opinion surveys in each of the member states. These surveys contain a number of questions, called 'trend questions', which are the same in every survey. Several of them deal with support for integration, thus enabling a systematic longitudinal study of the level of support in each country. In the current literature, variations in the level of citizens' support for the EU have generally been measured using four of these questions, referred to as 'benefits',[15] 'belonging',[16] 'dissolution',[17] and 'unification'.[18] However, these questions have been interpreted and used in a variety of different ways. The most commonly mobilised question deals with support for one's country belonging to the EU. In a number of major studies, the dependent variable, that is, the empirical legitimacy of the European system, is measured purely on the basis of this one indicator (Gabel 1998). However, other researchers have instead operationalised support for integration on the basis of several indicators combined (Anderson and Kaltenhaler 1996; Cautrès and Grunberg 2007; Gabel and Palmer 1995; Hooghe

---

the governed' (Scharpf 2007). The two exceptions to this are elections to the European Parliament and referendums, which are also very widely studied (*see* Atikcan 2010; Blondel, Sinnott, and Svensson 1998; Franck and Boldrini 2006; Hobolt 2009, among others).

15. 'Taking everything into consideration, would you say that (your country) has on balance benefited or not from being a member of the European Community (Common Market)? Benefited, not benefited, don't know'.

16. 'Generally speaking, do you think that (your country's) membership of the European Community (Single Market) is: a good thing; a bad thing; neither good nor bad; don't know?'

17. 'If you were told tomorrow that the European Community (Single Market) – European Union – had been scrapped, would you be: very sorry about it; indifferent; very relieved; don't know?'

18. 'In general, are you for or against efforts being made to unify Western Europe? Are you: for–very much; for–to some extent; against–to some extent; against–very much; don't know?'

and Marks 2004; McLaren 2002). These different operationalisations obviously raise problems of comparability.

From the 1990s onwards, and following the so-called break in the permissive consensus, a second distinction emerged as decisive in the framework of the analysis of opinions regarding European integration. Another dichotomy, differentiating this time between inputs-based support and outputs-based support, came to complement the distinction between explicit and diffuse support (Belot and Cautrès 2008). Here one sees the normative political theory developed by Fritz Scharpf, already mentioned, which brings together two distinct and complementary approaches to legitimacy. The input-oriented approach emphasises legitimacy going into the system, whereas the output-oriented approach focuses on the results of the system. Thus the first refers to the idea of government by the people whereas the second poses the question of government for the people. The apparent link between the theoretical framework developed by the German sociologist Fritz Scharpf and the notion of inputs-based support, including the question of belonging to the political community, and outputs-based support, goes some way to explaining the dominance of this paradigm within European studies. For once, normative theory and empirical studies appear to be engaged in a genuine exchange.[19]

Within the academic sphere, a consensus developed during the first affirming that the legitimacy of the EU was, above all, based on performance or outputs-based support – as envisaged by (neo-) functionalist theory. Citizens perceive (or are assumed to perceive) the integration process as legitimate to the extent that it produces policies that they see as having a positive impact, particularly in economic terms.

The work of Matthew Gabel is particularly important here, paving the way for an analysis of support in utilitarian terms (Gabel 1998; Gabel and Palmer 1995). He defends the idea that individual attitudes towards European integration are the result of a rational calculation in which everyone weighs the economic costs and benefits of what they personally expect from integration. Although this assessment was initially near universal, the conclusions drawn from it varied considerably. Certain commentators affirmed that the European political system can survive in the long term with only this utilitarian support. Others, however, consider that legitimacy based on *outputs* is as fragile as it is fluctuating and that only legitimacy from *inputs*, based on the construction of a political community, would guarantee the stability of the European political system.

Faced with the limitations of these explanations in terms of economic preferences, other authors have questioned the role of identity and belonging to a political community as determining factors in citizens' support for European integration.[20] As Sophie Duchesne argues

---

19. Interactions between normative theories and empirical studies are in fact relatively few and far between. I will come back to this point in the conclusion of this chapter.

20. For an overview of the literature on European identity, *see* the special issue of the review *Politique Européenne* edited by Sophie Duchesne and, in particular, her introduction (Duchesne 2010).

in the space of a decade, research dealing with the relationship between citizens and the political system born out of European integration, have generally swapped an attitudes based approach for questions relating to identity (Duchesne 2006).

This approach is not new[21] but European studies nonetheless began showing a veritable passion for identity from the end of the 1990s (Duchesne 2010). From this point, the idea that the affective relationship of Europeans to the new Union would gain strength and even compete with ties to their national political communities, began to spread rapidly in the literature (Duchesne 2006). These questions of changing identities then paved the way for the third period, and resistance to European integration. This is because national identity was presented as a factor explaining the rejection of European integration by some citizens (Carey 2002).

However, numerous authors have questioned the idea that European identity develops in opposition to national identity; instead they suggest that these two identities are cumulative. There are many different models that seek to explain the complementary relationship between European and national identity. Sophie Duchesne and André-Paul Frognier, for example, suggest that we distinguish between the sociological and political dimensions of territorial identity and consider the relationship between European and national identity in this duality (Duchesne and Frognier 1995, 2002, 2008). The bi-dimensional nature of territorial attachments allows these authors to explain why we observe an antagonism in the measures of attachment to Europe and its nations during national public debates on Europe, when outside these periods of politicisation we don't. Juan Diez Medrano and Paula Gutierrez describe the interaction between these different levels of identity in terms of nested identities (Diez Medrano and Gutierrez 2001), whereas Thomas Risse prefers the metaphor of the marble cake (Risse 2003). The multi-dimensional nature of these identities may also be used to distinguish them; Joachim Schild, for example, differentiates the affective dimension of national identity from the primarily evaluative dimension of European identity (Schild 2001). For his part, Michael Bruter proposes a distinction between the civic and cultural dimensions of European and national identities (Bruter 2004, 2005).

From the mid-1990s, there were two distinct trends in European research. One pursued the exploration of support for integration with specific attention to utilitarian strategies that may be behind positive and negative attitudes. The other investigated the possible development of an affective dimension in attitudes towards Europe through the analysis of changing identities.[22] The Eastonian

---

21. Sophie Duchesne and André-Paul Frognier posed the question of European identity as early as 1995. Their article both interrogated the concept and situated it within a scientific context still marked by the permissive consensus model, which was then only just beginning to be questioned (Duchesne and Frognier 1995).

22. Here one can mention two articles, one by Matthew Gabel and another by Liesbet Hooghe and Gary Marks, which are particularly characteristic of this period. They set up an opposition between these two perspectives to test them using empirical data (Gabel 1998; Hooghe and Marks 2004).

paradigm provides a framework that allows for this double investigation, of both affective and utilitarian support. The conceptual slip between support and identity, and the shift in concern that results from this, was accompanied by a change in indicators. The so-called Moreno question – 'do you feel only [nationality], [nationality] and European, or just European?' – became a standard question in the Eurobarometers from 1992.[23] The parallel evolution of concepts and indicators again suggests the inextricable entanglement between political and university spheres on one hand and normative and empirical theories on the other.

Beyond the near-universal use of the Eastonian paradigm of support, these analyses also often have in common that they provide a comparison over a large number of countries – given that they tend to mobilise Eurobarometer-type survey data. As a result they emphasise a series of factors – both at the individual and systemic level – explaining variation in citizens' support for European integration in different member-states. The objective is clearly to explain the different levels of support for integration because behind majority support is a diverse ensemble of individual and national situations. The use of the Eurobarometers has thus guided work in this area through the imposition of a research object: the search for the factors that determine support for integration in order to explain the decline in this support in the post-Maastricht era (Belot 2005: 154–58). However, explanations diverge on factors as diverse as: expectations in terms of benefits at the individual and collective level (Anderson and Reichert 1995; Gabel and Palmer 1995); the performance and structure of the national economy (Anderson and Kaltenhaler 1996; Eichenberg and Dalton 1993); assessment of the national political system and economy (Anderson 1998; Brigenar and Jolly 2005; Kitzinger 2003); cognitive mobilisation and post-materialist values (Janssen 1991); geographical distance (Berezin and Díez-Medrano 2008); and, more recently, the perception of cultural threat, fear of immigration and the loss of social benefits (McLaren 2002).

Above and beyond the controversies that have swept the field of European studies, research conducted since the 1960s has brought out a series of explanatory factors at the individual level that have proven stable and verifiable over the years. At the individual level, debates have mainly concerned socio-political structures of support for the EU. Many authors have indeed demonstrated that citizen support appears to be determined by both sociological and political criteria. Firstly, an important point is that most studies recognise the existence of certain sociological traits behind the European idea. Studies conducted since the 1960s agree that support for European integration is more particularly developed among 'elites'. Thus, support for European construction is more frequent for social groups that are not only more educated but also in higher-status professions and with more income. Moreover, these effects are not only linked to each other; they reinforce each other (Belot and Cautrès 2006). Although this observation is straightforward, the theories put forward to explain it are many and varied (Belot 2002).

---

23. For a detailed discussion of the way the notion of identity has been conceptually adapted to Europe, and the question of the indicators used, *see* Duchesne 2006.

Level of education and, by extension, formal knowledge and social status are not everything, however. Political variables also have a role to play. Political competence is also important because, when we control for level of education, interest in politics plays a significant role in determining support for the idea of Europe. Indeed, it seems that interest in politics and political competence 'allow individuals to appropriate this political object, the EU, which is in perpetual flux and of which the boundaries appear rather blurry' (Belot and Cautrès 2008: 161). In the production of attitudes towards Europe there is a political effect that plays out beyond the impact of sociological structures. Janssen demonstrates this, partly throwing Ingelhart's theory into question, with his conclusion that post-materialist individuals do have a more favourable attitude towards the EU than materialists, not because of diverging values but simply because they are more politically competent (Janssen 1991).

Moreover, certain studies have argued that ideological position is a decisive factor in explaining support for European integration. According to this perspective there is a direct link between party preference and attitudes towards Europe. As a result, some authors have recently identified the emergence of a cleavage between the supporters of pro-European parties on one hand and, on the other, those who support the extremes (left or right), which are generally more critical of the integration process (Hooghe, Marks, and Wilson 2004).

By emphasising the sociological and political forces that determine support for European integration, these studies shed light on the similarities between the different member-states. However, most of these authors agree that nationality remains the strongest determining factor in explaining attitudes towards Europe, given that support for the EU varies considerably from one state to another. There is therefore a strand of the literature that emphasises the importance of the national context in understanding processes of support for Europe. Following this, a number of authors attempted to identify factors that would explain this cross-national variation. The economic approach, for example, insisted that countries that benefited most from integration – particularly through Community funds – would be the ones whose citizens would be most favourable to integration. The corollary of this is that the citizens of the countries benefiting the least in economic terms, the 'net contributors' to the Community's budget, would be the least inclined to support the process (Anderson and Reichert 1995).

For Christopher J. Anderson and Karl Kaltenthaler, the national variations observed are in fact the result of a combination of three factors, namely, the economic conditions of the country, the moment and circumstances of its accession and the duration of its EU membership (Anderson and Kaltenhaler 1996). Firstly, if the national economy is performing well, citizens will judge European integration in a positive light because this integration is intended to increase economic prosperity. If, on the other hand, the national economy is struggling, they will tend to regard integration more critically and question whether this construction is useful for ameliorating the state of their national economy. These authors then argue that the timing and the circumstances in which a country becomes a member of the EU are good indicators of citizens' support for integration. Thus, the six founding members have the highest levels of support, whereas countries that entered the Union during the 1970s presented strong domestic opposition to the membership application, which explains their later membership. Finally, the last countries to enter have intermediate levels of support. The authors defend the hypothesis that there is a process of national socialisation that leads to greater awareness and appreciation of the benefits of the integration process and which leads to an increase in the level of support over time.

Notwithstanding these interesting results, quantitative analyses are of limited use when it comes to analysing the national variable in all its complexity. Indeed, studies of public opinion have shown themselves unconvincing when it comes to explaining levels of support. Yet the stakes are high. Some authors suggest that these differences between countries are due to the distinct national history and culture of each one, thus marking a qualitative turn in the study of citizens' attitudes towards the European Union. Marco Cinnirella, for example, used interviews with students in Italy and in the United Kingdom to analyse the relationship between a feeling of national belonging and attitudes towards integration. He showed that, in the UK, affirming one's national identity is considered incompatible with the recognition of European identity (Cinnirella 1997). Céline Belot, for her part, provides a study of the sociological processes that underlie young French and British people's support for the European political system (Belot 2000). Based on individual interviews, her research looks not only at the level of support for integration but also at the different types of support. Juan Diez Medrano, in analysing different conceptions of 'Europe' (using qualitative material), explores variations in opinion between German, Spanish and British citizens. He emphasises that attitudes towards integration reflect, above all, cognitive perceptions that are culturally and, especially, nationally based and which 'frame' the way in which ordinary citizens think about the EU (Diez Medrano 2003). Beyond their similarities, German, Spanish and British citizens have developed different ways of looking at European integration, which stem from their perceptions of their national cultures, their collective memories and their different common concerns.

In conclusion, this second period was marked by the Eastonian paradigm and the notion of support that it used. The Eurobarometers and the data that they have produced influenced research in this area by imposing an (overwhelmingly) dominant level and framework of analysis. This framework was based on the Eastonian notion of support and implies a particular research question, namely, the search for factors that are decisive for this support. The concepts of legitimacy and political support have long been intrinsically, although too often implicitly, linked. Moreover, the claims of the legitimacy crisis or, more specifically, the democratic deficit of the EU have found an echo in the constant decline of popular support for European integration in the post-Maastricht era, as well as in low levels of participation in European elections. To the indirect legitimacy based on system performances or outputs can be added a direct and democratic form of legitimacy based on inputs. The latter brings with it normative questions linked to the accomplishment of democracy and the construction of a political community at the European level. It also mobilises studies that interrogate the possible development of the affective aspect of attitudes towards the EU, through an analysis in terms of changing identities.

Thus, although before the 1990s only a handful of studies were interested in studying the empirical legitimacy of European integration, today there are many researchers who focus on citizens' attitudes to this integration. Their work aims to understand and explain the subjective dimension of European construction: how the EU is perceived by its citizens. It was necessary to wait for the bitter debates surrounding the Maastricht Treaty and the accusations of a legitimacy crisis and a democratic deficit to pass for the citizen fully emerge into the process of legitimising the construction of Europe. The break in the permissive consensus and the search for direct legitimacy in the EU have propelled the citizen into the European spotlight – both politically and academically. In spite of the absence of a clear consensus on whether democratisation of the Union is necessary, possible or even desirable, it is now clear that Europe will need informed citizens capable of accessing their political leaders – citizens who are able to influence, to reject or even to overthrow the decisions made in their name.

The constraining dissensus model and the analysis of euroscepticism

The double 'no' to the project for a Constitutional Treaty expressed in the French and Dutch referendums in 2005, followed by Ireland's rejection of the Lisbon Treaty, helped revive questions about the legitimacy of the European project and its relation to its citizens. For a number of years, the EU has been trapped in a quagmire of questions relating to the reach of the European project. To explain this, many specialists have invoked the rise of euroscepticism, as a corollary of the break in the permissive consensus. Euroscepticism is a thesis that is widely accepted both at the level of studies of public opinion (Franklin, Marsch and McLaren 1994; Gabel and Palmer 1995; Vasilopoulou 2013; Wessels 2007, among others), and in studies of political parties (Hooghe 2007; Taggart and Szczerbiak 2012, to mention only a few). The beginning of the twenty-first century thus saw the emergence of a third phase in the analysis of citizens' attitudes to integration, marked by the emergence of studies on euroscepticism (Leconte 2010). This notion, problematic because rarely defined and often conflating diverse realities, has become very common in the literature in recent years and, in particular, in the context of thinking about the future of European integration.[24] The current European crises and their analyses fall into this third period marked by euroscepticism.

The term was used for the first time by *The Economist* on 26 December 1992, as a way of describing German public opinion; it refers to a state of doubt or incredulity regarding European integration. Euroscepticism covers a range of positions that are critical of integration, including complete opposition. Its most

---

24. Two major European journals have dedicated a special issue to the question of euroscepticism: *European Union Politics* 8(1), March 2007 and *Acta Politica* 42(3), September 2007). The *Revue internationale de politique comparée* also dedicated an issue to the question of resistance to European integration (15(4), 2008).

visible manifestations are the emergence and/or reinforcement of political parties that challenge the integration process within member-states and challenges to governments during referendums on the ratification of European treaties.

The constraining dissensus model: looking for the politicised citizen

As far as theories of integration are concerned, the extent and the intensity of resistance to the integration process in the wake of the Maastricht Treaty were unexpected (Hooghe and Marks 2008). Indeed, the neo-functionalists had assumed that deepening European integration would lead to more support for, not more opposition to, the process of political integration. Given the predicted gradual shift of political loyalties to the supranational centre, there was to be a 'spillover' effect, with the benefits of integration passing from some individual interests to the whole society. The intergovernmentalists, on the other hand, continued to ignore public opinion because, for them, governments and not citizens determined the meaning and reach of the European project.

Unsurprisingly, resistance to European integration attracted particular attention from European specialists, who were torn between their perplexed fascination at the way in which this new political system was evolving before their eyes and the desire to contribute to its consolidation (Leca 2009). European studies provided a site for several attempts to re-theorise the integration process and, by extension, to legitimise it (Bartolini 2005; Hooghe and Marks 2008). Thus, Stefano Bartolini, in his book *Restructuring Europe*,[25] characterised European integration as a historical stage representing a sixth phase in European political development (Bartolini 2005). In the penultimate chapter, the author provides a sophisticated interrogation of the possibility of politicising European issues and, in the conclusion, he goes as far as to warn against the politicisation of the European public. In the context of *Notre Europe*, Stefano Bartolini launches into a debate that opposes him to Simon Hix on the specific question of the politicisation of European integration. Where Bartolini sees it as a poison, Hix perceives politicisation as the remedy to the legitimacy crisis (Hix and Bartolini 2006). On the sidelines of this debate, other theorists have emphasised the very unequal benefits that different segments of the population gain from European integration as a potential source of conflict and politicisation. Neil Fligstein, for example, uses survey data to develop the theory of a rising political conflict between the winners and losers in European integration, in his book *Euroclash* (2008). The team working with Hans-Peter Kriesi envisaged the issue in terms of the emergence of a cleavage around the consequences of globalisation (Kriesi *et al.* 2008).

But this third period is particularly marked by the development of another theory of integration, put forward this time by Liesbeth Hooghe and Gary Marks. Post-functionalist theory, as it was called, defended the idea of a shift from the

---

25. The six phases are as follows: state construction; development of capitalism; construction of the nation; democratisation; development of the welfare state; and, finally, European integration.

permissive consensus to a constraining dissensus (Hooghe and Marks 2008). It is based on the idea that the increased visibility of Europe has led to a polarisation of opinions about integration. All the debates on the treaties – from Maastricht to Amsterdam and Nice and, finally, the Constitutional Treaty – helped politicise European space. Although resistance to the integration process has always existed, it became fundamentally institutionalised. These two authors stress that 'the decisive change is that the elite has had to make room for a more Eurosceptical public' (Hooghe and Marks 2008: 9). On this point, greater polarisation of public opinion on the European issue was going to have an impact on party systems at the national level. Indeed, parties adopting anti-European[26] platforms found the electoral base needed for their future development, thanks to this polarity of opinions (Steenbergen, Edwards and De Vries 2007). Thus, the polarisation of attitudes creates electoral incentives for the parties situated at both extremes. Similarly, in the event of a new European issue or even a new cleavage emerging, traditional centrist parties that had not yet adapted to it might be confronted by both internal divisions and external pressure to take a position on this new European issue (Down and Wilson 2008: 27). Indeed, given that national political parties derive their internal cohesion from issues other than European integration, their leaders and members may have developed different preferences regarding Europe, which might generate horizontal and vertical integration problems (Bartolini 2005: 310). In light of what was observed in France and the Netherlands during the debates around the referendums on the Constitutional Treaty, it seems that issues linked to the EU have the potential to divide the traditional party base in many member-states. Traditional parties also appear less adept at mobilising their supporters in this kind of referendum, compared to simple national elections (van der Eijk and Franklin 2004). European referendums are thus periodic demonstrations of the directly observable impact of Europe on the electorates (Atikcan 2010; Hobolt 2009). Given this, European issues could become centred around the emergence of a new stable cleavage, which would divide parties' national electorates (Bartolini 2005: 310). Studying the link that develops (or not) between European integration and mass public opinion has thus become an issue of substantial importance in understanding the European political landscape.[27]

Thereafter, the elitist perspective defended by both the intergovernmentalists and the neo-functionalists, which argues that European integration is largely a non-issue for the public, no longer held water in the post-Maastricht era. Indeed, Hooghe and Marks consider that the three basic tenets on which this elitist perspective is based are no longer applicable today (Hooghe and Marks 2008:

---

26. Taggart puts forward a detailed classification of political parties around the European question. He distinguishes between: (1) single-issue eurosceptic parties; (2) classic protest parties that tend towards euroscepticism; (3) established parties that defend a majority eurosceptic position; and (4) eurosceptic factions present within traditional parties that otherwise support the European integration process (Taggart 1998).

27. Of course, the literature on this subject is extensive and opinions differ as to the impact that European integration has or not on national political systems.

6–7). First, citizens' attitudes towards integration can no longer be considered superficial and seen as not structuring electoral motivations in party organisation. Second, European integration is no longer a non-issue for the general public and, as a result, does influence party competition. Third, the problems raised by European integration are not problems in themselves but only become so when linked to the fundamental conflicts that structure national politics, particularly according to a left–right axis. The underlying central hypothesis, which is widely shared, is that the vague consensus has been replaced by public opinion that is more polarised and both more politicised and more critical about the integration process. This polarisation, the result of the deepening of the integration process and the politicisation of European issues that has accompanied it, means that European governments are now obliged to take citizens' opinions into account – even when they are eurosceptic. On this last point, it is widely accepted that the underprivileged sections of the population are the least supportive of the integration process because they don't benefit from it (Fligstein 2008).

The place of the citizen within the legitimation process of the European construction has only increased, meaning that understanding citizens' attitudes is now more important than ever. Increasing use of referendums has impact beyond national party systems; it also constantly accentuates the importance of the role of the citizen.

Eurosceptic citizens: interrogation in terms of lack of support

The study of citizens' attitudes had, up until this point, been primarily concerned with factors determining their support for the EU; now the focus is on patterns of rejection of integration (Belot and Cautrès 2008: 163). The concept of euroscepticism has become part of a school of thought that allows for resistance to European integration. The conceptual slippage from support to rejection contained in the term euroscepticism has the advantage of bringing to light the shift in perspective that happened in the discipline from the beginning of the 2000s, illustrating a turning point in political science studies dedicated to the EU. Once again, the Eastonian paradigm provides the analytical framework (Wessels 2007); the category of interest simply shifts from 'belonging to the EU is a good thing' to 'belonging to the EU is a bad thing'. Support for integration and euroscepticism are two ends of the same continuum.

Here too, among studies dealing with citizens' attitudes, the search for the factors determining the rejection of integration is at the centre of the inquiry. Given that resistance is most often defined as lack of support, the decisive factors can be seen as the corollary of those presented above.[28] The use of an indicator of net support – the difference between positive and negative answers to the questions above – enables us to make the connection empirically between these two concepts

---

28. For a detailed presentation of these explanatory factors, *see* the article by Lauren McLaren (McLaren 2007).

and thus between these two periods of study. In explaining the determining factors of resistance, some authors underline the importance of lack of knowledge about European construction (Karp, Banducci and Bowler 2003); others suggest using dissatisfaction with the performance of national governments as an indicator of citizens' negative opinions about the EU (Anderson 1998). Poorly functioning national democracies, concerns about the loss of national identities and symbols (Carey 2002; Hooghe and Marks 2004; McLaren 2002) and the calculations of personal costs and benefits linked to European integration (McLaren 2007) have all been put forward as decisive factors in the development of euroscepticism.

In addition, and partly in order to address criticisms of this concept, several authors have tried to construct typologies of euroscepticism (Leconte 2010), first in the study of political parties[29] and then in studies analysing citizens' attitudes.[30] The most common criticism levelled at this concept is that it fails to capture the complexity and diversity of attitudes of resistance to integration.[31] These attempts at typologies thus primarily aim to break down the concept of euroscepticism (Déloye 2008). The study of resistance to European integration thus aims to

[...] listen, in order to better understand a European revolution, which was initially silent because of the 'permissive consensus' that accompanied the beginnings of the EU, but which has become deafening because of the political implications it has provoked (implications bearing with them a dynamic of 'politicisation'). Deafening also because of the various ideological counter-offensives, which, not always converging, now accompany it (Déloye 2008: 681).

By way of conclusion, we can say that, during this last period, the citizen has indeed taken a role centre stage, in that the citizen is now seen as a politicised figure (or at least polarised on European issues) and that his or her opinions are seen as a constraining force on the integration process. Given that the Eastonian paradigm is again the central framework for analysis, one must agree that its omnipresence explains certain weaknesses or oversights in the study of citizens' opinions about the integration process (Belot and Cautrès 2008: 160); these weaknesses and oversights are what I seek to address in this book.

A citizen for whom Europe constitutes a concrete reality that he or she is able to evaluate, criticise and even challenge emerges. The various referendums and mobilisation by political parties, especially the extreme left and the extreme right, have made the EU a salient issue in the eyes of the citizen. This politicisation is manifested in rising euroscepticism, both at the level of political parties and for citizens themselves (De Wilde and Zürn 2012). The image of the politicised

---

29. The classic distinction between soft and hard euroscepticism can be cited here.
30. An interesting distinction was developed by Bernard Wessels (Wessels 2007).
31. This is why the French literature often refers to resistance to integration instead of euroscepticism; using terms that are more inclusive and which convey the plurality of opposition to the process (Crespy and Verschueren 2009).

European citizen serves as a model for the legitimation of a European project that is confronted with unexpected challenges. These challenges seek to modify its reach, its intensity and/or its direction, to recast its still uncertain borders or even (more rarely) interrupt the process all together. The emergence of a critical citizen is at the centre of the legitimation process, which must now happen through the politicisation of the European sphere.[32]

Models of legitimacy and empirical analyses that are products of their time

The question of the legitimacy of the EU is defined in empirical terms as citizens' acceptance of the European political order and, by an unfortunate simplification, as citizens' support for the European integration process. Anyone who sets out to study this is necessarily confronted with the substantial corpus of normative theories concerning European integration. As this chapter has shown, although there are few explicit connections between the models of legitimacy suggested by normative and empirical work, there are numerous implicit connections. The amount of European literature on both the question of democratic legitimacy and the empirical study of public opinion is striking. Here it is worth remembering Max Weber's warning not to confuse the beliefs and attitudes that shore up the legitimacy of a regime within a political community with legitimation defined as an ensemble of actions by which elites (in a broad sense) tend to establish and proclaim their legitimacy. In other words, legitimation should be defined as the way political leaders and other dominant groups preserve the image of political power in agreement with the fundamental values of the political community in question.

It is widely acknowledged that European political elites and senior public servants are continually trying to produce or reinforce certain principles of legitimation for European construction, particularly through top-down institutionalisation of channels of representation, mainly electoral. However, the energy that numerous European specialists invest in justifying the need to democratise the European system, or in the search for new standards and principles of legitimacy, although less often emphasised, is nonetheless remarkable. As Stefano Bartolini notes, 'there are few historical examples of politicians, bureaucrats, and scholars searching so frenetically for "democracy" and "legitimacy" that no citizen has demanded' [as in the EU context] (Bartolini 2005: 407). From the beginning, the European Communities were born and constructed by an ensemble of European political actors and academics who developed the framework we use to comprehend and legitimise this new type of political order. This framework can be best seen in the analogies used to characterise the institutional and political transforma-

---

32. Yet no consensus exists as to the need or appropriateness of politicising the European sphere. In reference to this, *see* the debates surrounding *Notre Europe*, following Hix and Bartolini's publications already mentioned. Other European specialists also participated in this debate, notably Magnette (2006) and Quermonne (2006).

tions in Europe: 'democratic deficit', 'good governance', 'European Constitution', 'open method of co-ordination' or the 'European social model'. These are all contributions by academic players to help formulate and legitimise reform projects (Cohen and Vauchez 2007; Georgakakis and De Lasalle 2007). The involvement of the academic sphere in the creation and the development of the Eurobarometers as a tool for the institutionalisation of European public opinion is also part of this strategy of co-operation and legitimation between two spheres of activity: the European politico-administrative world and the world of academia (Aldrin 2010, 2011). Given this, the overview of the European-studies literature presented in this chapter probably tells us more about the representations of leaders and their most frequent interlocutors regarding the foundations of legitimacy than about why groups and individuals effectively consent to and support the exercise of political power (Lagroye, François and Sawicki 2006: 448). In this, I fully agree with Claudia Schrag Sternberg's conclusions that, 'Parallel to Rodney Barker's argument about national governments (2001), the "rulers" in EU politics risked justifying their rule and the EU in their own eyes more successfully than in the eyes of their subjects' (Schrag Sternberg 2013: 205).

It is therefore important to identify and apprehend the different models of legitimacy in the European political order. As this chapter has shown, the study of citizens' attitudes towards the European integration process has undergone three main stages; each marked by a different vision of legitimacy for the European political system and each a product of its time. It is above all the role of the citizen within this legitimation process that has varied over time. The citizen was initially a shadow figure, taking on an active role in the aspiringly democratic legitimation process only after Maastricht and in response to accusations of a democratic deficit levelled at the European construction process. Support from elites was clearly no longer sufficient and citizens' participation became essential for the legitimacy of the process; it was not only desired but actively sought by European actors. More recently, the figure of the participative citizen was replaced by the need for a citizen who was politicised (but not too much!) on European questions. The idea was that the limited (but desirable) political participation of the citizen should be accomplished through politicisation, which certain actors see in the beginnings of new forms of resistance to integration.

In this, I follow Johan P. Olsen that the role of European citizens within European governance depends very much on the way in which the future European political order is envisaged (Olsen 2003). Today, more than ever, the citizen is at the centre of the debates between elites – political or academic – on how the future of the EU is to be envisaged and defined. This increasingly important reference to the citizen, both by European actors and theorists, is evidently not neutral. The place of the citizen is emerging as a key issue in debates between political actors regarding the future of the European project. We have come far from Monnet and his successors' desire to avoid the possibility of a heated public debate emerging around the European question (Lindberg and Scheingold 1970: 70).

The way the future of this 'unidentified political object' is envisaged thus plays an essential role in the place of the citizen within it. In this regard, it is necessary to note that this envisaged future was clearly not the same at the beginning of the 1970s, when Lindberg and Scheingold put forward their permissive consensus model, as it is today with the model of constraining dissensus proposed by Hooghe and Marks. In the 1960s, the simple continuity of the European system was still in question; its future was uncertain, yet to be built. Re-reading the texts from this period today, it is clear that their authors believed that the demise of the young European system was entirely possible. Today, for certain scholars, its future development appears to be dependent on its possible politicisation. Analysing the present is thus clearly very complex, given that the actors and commentators cannot overlook their conceptions of the integration process when faced with a future that constitutes the backdrop of their present.

As we have seen, both the theoretical models and the empirical studies are profoundly marked by their time. They are based on normative and political premises, particularly concerning the role that the European citizen should play in legitimising the European integration process. One can see that, beyond these theoretical debates (between perspectives that in fact are more complementary than contradictory), the real issue concerns the justification of European integration, which is inevitably conditioned by its present and its future and has thus varied significantly over the course of European construction. Thus it is a characteristic of the European integration project that its goal is still to be clearly defined, let alone attained. If the European project remains fundamentally undefinable, yet with massive political effects, the same must be said for the place of the citizen in this process.

The legitimacy of a political order is a complicated notion, perhaps more so in the European context. It is therefore not surprising to note that no consensus has been found within European studies regarding the meaning and the reach of European legitimacy. On the contrary, there are a multitude of different approaches to this issue, some of which have been sketched in this chapter. Dealing with the full complexity of the literature on the legitimacy of the EU is beyond the scope of this book but this chapter aimed to demonstrate that this question is at the heart of discussions on the EU seen as a political system in progress. As this new entity emerges in the shape of a political system, the question of its legitimacy is projected on to the political and academic agenda. It thus seems that the time has come for the theoretical revival that political research on the EU needs, or for an attempt to move past questions that have become too familiar to be insightful and, to an extent, already adequately answered.

Chapter Two

Revising the 'End' of the Permissive Consensus

> The other side of support is discontent, although neither discontent nor scepticism is an exact opposite of support because non-support may also include indifference (Wessels 2007: 290).

The previous chapter outlined the evolution of citizens' attitudes in light of normative debates on legitimacy that have accompanied the European project from its inception. It showed how from a simple spectator or a 'shadow citizen', the European citizen has become a decisive actor in the legitimisation of European integration (Belot 2000: 19). This second chapter comes back to the existing survey data, in order to provide an analysis over the long term. By doing so, it aims to distance the results observed from the normative contexts of each period as much as possible. I provide a reinterpretation of the data here as a way to distance the observations from the story generally told by Europeanists, who often directly seek to contribute to the consolidation of the European political system. The objective here is to pave the way for new reflection in the study of citizens' attitudes towards the European integration process today. In a time of so-called crisis, a long-term perspective seems obviously required. In order to assess what has changed, one needs to know first what was.

In dealing with the European project, social scientists find themselves thrown into a process of creation 'in real time'; they have to address the difficulty of working in the present on the present (Abélès 1997: 37). As the authors of *Europe's Would Be Polity* have argued 'Anybody who writes about a phenomenon that is contemporary and that changes constantly is bound to encounter problems of perspective and timing' (Lindberg and Scheingold 1970: v). Re-reading the past in light of the present should provide an analysis with greater perspective on this process and its effects on citizens: effects which are, for the moment, perceived but not easily evaluated. What is important here, in revisiting this survey data, is to interrogate the specific historicity proposed by European studies, in other words, the relation that this discipline has with the immediate history of European construction. In this, I hope to convince the reader that looking at this issue through some kind of interpretative 'filter' is inevitable: the current filter being a combination of politicisation and euroscepticism. In European studies, this is clearly also a normative filter because one of the current questions is whether politicising European integration could or should be a solution to its democratic deficit (*see* the debate between Hix and Bartolini and, more recently, articles by

De Wilde (Hix and Bartolini 2006; Bartolini 2005; De Wilde 2011; De Wilde and Zürn 2012). In this sense, euroscepticism is perceived as a 'good thing': the sign of a growing politicisation of the European integration process. In this regard, the enquiry will pay particular attention to the passage from the model of permissive consensus to that of constraining dissensus, as discussed previously. The existence and then the breakdown of this consensus have come to be recognised as near-absolute truths and are rarely, if ever, questioned.

As mentioned in the previous chapter, post-functionalist theory defends the idea that we have moved from a situation where permissive consensus dominated (Lindberg and Scheingold 1970) to a period marked by a constraining dissensus (Hooghe and Marks 2008). In particular, post-functionalist theory is based on the claim that the increased visibility of the European integration process results in a polarisation of opinions regarding regional integration (Hooghe and Marks 2008). Public debate surrounding the various treaties – Maastricht in 1992, Amsterdam in 1997, Nice in 2001 and then the Constitutional Treaty in 2005 – and more recently the financial and economic crises, all contributed to politicising European space whilst simultaneously increasing concerns about the integration process itself (De Wilde 2011; De Wilde and Zürn 2012). The central hypothesis underlying post-functionalist theory is that the vague consensus has been replaced by public opinion that is more polarised on the issues relating to European integration and characterised by increasingly critical attitudes towards this process. The increasing authority of the European Union and the politicisation of European issues that has accompanied it have, apparently, polarised opinions (De Wilde and Zürn 2012).

Although it is difficult to contest the sudden decline of citizen support from the beginning of the 1990s, to what extent can Maastricht be said to form a rupture in the permissive consensus? Can we talk of constraining dissensus and, by extension, of a polarisation of European public opinion? This second chapter aims to respond to these two questions, interrogating this dominant reading based on the breakdown of the permissive consensus. It will then proceed to systematically analyse the claim of increasing polarisation in European public opinion, within the framework of the process of politicising the EU (De Wilde 2011; De Wilde and Zürn 2012). Indeed, with the notable exception of a recent article by Down and Wilson (Down and Wilson 2008), inspired by the work of di Maggio and his team (di Maggio, Evans, and Bryson 1996) on the polarisation of Americans' attitudes, few studies have directly tackled the question of polarisation from an empirical perspective.[1]

---

1. In a recent article, Pieter De Wilde and Michael Zürn put forward certain empirical elements, with the aim of convincing the reader of the increasing polarisation of European public opinion (De Wilde and Zürn 2012). The weakness of their empirical demonstration – noted by the authors themselves as they specify in the text 'although this contribution falls short of thoroughly testing hypotheses derived from this model against empirical data [...]' (De Wilde and Zürn 2012: 146) – is so evident that it renders it impossible to take their demonstration seriously, on an empirical level at least.

Most recent research on changing opinion at the aggregate level is focused on the central measures of average or net support. Drawing on these studies and the classic operationalisation that they use, the first part of this chapter interrogates the cases of the breakdown in the permissive consensus, defined as a decline of average support visible in the re-analysis of survey data. It is the periodisation of changes in citizens' attitudes towards integration that is in question here; instead of the widely accepted division between the periods before and after Maastricht, I use a periodisation of three stages. The first part of the chapter is the first step in relativising the breakdown in the permissive consensus defined as a decline in the mean level of support.

From questioning the relevance of a reading based on the 'breakdown of the permissive consensus and rise in euroscepticism', the chapter then moves on to the analysis of the polarisation of opinion. First, I return to the definition of what polarisation of opinions refers to and emphasise the empirical and analytical distinction between this concept and that of declining support. In order to address the hypothesis of a constraining dissensus, I then examine the way this polarisation is measured (Down and Wilson 2008). Here, I draw upon theoretical, empirical and methodological questions to underline the rise in ordinary citizens' indifference and indecision regarding the integration process since the 1990s. The permissive consensus that dominated in the 1970s has not disappeared but its nature has probably changed. Far from having become overwhelmingly eurosceptic, citizens are instead now more ambivalent *and* more indifferent to European integration. Finally, using the 'neither-nor' category as a proxy and mobilising more recent data, I will argue that this has continued to be the case since the beginning of financial and economic crises.

The end of the permissive consensus?

In this section I will undertake a longitudinal analysis of the distribution of ordinary citizens' attitudes over the last 40 years, by constructing an index of support.[2] I will begin my analysis by exploring the average support for European integration. There is a twofold point in beginning with the presentation of an analysis in terms of average support. First, it means validating the index I have constructed and presenting a reading of existing data based on this index; this echoes the traditional analysis in validating the breakdown of the permissive consensus, for the countries where it existed. Second, it means interrogating this reading of citizens' attitudes towards European integration by constructing an alternative periodisation, which, this time, leads to us to relativise the breakdown in the permissive consensus. This section of the chapter thus re-examines the existing survey data to propose a new analysis over the long term; an analysis that differs from the reading most

---

2. Part of the analysis presented in this chapter was published in French in the journal *Sociologie*. Many thanks again to the anonymous readers for their precious comments and to the journal for partially publishing this text (Van Ingelgom 2012).

commonly accepted and recounted by European studies scholars. It allows me, by way of conclusion, to nuance the thesis of the breakdown in the permissive consensus. Indeed, in the eight countries that I analyse, only the Belgian, French and German cases showed an average level of support that was significantly lower in the post-Maastricht period than in the 1970s.

Data: the construction of a support index incorporating indifference and indecision

Here, I will use the variables from the *Mannheimer Eurobarometer Trend File 1970–2002*. The advantage of this file is that it provides data anterior to 1990,[3] and thus addresses the difficulties raised by the series of questions that begin after this date. The lack of more recent data in this data file is not of consequence in this part of the chapter. This is because here I am interested in gauging the appropriateness of the reading in terms of the permissive consensus and constraining dissensus in which the signature of the Maastricht Treaty and the events that surrounded it played a pivotal role. More recent data from 2011 will be introduced at the end of this chapter, to provide perspective. The analysis covers eight countries: the five founding states of the CEE[4] (Belgium, France, (West) Germany,[5] Italy and the Netherlands), as well as the three member states that joined in 1970s (Denmark, Ireland and United Kingdom). The data corpus is, consequently, not directly affected by the successive enlargements of the EU because, throughout this period, only the eight original countries are included in the analysis. Eurobarometer data is available for all of these countries since 1973. Moreover, the last section will broaden the geographic scope of this analysis, using 2004 data covering 25 member-states.

In anticipation of longitudinal analyses, I have constructed an attitude index based on the two trend questions that are typically used to gauge the attitudes. These two questions are as follows:

> Generally speaking, do you think that (your country's) membership of the European Community (Common Market) is: 'A good thing'; 'a bad thing'; 'neither good nor bad'?

> If you were told tomorrow that the European Community (Single Market) – European Union – had been scrapped, would you be: very sorry about it; indifferent; or very relieved?

---

3. There are of course other recent studies that also mobilise data from before 1990 (Anderson and Kaltenhaler 1996; Down and Wilson 2008; Eichenberg and Dalton 2007).

4. I have not included Luxembourg in the group of member states, because the size of the sample was insufficient to complete all the analyses necessary.

5. Future references to Germany refer to West Germany.

Table 2.1: Construction of the index of support for European integration

Dissolution question	Membership question			
	Good thing	Neither good nor bad	Bad thing	Don't know
Very sorry	2	1	9	9
Indifferent	1	0	-1	9
Very relieved	9	-1	-2	9
Don't know	9	9	9	9

The scale was constructed in order to conduct a systematic and longitudinal study of the evolution of the dispersal of citizens' attitudes towards European integration.[6] The combination of these two questions seemed relevant for the examination of the absence of salience emphasised in recent qualitative studies (*see* Introduction and Chapter One). The response categories of the 'membership' and the 'dissolution' questions explicitly include a middle-of-the-road category expressing respectively indecision and indifference. This is not the case for the 'benefit'[7] and 'unification'[8] questions (Niedermayer 1995: 55). If respondents can only choose between positive or negative answers, it is impossible for them to express the lack of salience of the EU, their indifference or ambivalence; their only options are to respond by answering 'I don't know' or not to answer the question at all. Therefore, if a median category is not offered to respondents, a higher proportion of positive or negative answers, and a greater apparent polarisation of attitudes, is to be expected.

I have assigned different values to this index from those proposed by the Mannheim Centre, in order to facilitate the presentation of the results. In concrete terms, the five categories of the new indicator are as follows: -2 = strong opposition to the European integration process (8.1 per cent of the overall population, including missing data, N= 377.600); -1 = moderate opposition to integration (7.2 per cent); 0 = indifferent *and* undecided regarding the integration process (17.7 per cent); 1= moderate support for integration (22.1 per cent); 2= strong support for European integration (45 per cent).

Negative values were thus attributed to modalities indicating a certain opposition to integration and positive values were reserved for values indicating

---

6. The operationalisation and the frequencies of modalities of the index can be found in Appendix One.

7. 'Taking everything into consideration, would you say that (your country) has, on balance, benefited or not from being a member of the European Community (Single Market): benefited; not benefited; don't know?'

8. 'In general, are you for or against efforts being made to unify Western Europe? Are you: for–very much; for–to some extent; against–to some extent; against–very much; don't know?'. The 'unification' question contained an indifferent category for the first time, when the respondents were offered the category 'indifferent' (Niedermayer 1995: 55).

support. Zero indicates both positions of indifference and ambivalence. Finally, missing data were coded with the number nine and excluded from the analysis. Among the missing data I included responses for which I couldn't be sure whether the overall orientation was positive, negative or indifferent. This therefore includes the 'I don't know' category.[9] I could have considered these responses as neutral but the uncertainty associated with this assumption was too high.[10] Indeed, this category of response can indicate neutrality, indecision, indifference or simply a non-attitude. I also chose to exclude those individuals presenting extreme variation in their answers.[11] My operationalisation differs in this from the recent work by Marco Steenbergen and Catherine E. de Vries, as well as from that of Florian Stoeckel, which focus on ambivalence defined as variation in responses (de Vries and Steenbergen 2013; Stoeckel 2013).

Using this attitude index offers several significant advantages for the analysis. Firstly, the two questions used to construct the index were present as early as 1973, from the first regular Eurobarometers: up until 2004 for the question on dissolution and up until the present for the question on membership. Their formulation has also remained the same, ensuring that they continue to be comparable. Secondly, they both have a median category, undecided or indifferent respectively. The particular construction of the index leads me to focus on the group of citizens who see themselves as both indifferent and ambivalent about their country's membership of the Union. Indeed the zero category in the index refers to an attitude which combines *both* indifference and indecision. Thus I do not consider it to be a non-attitude (Converse 1964; Zaller 1992). In fact, this category of attitudes is particularly demanding because only those individuals who don't manifest any evaluations at all, positive or negative, were included in it. Combining these two questions thus allows controlling the stability and intensity of the mean attitude to make sure that it is not simply a non-attitude (Converse 1964). In choosing this solution, I ensured that the undecided and indifferent category constructed for the index was both robust and demanding. In terms of percentages, this leads me to examine a category of undecided and indifferent citizens that is smaller than if I had restricted myself to a single question.[12] This intermediary category is also essential to the study of the (non-)polarisation of opinions and their evolution; a binary indicator would not allow us to observe the process of polarisation,

---

9. On the methodological and theoretical decision to not include the 'don't know' category within our analysis, *see* the text by Paul Di Maggio, John Evans and Bethany Bryson (1996).

10. On this point, I distance myself from Oskar Niedermayer, who considers the 'don't know' category as a neutral category that he assimilates to the 'neither-nor' and 'indifferent' categories (Niedermayer 1995: 55).

11. I wish here to thank Lieven de Winter for his insistence that I don't consider expressed ambivalence as equivalent to ambivalence defined in terms of variation in responses. The analyses presented in this chapter vary little in purely numerical terms from earlier publications on this issue (Van Ingelgom 2010, 2012). However, the rest of past results are corroborated by these analyses.

12. The percentages can be found in Appendix One.

Figure 2.1: Evolution of support for EU membership, net support and the support index (1973–2002, EU8)

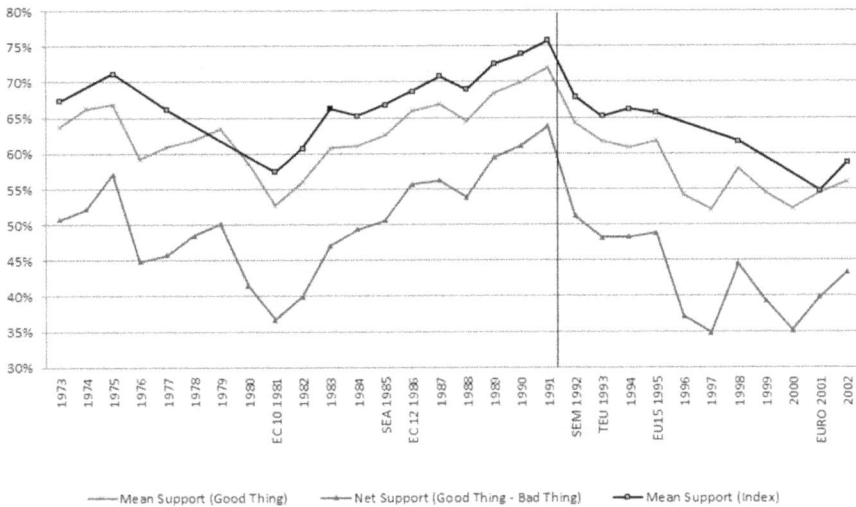

Data: Mannheim Eurobarometer Trend File (1973–2002).
Notes: EC10, EC12, EU 15 = enlargement of the EU to 10, 12 and 15 member states; SEA = Single European Act; SEM = Single European Market; TEU = Treaty on European Union; EURO = introduction of the Euro.

because a decrease in one category would mean an automatic increase in the other. Finally, the combination of these two questions gives a clearer perspective of the intensity of these attitudes, allowing us to distinguish two degrees of acceptance or opposition as well as to gauge how robust the median attitude is.

Figure 2.1 charts the evolution of traditional indicators of support and net support for European integration between 1973 and 2002, as well as the evolution of the index of support for the eight countries studied here. The average support indicator reflects the average percentage of citizens who declare that 'our country's membership of the EU is a good thing'. Net support is calculated by subtracting the respondents who declare that their country's membership is a bad thing from those who think it is a good thing. Finally the evolution of my index is calculated using the sum of the percentages of the 'strong support' and 'moderate support' categories.

As we can see in Figure 2.1, the support index follows almost exactly the same curve as the indicators of average support and net support that are generally used. This enables us to validate it as an indicator of support. More specifically, we can see the existence of the permissive consensus discussed by Léon Lindberg and Stuart Scheingold (Lindberg and Scheingold 1970) before 1991 and the trends of the three indicators after this year reflect the widely accepted story of its breakdown. At the beginning of the 1970s, a little more than half of the citizens of the original member-states supported the European integration process. In 1973, 63.5 per cent considered that their country's membership of the then European Community was a good thing. But, following the petrol crises in 1974 and 1981 and Greece's membership in the same year, the level of support was at a low of 52.5 per cent. Average support then increased markedly until the beginning of the 1990s. These observations were predicted by functionalist theory and by economic models of European integration. These approaches supposed that, as European economies and trade became increasingly interconnected, support for integration would increase. This is how the peak of support for integration at the end of the 1980s has been interpreted (Eichenberg and Dalton 2007). Early in 1991, average support was 20 per cent above the average observed before the adoption of the Single European Act, increasing from 52.5 per cent in 1981 to 72 per cent in 1991. Concerning the ratification of the Maastricht Treaty, if we compare citizens' support between 1991 and 1993, just before and just after Maastricht, we can clearly see a decline in the consensus – where this is defined in terms of average support. The European average for the eight countries analysed dropped from 72 per cent to 61.5 per cent during this period. The same is true for the indicator of net support, which drops from 61 per cent in 1991 to 48 per cent in 1993. The end of the permissive consensus model was widely proclaimed, as a result of the evolution of these indicators of support (Franklin, Marsch and McLaren 1994; Niedermayer and Sinnott 1995). In the next section, I will provide a systematic analysis of this interpretation.

An analysis in terms of average support

In order to systematically identify the changes in the distribution of attitudes towards European integration over time, the means of the new indicator of support have been calculated for each country for each year.[13] The values are coded from -2 (for strong opposition) to 2 (for strong support); as a result the mean varies between -2 and 2. Figure 2.2 presents the evolution of averages of this index of support for European integration between 1973 and 2002.

The average for the eight countries together shows an evolution that is similar to that described above, falling from 1.11 in 1991 to 0.53 in 2001. Although the overall average remains positive throughout the period under consideration, it masks different national realities and points to the importance of the national variable already emphasised (*see* Chapter One). Thus in 1973, just as the German average peaked at 1.38, the British average was scarcely at -0.31.

In order to conduct a systematic study of the evolution in the average over time, a linear regression analysis (OLS regression) was performed for the eight

---

13. These figures can be found in Appendix One. The variance and the kurtosis were also calculated; I will come back to these below.

Figure 2.2: Evolution of (national) means of the index of support for European integration (1973–2002, EU8)

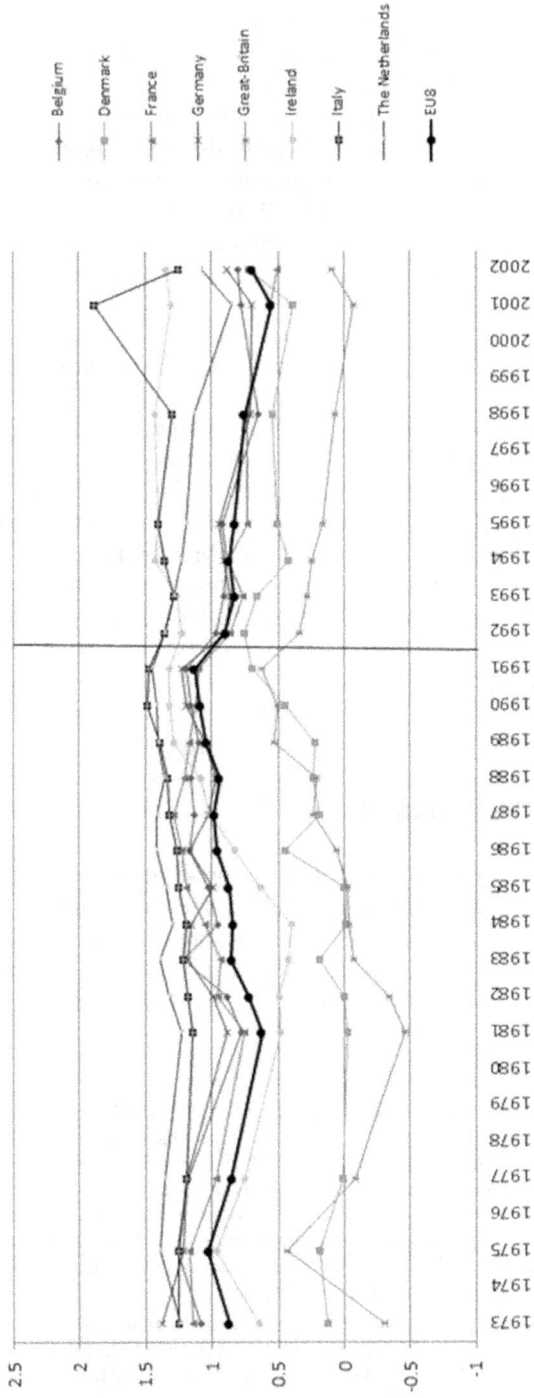

Source: Mannheim Eurobarometer Trend File (1973–2002).

countries, both individually and at an aggregate level. This analysis allows observing average annual changes. The model, which is taken from Down and Wilson, permits us to compare changes in the distribution, as well as the average annual changes in distribution of data, before and after the Maastricht Treaty (Down and Wilson 2008: 33). Logically, the regression analysis constrains the data with a view to specifically testing the hypothesis of a break in the permissive consensus following Maastricht.[14] My analysis aims to provide a complementary perspective to that offered by Downs and Wilson in the original model, by proposing a dependent variable that is substantially different from the one they used. The equation below was estimated for each country by linear regression, using the mean as the dependent variable:

$$\text{Mean} = \alpha + \beta 1 \text{ Year} + \beta 2 \text{ Maastricht} + \beta 3 \text{ Maastricht x Year} + \varepsilon$$

The variable 'Year' is a trend variable, coded as the year of analysis minus 1970. The variable 'Maastricht' is a dummy variable, coded 0 for each year after 1992 and 1 for year prior to 1991. In undertaking this, the data are thus constrained in order to test the hypothesis of a rupture in the evolution of attitudes following the events of Maastricht. The variable 'Maastricht x Year' introduces interaction between the two preceding variables. More specifically the coefficient $\beta 1$ corresponds to the average annual change in the dependent variable before the events of Maastricht. A positive coefficient corresponds to a positive slope and thus an increase in average support. Inversely, a negative coefficient corresponds to a negative slope and thus to a decline in the dependent variable. The coefficient of the interaction variable $\beta 3$ represents the difference between the slopes before and after Maastricht. As a result, the slope of the post-Maastricht curve is equal to the sum of $\beta 1$ and $\beta 3$. The interpretation of the coefficient $\beta 2$ isn't used in this analysis.[15]

Looking at Table 2.2, we can see that in the pre-Maastricht era the average level of support ($\beta 1$) increases significantly each year in three countries, Denmark, Ireland and Great Britain. For the other countries, and for the eight overall, we observe no significant change, however. In the post-Maastricht era, the analysis shows a significant decline in the average level of support in France, the

---

14. This data constraint is indeed logically guided by the hypothesis that the authors set out to test, i.e. the breakdown of the permissive consensus. We will see below that the data can be constrained in other ways by using a structure in three time periods. The idea here is to test whether the situation that prevailed in the 1970s and which was described as a permissive consensus was still operating in the 1990s and beyond. Dividing the time into three periods responds to a different initial question, but also responds to a different evolution in the trend curves, which we can see more clearly because of this division into two points. Another way of dividing these periods is possible and, indeed, desirable, as we will see at the end of the chapter.

15. Technically, this figure corresponds to the difference between the constant of the model, α, which corresponds to the value expected of the dependent variable in 1970, calculated on the base of the pre-Maastricht slope, $\beta 1$, and the expected value of the dependent variable in 1970s calculated on the base of the post-Maastricht slope, the sum of $\beta 1$ and $\beta 3$ (Down and Wilson 2008).

Table 2.2: Analysis of means of the index of support for European integration (1973–2002, EU8)

Mean	Pre-Maastricht slope	Maastricht	Year X Maastricht	Constant	Post-Maastricht slope	N
	β1	β2	β3	A	β1+β3	
Belgium	0.002 (0.006)	0.294 (0.363)	-0.021 (0.015)	1.064** (0.093)	-0.019	21
Denmark	0.022* (0.009)	0.888 (0.497)	-0.030 (0.020)	-0.101 (0.127)	-0.008	21
France	0.008 (0.006)	0.607 (0.357)	-0.041* (0.014)	0.985** (0.091)	-0.033*	21
Germany	-0.008 (0.006)	-0.041 (0.341)	-0.005 (0.014)	1.228** (0.087)	-0.013	21
Great-Britain	0.036* (0.012)	1.402 (0.713)	-0.068* (0.029)	-0.393* (0.183)	-0.032*	21
Ireland	0.033* (0.012)	0.835 (0.709)	-0.028 (0.029)	0.378 (0.182)	0.005	21
Italy	0.013 (0.007)	-0.230 (0.395)	0.007 (0.016)	1.102** (0.101)	-0.002	21
The Netherlands	0.007 (0.003)	0.890** (0.191)	-0.045** (0.008)	1.259** (0.049)	-0.038**	21
EU8	0.012 (0.006)	0.739* (0.323)	-0.039* (0.013)	0.752** (0.083)	-0.027*	21

Data: Mannheim Eurobarometer Trend File (1973–2002) * $P < 0.05$ ** $P < 0.001$

Netherlands, Great Britain and for the eight countries on an aggregate level. These analyses thus partially support the thesis of the break in the permissive consensus and corroborate the results from older studies that indicate the average level of support was lower during the 1990s than during the previous period (Down and Wilson 2008; Eichenberg and Dalton 2007).

A play in three acts?

However, these analyses are based on the classic scenario discussed above, which distinguishes between pre- and post- Maastricht periods. If one observes this data over the long term, one is obliged to reconsider the extent of the break in the permissive consensus. Returning to Figures 2.1 and 2.2 enables us to see that the level of support observed coming out of the process of ratifying the Maastricht Treaty is not substantially different from that observed at the beginning of the 1980s. I thus suggest an alternative organisation of the time periods, structuring the analysis around three periods roughly covering the last three decades of the data file, that is, 1973 to 1981, from 1982 to 1991 and from 1992 to 2002. This organisation of time periods allows us to use the data in new ways, in order to test the hypothesis of the permissive consensus differently. In this, I am looking to see whether the dominant situation in the 1970s, the period during which the permissive consensus model was developed, is different from that observed in the post-Maastricht period and which supposedly signalled the end of this model of citizens' attitudes.

Table 2.3 reports the mean of means of each comparative period, as well as the difference observed between the periods and the significance of the *F-Test* used. In order to make the results here more readable, I have underlined the differences in average that show a significant (*F-Test*) drop in the average of averages between the two periods.

If we compare the first period to the second, we can see a significant change in terms of the level of average support. The comparison of the second and third periods, just before and just after Maastricht, indicates a significant decline in the level of average support in Germany (-0.25), in Belgium (-0.25), in France (-0.40) and in the Netherlands (-0.22). On the other hand, a significant increase can be observed in Denmark (+0.33) and in Ireland (+0.46). No significant change was observed in Italy or in Great Britain. Although the decline in the average level of support was also significant for the eight countries at the aggregate level (-0.17), only half of these countries actually presented a sharp decline in average support between the decade preceding Maastricht and that following it.

The comparison between the first period (the closest to the origins of the permissive consensus model) and the third period (after Maastricht), shows that most of the countries studied showed a level of support that was not significantly below that of the 1970s. It is only in Germany (-0.32), Belgium (-0.23) and France (-0.29) that the difference between the two periods is both negative and significant. On the other hand, Denmark (+0.49) and Ireland (+0.63) both show averages that are significantly higher for the post-Maastricht period compared with the permissive consensus period.

Thus, this consensus in terms of the level of support doesn't seem to have totally disappeared today as a large majority of citizens in the eight oldest countries support the process as much as they did in the 1970s. Only three countries, Germany, Belgium and France, saw a significant drop in support compared to the situation at the beginning of the 1970s. The importance of the Franco-German pair cannot be neglected here, particularly in understanding the hypothesis of a stronger polarisation of opinions. In the Danish, English and Irish cases, the permissive consensus did not exist when they entered the Union, so there is no reason to talk of its breakdown.

One can thus tentatively conclude that, although one can't deny the impact of Maastricht on the European political system, both on an institutional level and in terms of citizens' attitudes, it seems to have slowed the enthusiasm for integration rather than 'broken' the permissive consensus. This echoes the results obtained by Richard Eichenberg and Russell Dalton (Eichenberg and Dalton 2007). In an analysis of Europe overall, these authors demonstrated a general tendency for

Table 2.3: Analysis of the means of the index of support for European integration (1973–2002, EU8)

Means	Mean of means (by ten-year period)			F-Test (Anova)			N
	µ P1	µ P2	µ P3	P2-P1	P3-P2	P3-P1	
Belgium	1.07	1.09	0.84	0.02	**-0.25****	**-0.23***	21
Denmark	0.08	0.24	0.57	0.16	**0.33***	**0.50****	21
France	1.01	1.12	0.72	0.11	**-0.40***	**-0.29***	21
Germany	1.16	1.09	0.84	-0.07	**-0.25****	**-0.32***	21
Great Britain	-0.10	0.17	0.16	0.27	-0.01	0.26	21
Ireland	0.71	0.88	1.34	0.17	**0.46***	**0.63****	21
Italy	1.21	1.31	1.41	0.10	-0.10	0.20	21
The Netherlands	1.30	1.38	1.16	0.08	**-0.22****	-0.14	21
UE8	0.84	0.94	0.78	0.10	**-0.16***	-0.07	21

Note: P1 = 1973–1981, P2 = 1982–1991, P3 = 1992–2002
Data: Mannheim Eurobarometer Trend File (1973–2002) * $P < 0.05$ ** $P < 0.001$

support for integration to be high before Maastricht and to decline significantly between 1991 and 1992, followed by a period with no significant change. These authors suggest that, although the aggregate level of support is lower in the 1990s than it was the previous decade, it remains higher in most countries than it was in the 1970s (Eichenberg and Dalton 2007). Similarly, this initial analysis also confirms Ian Down and Carole J. Wilson's results on the basis of another indicator (Down and Wilson 2008: 34–6). Finally, constraining the data by dividing it into three time periods corresponds better to the evolutions that we observe in Figures 2.2 and 2.3.

Towards the polarisation of European public opinion?

In addition to the breakdown of the permissive consensus, defined as a drop in average support, another understanding of the end of this consensus can be found in the literature. This corresponds to an increase in disagreement within the population (Down and Wilson 2008). At the heart of thinking about the politicisation of the European integration process is the question of the polarisation of opinions (De Wilde 2011; De Wilde and Zürn 2012), which supposes an increase in the percentage of so-called 'eurosceptic' citizens. The polarisation of citizens' attitudes as a corollary to the politicisation of the process is thus at the heart of major debates in European studies today (De Wilde and Zürn 2012). The hypothesis of an increase in the polarisation of opinions thus needs to be tested. In this section of the chapter, I will test this hypothesis using the support index and data up until 2002. As already mentioned, the final section of this chapter will broaden these results on a geographical but also temporal level, using more recent data and providing a perspective from 2011.

The polarisation of attitudes: an essential conceptual and empirical clarification

Two elements must be analysed in order to understand the attitudes of citizens towards European integration in this context: the average level of support, a sign of the permission accorded to the elites as to the pursuit of integration, and the degree of agreement or disagreement reflecting the consensus or dissensus in the population. At a time when the polarisation of the European political order and, by extension, the increase in euroscepticism are at attracting a lot of public attention, an analysis of the dispersal of attitudes is central (Down and Wilson 2008).

In this perspective, one can easily imagine that the drop in support observed in the post-Maastricht era reflects a significant division of European public opinion, as commonly assumed, in particular by the constraining dissensus model. The decrease in support would thus be accompanied by an increase in opposition, in other words, more euroscepticism. In this case, attitudes would indeed be more dispersed, the distribution of opinion even becoming bimodal, suggesting a veritable decline in consensus and, in the most extreme case, a polarisation of European opinion (De Wilde and Zürn 2012). Concretely, this polarisation would be the result of a shift of part of these positive responses to negative categories, generally considered as regrouping eurosceptic citizens.[16] To this extent, it is doubtful that the average level of support is really a useful measure for observing polarisation. Indeed, a drop in the average level of support could be accompanied by an increase, a decrease or even no change at all in the dispersal of attitudes. It is necessary to check whether a decrease in categories of support leads to an increase in categories of opposition and thus to more polarisation. This displacement could also be to the advantage of a neutral category, in which case it would be a mistake to talk of polarisation of opinion. On this point, the construction of our index to include a median category reflecting an attitude of indecision and indifference is indeed fundamental.

In this second section, we will be studying the distribution of attitudes more fundamentally based on their dispersal (Down and Wilson 2008). The average has been very widely used by specialists in European studies. Indeed, with the notable exception of a recent article by Down and Wilson (2008), few studies directly addressed the question of polarisation in empirical terms. In light of this research, I propose to use the classic distribution and dispersal methods of variance and kurtosis.[17] The distribution of public opinion faced with a particular question

---

16. Remember that I have decided to not include the 'don't know' answers in my analysis. However, I can emphasise the fact that this exclusion has no bearing on the results given that this category declines over the period that is of interest here (*see* Figure 2.6).

17. These measures were also used by Ian Down and Carole Wilson, in their 2008 article, which was inspired by Paul di Maggio, John Evans and Bethany Bryson's article of 1996, which I referred to in reference to the detailed explanation of variance and kurtosis. In a very different domain, that of the comparison of legislative production, Frank R. Baumgartner and Bryan D. Jones and the team working with Sylvain Brouard in France also suggest we use the measure of kurtosis to observe the 'pointiness' of a distribution and, in so doing, observe the dynamic of legislative agendas (Brouard *et al.* 2009).

is indeed a measure of polarisation because the opinions expressed are diverse, differentiated in terms of their content and relatively well balanced between the extremes of the range of opinions (di Maggio *et al.* 1996). In replicating the analysis proposed by these authors with the new indicator and in enlarging the analyses to the periodisation constructed in previous section, I demonstrate how the traditional measures of dispersion can be useful. The empirical object of this chapter thus allows us to document the methodological stakes in using the measures of variance and kurtosis to study opinions and attitudes – stakes that transcend European studies. The relevance and validity of these measures can be found in the ability of these analyses to shed light on the growing non-polarisation of attitudes towards the EU. This evolution is in fact difficult to observe with other measures and has, consequently, been neglected in spite of its importance.

Dispersion as an indicator of polarisation

Variance is the most common measure of dispersion.[18] Polarisation is defined here as an increase in variance over time (Down and Wilson 2008). This measure is affected by the proportion of responses expressed, because it represents the sum of deviations from the mean. The greater the dispersal of opinion, or even polarisation of opinions in extreme cases, the more the variance increases. Variance is a good measure of dispersion but it does not give us an idea of the shape of the distribution – particularly its 'pointiness' (Brouard *et al.* 2009: 397). Kurtosis,[19] on the other hand, is both sensitive to the proportion of responses at both extremes and able to also take into account the movement of the distribution from the centre towards the extremes and *vice versa*. Where variance enables us to analyse the dispersion of attitudes, kurtosis enables us to evaluate the movement from or towards bi-modality in the distribution (Down and Wilson 2008). Indeed, the polarisation of public opinion can be seen when different responses to a single question form two distinct poles, with the modalities between these poles remaining relatively rare.

In concrete terms, a normal distribution (in the statistical sense), has a kurtosis of 0. A distribution that is pointier than normal, suggesting a high degree of consensus and thus a weak polarisation, would have a positive kurtosis. Inversely, a distribution that is flatter than normal would have a negative kurtosis, -1.3 in the case of a perfectly flat distribution. Finally, for a distribution that is purely bi-modal, where the population is perfectly polarised on a particular question, the kurtosis would be close to -2. In case of bi-modality, a situation of polarisation or perfect dissensus in public opinion would be represented by a kurtosis value between -1.3 and -2 coupled with a high variance. Perfect consensus, on the other hand, would be represented by a variance near zero and a kurtosis tending towards infinity. Combining the measures of variance and kurtosis allows us to document the situation and evolution of citizens' attitudes regarding European integration in

---

18. The formula for the variance is: $s^2 = \sum (x-\mu)^2/N-1$, where μ is the mean.

19. The formula for kurtosis is: $K = \sum (x-\mu)4/N\sigma4-3$, where μ is the mean and σ the standard deviation. Subtracting three enables to ensure that the normal distribution takes the value zero.

terms of distribution and polarisation. This is illustrated by the examples from our support index in Figure 2.3.

The case of the Netherlands in 1991 combined a low variance (0.63) and a high positive kurtosis (4.39), a configuration that is close to consensus, whereas the Danish case in 1973 illustrates a situation of dissensus combining a large variance (2.85) with a negative kurtosis, below -1.3 (-1.68). The situation in France in 2002, with a kurtosis between 0 and -1.3, reflects a distribution that is characteristic of non-polarisation of attitudes, where the indifferent and undecided categories include the mode of the distribution.

The advantage of using variance and kurtosis can be seen in the fact that the distributions of opinion in Denmark in 1973 and France in 2002 have means that are relatively low and similar – 0.51 and 0.31 respectively. In these two cases, using only an average might lead us to conclude that there was, respectively, an absence and a breakdown in the permissive consensus, especially since it is well known that Denmark remains, along with Great Britain, among the most 'eurosceptic' countries. Yet the distribution of French citizens' attitudes in 2002 and those of the Danish in 1973 reflect vastly different realities. In the former case the distribution of attitudes can be described as non-polarised, whilst in the latter a clear polarisation of attitudes is apparent. In Denmark, debates about membership were particularly intense during this period and this can be seen in the strong cleavage in Danish citizens' attitudes to the European question at the time.

Figure 2.3: Illustration of measures of variance and kurtosis (index)

Consensus **The Netherlands** **(1991)**	**Dissensus** **Denmark** **(1973)**	**Non-polarised** **distribution** **France** **(2002)**

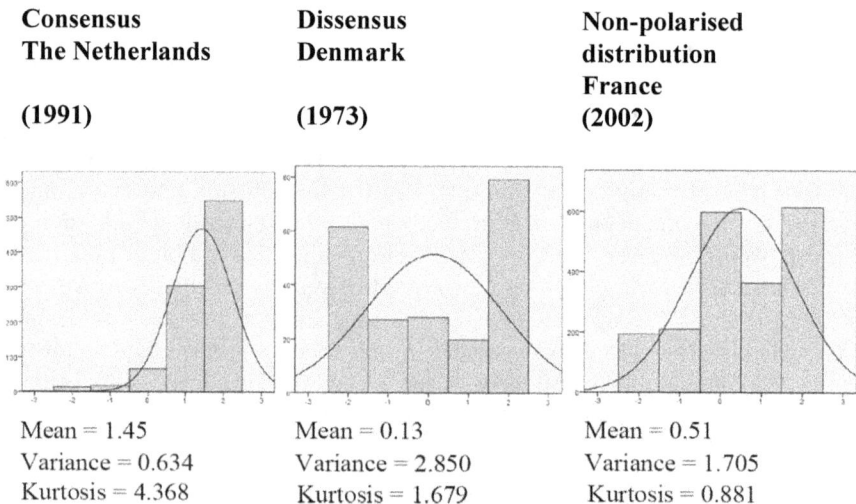

Mean = 1.45	Mean = 0.13	Mean = 0.51
Variance = 0.634	Variance = 2.850	Variance = 1.705
Kurtosis = 4.368	Kurtosis = 1.679	Kurtosis = 0.881

Source: author's own calculation; Mannheim Eurobarometer Trend File (1973–2002).

An analysis in terms of variance and kurtosis

I have calculated the variance and the kurtosis for each year and for each country between 1973 and 2002. Figures 2.4 and 2.5 illustrate the evolution of these measures over time.[20] The variance and kurtosis curves are similar in the post-Maastricht era, showing remarkable lack of change. As was the case for the mean, a regression model has also been estimated for each of the eight countries individually, as well as at the aggregate level. As a reminder, the equation is as follows:

Variance/kurtosis:

$$= \alpha + \beta 1 \text{ Year} + \beta 2 \text{ Maastricht} + \beta 3 \text{ Maastricht x Year} + \varepsilon$$

I will demonstrate here, using the measures of variance and kurtosis, that the post-Maastricht situation is in fact much more complex that suggested by the constraining dissensus model. Let's begin with the variance.

In the period leading up to the ratification of the Maastricht Treaty, six out of our eight countries (Belgium (-0.01), the Netherlands (-0.01), Italy (-0.01), Denmark (-0.02), Ireland (-0.05) and Great Britain (-0.04)) showed a significant annual drop in the variance of attitudes towards integration according to the index used here ($\beta 1$). In other words, in every country except France and Germany, as well as at the aggregate level (-0.02), one can see a decrease in the dispersal of opinions between 1973 and 1991. These results partially confirm the hypothesis of the permissive consensus and its breakdown, but only for the countries where this consensus was established at the beginning of the 1970s. In the Danish, English and Irish cases, speaking of a break in the permissive consensus is nonsensical, given that this consensus did not exist. However, if one cannot deny the significant drop in support and the increase in the variance that accompanied it following the events of the early 1990s, I can point out that these elements did not tend towards an increase in dissensus, marked by an increase in the variance (($\beta 1+\beta 3$) in the post-Maastricht period. Indeed, only in the Netherlands (0.04) and Italy (0.01) is there a strong positive slope in the variance for this period. In other words in the post-Maastricht era, in the majority of countries studied here, no significant change in the variance occurred.

More precisely, if one compares the first and second periods, the variance decreased significantly in the Netherlands (-0.14), Italy (-0.14) and Great Britain (-0.37) and increased significantly in Germany (+0.17). Germany remains an isolated case. If one then considers the shift from the second to the third period (pre- and post- Maastricht) one can see that the average annual variance increases substantially in the five oldest member states, as well as for the eight countries together (+0.19). It decreases in Denmark (-0.19), however, and in Ireland (-0.66). These results confirm those presented above in the regression analysis, and also partly confirm the results of Down and Wilson.

---

20. Appendix One contains the calculations for the values of variance and kurtosis for each year, each country and for the eight countries considered together at aggregate level.

Figure 2.4: Evolution of the variances of the index of support for European integration (1973–2002, EU8)

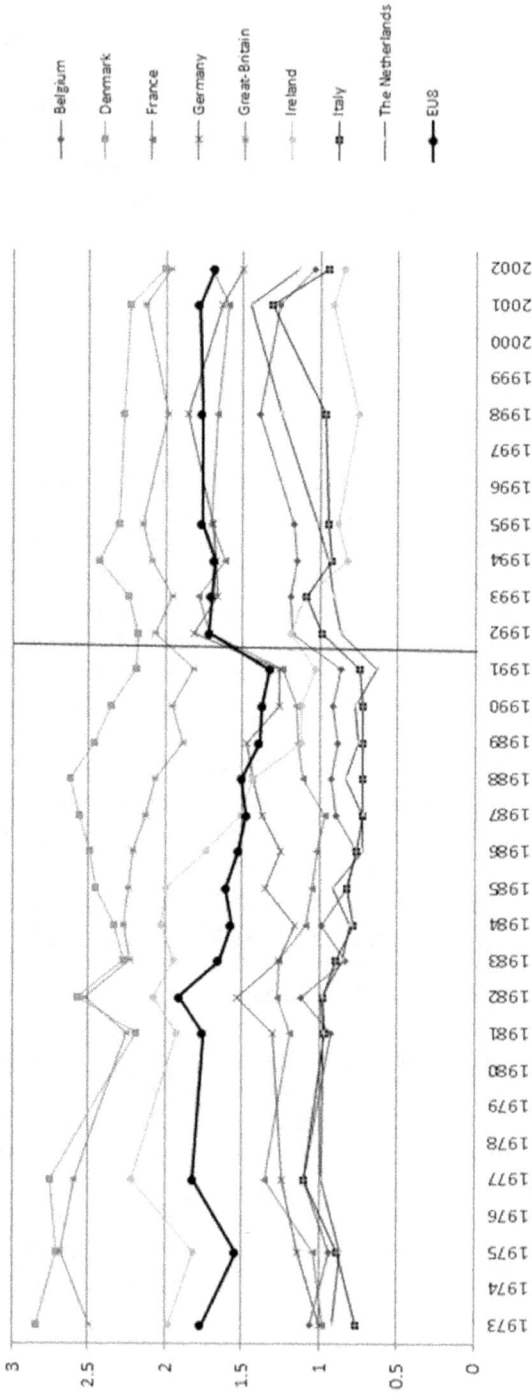

Source: Mannheim Eurobarometer Trend File (1973–2002); Author's own computation based on data from Mannhein Eurobarometer Trend File (1973–2002).

Table 2.4: Analysis of the variances of the index of support for European integration (1973–2002, EU8)

Variance	Year (Pre-Maastricht gradient) β1	Maastricht β2	Year X Maastricht β3	Constant A	Post-Maastricht gradient β1+β3	Mean of variances per ten-year period			F-Test (Anova)			N
						μ P1	μ P2	μ P3	P2-P1	P3-P2	P3-P1	
Belgium	-0.011* (0.005)	0.141 (0.280)	0.010 (0.011)	1.077** (0.072)	-0.001	1.01	0.90	1.20	-0.10	0.29**	0.19*	21
Denmark	-0.023* (0.008)	-0.109 (0.444)	0.006 (0.018)	2.803** (0.174)	-0.017	2.63	2.43	2.24	-0.20	-0.19*	-0.39*	21
France	0.001 (0.006)	0.752* (0.315)	-0.008 (0.013)	1.118** (0.081)	-0.007	1.14	1.13	1.68	-0.01	0.55**	0.55**	21
Germany	0.014* (0.006)	1.022* (0.333)	-0.030* (0.013)	1.090** (0.085)	-0.016*	1.17	1.33	1.68	0.17	0.35**	0.51**	21
Great-Britain	-0.043* (0.005)	-0.713* (0.301)	0.041* (0.012)	2.828** (0.077)	-0.002*	2.50	2.13	2.05	-0.37	-0.08	-0.45**	21
Ireland	-0.054* (0.012)	-0.896 (0.681)	0.031 (0.027)	2.446** (0.174)	-0.023	1.99	1.60	0.93	-0.39	-0.67**	-1.05**	21
Italy	-0.013* (0.006)	-0.284 (0.322)	0.024 (0.013)	1.005** (0.082)	0.011*	0.93	0.79	1.03	-0.14	0.24**	0.09	21
The Netherlands	-0.014* (0.005)	-1.141** (0.271)	0.059** (0.011)	1.030** (0.069)	0.045*	0.94	0.80	1.09	-0.14	0.29*	0.15	21
EU8	-0.023** (0.005)	-0.236 (0.309)	0.025 (0.012)	1.899** (0.079)	0.002	1.72	1.53	1.73	-0.19	0.20*	0.01	21

Source: Mannheim Eurobarometer Trend File (1973–2002); Author's own computation based on data from Mannheim Eurobarometer Trend File (1973–2002).

If we compare the 1970s to the period following the ratification of the Maastricht Treaty, the average variance only increases significantly in France (+0.55), in Belgium (+0.19) and in Germany (+0.51). This shows that there is an increase in the dispersal of citizens' attitudes in these countries, which could be interpreted as a polarisation of these attitudes. I will come back to this interpretation below. On the other hand, the dispersal decreases in Denmark (0.40), Ireland (-1.05) and in Great Britain (-0.45), where the average variance was lower in the post-Maastricht era than it was during the permissive consensus period. In the case of the Netherlands and Italy, no significant change occurred during these periods.

Thus it is only in three out of the eight cases that one can see an increase in the dispersal of opinions measured by an increase in the variance after Maastricht compared with the 1970s. At the same time, for the same number of countries, three out of eight, one can see an inverse trend, a decrease in the variance between the two periods; an observation which once again throws into doubt the thesis of the development of dissensus amongst citizens regarding the integration process. To sum up, the general trend, measured by the evolution of the variance alone, is of an increase in consensus in the period that preceded Maastricht, followed by a significant decline. This is observed by an average variance that is significantly higher in the post-Maastricht era (Down and Wilson 2008).

However, here we are also concerned with the value of kurtosis, in order to gauge the 'pointiness' or the bi-modality of the distribution. Looking at Table 3.4, we can see that the results for the kurtosis essentially reflect those of the variance. Indeed, a significant increase (or decrease) in the variance corresponds, with a few exceptions, to a significant decrease (increase) in kurtosis.[21] In five countries out of eight, and for the countries at the aggregate level, the slope of kurtosis is positive and significant in the pre-Maastricht period. This confirms the trend towards more consensus within these European populations. In France, Belgium and Germany on the other hand, this evolution is not statistically significant.

It is nevertheless important to be careful when interpreting these results because the measure of kurtosis does not refer to a linear evolution, which would extend from dissensus (for the negative values) to consensus (for the positive values). As emphasised, a kurtosis between 0 and -1.3 reflects a distribution of attitudes characterised by non-polarisation; in other words, it reflects a flat distribution in which the median category is particularly important. This kurtosis value is thus at the heart of the issue here, because it reflects a situation in which the undecided and indifferent category increases. Keeping this in mind, let's now analyse the kurtosis values according to the three distinct time periods.

Using these three time periods provokes a series of observations, which significantly nuance the increase in polarisation of opinions in the post-

---

21. These examples are linked to the fact that, unlike Ian Down and Carole J. Wilson, we are working here with five categories and not three, which allows for a greater dispersal of opinion. Thus, in our case, the increase in dispersal is not necessarily associated with an increase in bimodality and thus a decrease in kurtosis (Down and Wilson 2008: 42).

Figure 2.5: Evolution of kurtosis of the index of support for European integration (1973–2002, EU8)

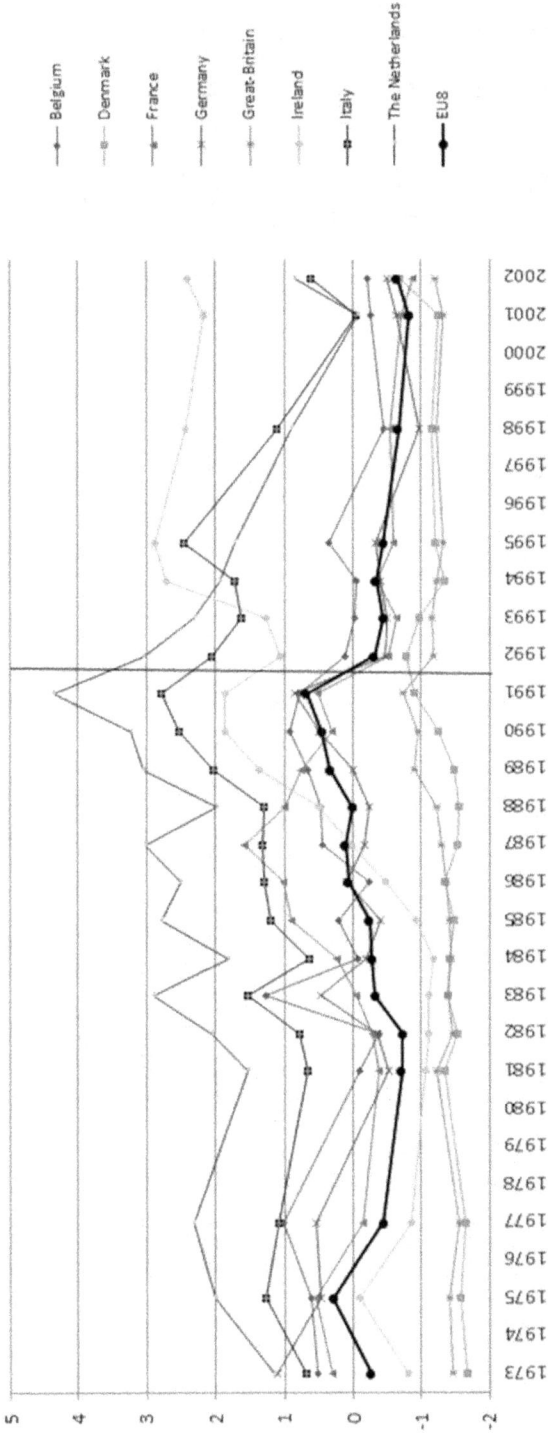

Legend:
- Belgium
- Denmark
- France
- Germany
- Great-Britain
- Ireland
- Italy
- The Netherlands
- EU8

Source: Mannheim Eurobarometer Trend File (1973–2002); Author's own computation based on data from Mannheim Eurobarometer Trend File (1973–2002).

Table 2.5: Evolution and analysis of kurtosis for the index of support for European integration (1973–2002, EU8)

Kurtosis	Year (Pre-Maastricht gradient) β1	Maastricht β2	Year X Maastricht β3	Constant A	Post-Maastricht Gradient β1+β3	Mean of kurtosis (per ten-year period)			F-Test (Anova)			N
						μ P1	μ P2	μ P3	P2-P1	P3-P2	P3-P1	
Belgium	0.002 (0.022)	0.614 (1.276)	-0.043 (0.051)	0.415 (0.327)	-0.041	0.52	0.41	-0.07	-0.11	-0.48*	-0.59*	21
Denmark	0.023* (0.010)	0.602 (0.563)	-0.020 (0.023)	-1.758** (0.144)	0.003	-1.56	-1.39	-1.05	0.17	0.33*	0.51*	21
France	0.043 (0.022)	0.322 (1.282)	-0.073 (0.052)	0.141 (0.328)	-0.030	0.08	0.60	-0.61	0.51	-1.20**	-0.69*	21
Germany	-0.025 (0.022)	-0.492 (1.249)	0.005 (0.050)	0.503 (0.320)	-0.020	0.40	0.06	-0.54	-0.34	-0.60*	-0.94*	21
Great Britain	0.033** (0.007)	0.629 (0.419)	-0.038* (0.017)	-1.720** (0.107)	-0.005*	-1.42	-1.21	-1.23	0.21	-0.02	0.19*	21
Ireland	0.131* (0.041)	2.006 (2.358)	-0.053 (0.095)	-1.925* (0.604)	-0.078	-0.70	0.08	2.13	0.79	2.05**	2.84**	21
Italy	0.081* (0.025)	6.039** (1.445)	-0.268** (0.058)	0.254 (0.370)	-0.185*	0.93	1.54	1.36	0.61	-0.18	0.43	21
The Netherlands	0.108* (0.027)	6.956** (1.555)	-0.352** (0.063)	0.997* (0.398)	-0.244**	1.75	2.77	1.52	1.02*	-1.24*	-0.23	21
EU8	0.041* (0.016)	1.256 (0.909)	-0.084* (0.037)	-0.632* (0.233)	0.043*	-0.28	0.01	-0.52	0.29	-0.53*	-0.24	21

Source: Mannheim Eurobarometer Trend File (1973–2002); Author's own computation based on data from Mannhein Eurobarometer Trend File (1973–2002).

Maastricht era. The values that are underlined show a significant decrease in the measure studied here: they alone corroborate the thesis of the breakdown of the permissive consensus in the post-Maastricht era, defined in terms of an increase in polarisation. One can see that they do not concern all of the cases. When one moves from the second to the third period, as the variance increases significantly in France, Belgium, the Netherlands and German, the average kurtosis decreases, confirming an increase in dissensus between these periods. Inversely, although the average variance increased in the Italian case following Maastricht, this result is not confirmed for the average level of kurtosis. Denmark and Ireland, on the other hand, show an increase in the average kurtosis (+0.33 and +2.05) between these periods. In other words, for these two countries, citizens' attitudes were less polarised after Maastricht than in the decade before, which is confirmed by the results of the analysis conducted here. Finally if we compare the 1970s, a decade at the heart of the permissive consensus model, to the post-Maastricht period, the hypothesis of a greater polarisation of citizens' attitudes towards the integration process is only confirmed in three out of eight cases: in France (-0.69), in Belgium (-0.59) and in Germany (-0.94). In the Netherlands and Italy the average kurtosis is not significantly different between these two periods, which is also the case for the eight countries aggregated.

Moreover, it is important to emphasise the values of the kurtosis in order to describe the evolution of the 'pointiness' of the distribution. In particular, regarding France, Belgium and Germany, it necessary to draw attention to the fact that, although the kurtosis decreases significantly between the two periods considered here, the average level of kurtosis reveals a situation that is far from bimodal and, thus, far from polarised. As we saw above, in the instance of a polarised situation the kurtosis would be between -1.3 and -2. However, here we observe that the average kurtosis levels were -0.61, -0.07 and -0.54 (respectively France, Belgium and Germany) for the post-Maastricht period (*see* Figure 2.3 for France in 2002), compared to 0.08, 0.41 and 0.39 for the 1970s. We also see the reinforcement of the median category over time, the indifferent *and* undecided position, which, for 2002, represents 28.7 per cent in France, 24 per cent in Germany and 27.8 per cent in Belgium. This leads to a flattening of the distribution (and a kurtosis close to -1.3), and not a situation close to bi-modality (a kurtosis between -1.3 and -2). In France, in 2002, the indifferent *and* undecided category covers a percentage similar to the strong support category, which is at 31.7 per cent (*see* Figure 2.3). On the other hand, in the Danish, Irish and British cases we see a more consensual situation in the post-Maastricht era than in the 1970s (*see* Figure 2.3 for Denmark in 1973). Thus, although Denmark and Great Britain had an average level of kurtosis below -1.3 in the 1970s, suggesting a certain trend towards the polarisation of public opinion, the value of their kurtosis is above the -1.3 mark. In Great Britain, in 2002 the neutral position on the index also included the mode, surpassing in number the category of fervent opposition, which was previously the largest category within the British population.

As a result, in the period following Maastricht, none of the countries studied here had kurtosis levels below -1.3, which is the sign of a decrease in polarisation of opinions. The events of Maastricht did therefore not bring about a greater polarisation in opinions over this period. Here, I echo the conclusions of Down and Wilson when they affirm that:

> Maastricht did not initiate a new trend of increasing dissensus in the member states. Maastricht may have been system transforming, both in the sense that the prior trend towards increased consensus ended and disagreement sharply increased, but it did not establish a new trend. In almost all member states, there was no significant difference in the dispersion of attitudes in 2002 from that in 1992 (Down and Wilson 2008: 40–2).

The events of Maastricht led to a flattening of most of the national distributions (a tendency which was confirmed in the post-Maastricht era) but without polarisation of opinions (Down and Wilson 2008). Using different time periods and data constraints, these analyses have enabled me to demonstrate that the permissive consensus, which dominated in the 1970s, has not totally disappeared, although it has probably changed in nature (*see* Chapter Five).

These results put into question the thesis of the 'break' in the permissive consensus. Although one does observe a radical decrease in support after Maastricht, this was essentially to the advantage of the intermediary category indifferent *and* undecided and was not the result of a massive shift to the categories of opposition. Maastricht led to a flattening of the distribution and not a polarisation of opinions as suggested in the literature. Indeed, if one looks more closely at the distribution of opinions in 1973 and in 2002 (Table 2.6), one can see the reinforcement of the undecided *and* indifferent category for all the countries which saw a significant change in their distribution. From this perspective, one can see a convergence in the level of consensus/dissensus observed in the eight countries studied here.

Neither eurosceptic nor europhile

Following from the previous section, we can say that, although fewer Europeans declare support for the integration process, this does not mean that the European public has turned against integration as such; rather, citizens are displaying increasingly indifferent and undecided attitudes towards it. The lack of polarisation in the distribution of citizens' attitudes is indeed an overwhelming phenomenon in the post-Maastricht era, even more than euroscepticism, as the data show an increase in the percentage of those who classified themselves as undecided and indifferent. The thesis of a transition from the permissive consensus model towards that of the constraining dissensus is incomplete and the politicisation model, which is based on polarisation of opinions, also appears erroneous (De Wilde and Zürn 2012; Hooghe and Marks 2008). Although euroscepticism has attracted much attention in the post-Maastricht period, indifferent and undecided citizens seem to be 'off the radar' as a result of the interpretation of the breakdown of the permissive consensus. The problem is that the vast majority of studies on citizens' attitudes towards European integration don't take into account, as such,

Table 2.6: Indifferent and undecided attitudes towards European integration by country (1973–2002, EU8)

Indifferent and undecided	1973	2002	Percentage change 1973–2002
Belgium*	19.6	27.8	+8.2
Denmark*	12.2	14.3	+2.1
France*	19.7	28.7	+9.0
Germany*	15.0	24.0	+9.0
Great Britain*	16.6	27.2	+10.6
Ireland	15.4	9.9	-5.5
Italy	16.3	18.3	+2.0
The Netherlands	15.9	15.4	-0.5
EU8	16.7	23.8	+7.1

Source: Mannheim Eurobarometer Trend File (1973–2002); Author's own computation based on data from Mannhein Eurobarometer Trend File (1973–2002)

* F-Test significant – P3-P1

this intermediary category characterised by indecision and indifference.[22] Instead, they assimilate it to opposition to the process of integration. However, this chapter shows that, as support declines, the indifferent and undecided category increases, and does so more rapidly than the category of opposition to the process. How can this increase in non-polarisation be explained, contrasting as it does with the mainstream diptych 'end of permissive consensus/growing euroscepticism'? Are the indifferent and undecided citizens different from their eurosceptic or europhile counterparts? This section aims to take a first step in the direction of exploring the indifferent and undecided attitudes before turning to a qualitative exploration of this category (*see* Chapter Five).

Indifferent and undecided: some descriptive results

Now that I have assessed the levels of indifferent and ambivalent citizens in the wake of the Maastricht Treaty, I will look more closely at this category and its evolution over this specific period. First of all, it is useful to look at the distribution of indifferent and undecided attitudes over time and across countries. Table 2.7 uses the index to show the evolution of indifferent and undecided attitudes by member state after Maastricht, and to compare these attitudes to the evolution of the opposition categories of our index (moderate and strong).

---

22. Some authors have recently examined the question of the ambivalence of citizens' attitudes towards European integration. For a quantitative approach, refer to the work Marco Steenbergen and Catherine de Vries (de Vries 2013; de Vries and Steenbergen 2013) or Florian Stoeckel (Stoeckel 2013).

Table 2.7: Indifferent and undecided attitudes towards European integration by country (1991–2002, EU8)

Undecided and indifferent	1991	1992	1993	1994	1995	1998	2001	2002	% change 1991–2002	% change oppositions 1991–2002
Belgium	16.0	20.9	21.1	23.8	19.7	33.4	26.6	27.8	+11.8	+4.2
Denmark	11.1	10.7	12.4	12.6	14.3	13.3	17.9	14.3	+3.2	-2.6
France	15.5	18.5	18.6	20.0	21.8	21.0	26.8	28.7	+13.2	+10.3
Germany	13.2	15.0	20.6	18.4	15.8	18.2	24.2	24.0	+10.8	+4.0
Great Britain	17.3	19.5	21.7	20.7	20.6	25.5	25.3	27.2	+9.9	+11.3
Ireland	9.1	10.2	10.7	8.1	8.4	8.3	11.8	9.9	+0.8	-2.6
Italy	10.1	10.6	12.2	13.4	11.0	14.1	24.2	18.3	+8.2	+1.3
The Netherlands	5.4	7.1	8.5	10.9	9.6	10.9	18.6	15.4	+10.0	+5.5
EU8	13.5	15.3	17.7	17.8	16.8	19.2	24.4	23.8	+10.3	+6.7

Source: Mannheim Eurobarometer Trend File (1973–2002); Author's own computation based on data from Mannhein Eurobarometer Trend File (1973–2002)

Table 2.8: Occupations and indifferent and undecided attitudes (1991–2002, EU8)

Undecided and indifferent	1991	1992	1993	1994	1995	1998	2001	2002	% change 1991–2002	% change oppositions 1991–2002
Self-employed	14.6	14.7	16.8	16.3	15.5	20.0	21.2	22.4	+7.8	+0.1
Managers	10.2	12.3	12.3	12.9	10.7	14.2	20.2	17.2	+7.0	+5.5
White collars	12.7	17.5	17.7	18.1	12.4	22.7	27.5	25.3	+12.6	+3.7
Workers	18.6	20.1	23.4	23.3	22.4	23.5	28.8	29.0	+10.4	+5.9
Inactive	15.4	17.8	20.5	19.3	20.0	20.6	26.0	24.7	+9.3	+8.6

Source: Mannheim Eurobarometer Trend File (1973–2002); Author's own computation based on data from Mannhein Eurobarometer Trend File (1973–2002)

In terms of variation over time, changes in percentages by country between 1991 and 2002 reveal a common pattern of net increase in the percentage of citizens that are undecided and indifferent towards European integration. Interestingly, the national variation in the level of indecision and indifference across member states is less clear. The public in Belgium, Italy, the Netherlands or Germany are the most pro-European, yet they record almost the same levels of indecision and indifference as the most consistently sceptical countries such as Great Britain or Denmark. Table 2.7 shows that the decline in support for European integration was based on quite different processes in different states. In France and Great Britain, declining support was based both on an increase in indifference and indecision and on growing opposition. In Belgium, Germany, Italy and the Netherlands, this decline was mainly due to growing indifference and indecision and partly to growing opposition. A completely different evaluation occurred in Denmark and Ireland, where declining support was exclusively based on growing indifference and indecision, given that opposition to EU integration is declining.

In order to further characterise the increase in indifferent and ambivalent attitudes in the post-Maastricht period, I am also interested in how the non-polarised distribution of citizens' attitudes varies across social groups, given that professional occupation has been demonstrated to be a determinant of support and euroscepticism (Cautrès and Grunberg 2007; Fligstein 2008; Gabel 1998; Gabel and Palmer 1995; Hooghe and Marks 2004).

Table 2.8 shows that white-collar employees, workers and inactive people are the most undecided and indifferent towards European integration. Moreover, indifference and ambivalence in these groups underwent the biggest increase between 1991 and 2002, going up +12.6%, +10.4% and +9.3% respectively. The percentages of citizens who are opposed to European integration increased over the same period by only +3.7%, +5.9% and +8.6% in these specific categories, which are usually considered to be the most eurosceptic.[23]

Exploring the indifferent and undecided attitudes of European citizens: another aspect of euroscepticism?

I will now turn to the indifferent and undecided category of citizens, using a multinomial logistic regression in order to test whether this attitude is in fact different from eurosceptic attitudes towards the EU. Indeed, if these citizens do not differ from their eurosceptic counterparts then there is no point taking them into account, as their attitudes could be assimilated into the eurosceptic category. On the contrary, however, empirical results presented in this section show that euroscepticism cannot be defined simply as non-support. This is an important difference, given that I have demonstrated that one may simultaneously observe declining support, and/or relatively stable or slowly growing scepticism, along with increasing indifference and indecision.

In order to quantitatively explore this indifferent and undecided category in a precise manner, I first propose to use individual-level survey data from the Standard Eurobarometer 62.0 (Autumn 2004). The fieldwork was carried out between October and November 2004 and is the latest fieldwork available using the 'dissolution question', which allows us to use the index including the indifferent *and* undecided citizens. In order to verify the validity of the regression analysis after the Constitutional Treaty ratification process, we ran another model using the data of the Standard Eurobarometer 66.1 (Autumn 2006) and the membership

---

23. For a broader validation of these figures using qualitative data, *see* the chapter written by Sophie Duchesne in *Overlooking Europe* (Duchesne 2013).

variable as dependent variable ('EU integration is a bad thing' as reference category). The fieldwork was carried out between September and October 2006, making this latter the third Eurobarometer survey conducted after the rejection by France and the Netherlands. I find very similar results, both in terms of predicting the impact of independent variables and of the explanatory power of the model (Nagelkerke $R^2 = 0.469$).

The data were weighted to represent the national composition of the EU25. Leading to similar results, the model was also tested on the eight long-term countries (EU8). However, and in order to generalise from my argument, I present the results for EU25. I have selected the index of support combining the items of dissolution and membership as the dependent variable. In order to be able to run a regression model, I no longer distinguish between moderate and strong modalities of supporters and opponents. In 2004, supporters (moderate and strong) were coded 1 (60.9 per cent of the sample), the respondents who present indifferent and undecided attitudes were coded 0 (22.1 per cent), and opponents (moderate and strong) were coded -1 (reference category, 17 per cent). Respondents who answered 'I don't know' were excluded from the analysis.[24] Given the original coding and the distribution of responses on the dependent variable, multinomial logistic regression was chosen as the estimation technique.

The coding of independent variables can be summarised as follows.[25] The extensive literature on the determinants of public support for the EU suggests a number of variables that should be included in the models.[26] This body of research can be summarised by the finding of five major groups of predictors: economic calculation, political cues, national evaluation, cognitive mobilisation and identity (*see* Chapter One). Firstly, I included a set of socio-demographic characteristics for sex, age, type of occupation and education. Specifically, economic rationality will be controlled for by using occupation and education variables (Gabel 1998; Gabel and Palmer 1995). As political cues have been found to drive support for European integration (Hooghe and Marks 2005; Steenbergen, Edwards and de Vries 2007), I also checked for political orientation by introducing a three-position left–right scale variable. Based on previous studies that have demonstrated that support for the EU co-varies with trust in the national authorities (Anderson 1998; Franklin *et al.* 1994), I included a measure of confidence in the national government. I also included the question asking whether they tend to trust the European Union. On the evaluative level and in order to test the hypothesis of a clash between winners and losers of European integration (Fligstein 2008; Kriesi *et al.* 2008) as well as the individual competitiveness hypothesis (Gabel 1998), two items

---

24. As already underlined, our purpose is not to study unstructured attitudes but to analyse the indifferent and undecided attitudes as structured attitudes. Consequently, the 'I don't know' category is less interesting in this respect.

25. Descriptive statistics for all variables can be found in Appendix Two, as well as additional information about the construction of the variables.

26. A test of the wide range of macro-level explanations of EU support is beyond the scope of this study.

were used: a question related to the evaluation of the life they live and a question about expected change in the household's financial situation over the next twelve months, as an indirect measure of individual material well-being. Building on the literature on the effects of cognitive mobilisation and political sophistication on political support (Inglehart 1970a; 1970b; Janssen 1991), I included two variables measuring knowledge and sophistication regarding the EU. The question 'Using this scale, how much do you feel you know about the European Union, its policies, its institutions?' was also included, re-coded into a dichotomous variable. I also used agreement or disagreement with the statement 'I understand how the European Union works' as an indicator of political sophistication. In order to check for the predictive effect of politicisation, two dichotomous variables reflecting the level on the opinion leadership index were included. The identity variable was measured by the items related to national and European pride. Finally, to control for the effects of perceived cultural threat (McLaren 2002), a dummy variable associating the meaning of the EU with the loss of cultural identity was included. Country-dummies are included in the model to test the impact of different national contexts.

The model is statistically significant as Nagelkerke R^2 is 0.478. Table 2.9 reports the odds ratios of the independent variables. Values above 1 denote a positive association between two variables; values below 1 signify a negative association; and the value 1 denotes statistical independence. For instance, the odds ratio of 1.248 for confidence in national government indicates that the odds that an individual who trusts the national government demonstrates indifferent and undecided attitudes are 1.248 times as large as the odds that an individual who does not trust the national government is indifferent and undecided about European integration.

First of all, the qualifiers undecided and indifferent cannot be assumed to be the same as eurosceptics or critical Europeans. The statistically significant positive effects of the evaluation variables confirm that individuals who are satisfied with the life they lead and tend to trust the national government are more likely to support the EU (respectively, $e^b = 1.726$, $p<0.001$ and $e^b = 1.635$, $p<0,001$) but also more likely to be undecided and indifferent about it (respectively, $e^b = 1.256$, $p<0.05$ and $e^b = 1.248$, $p<0.05$). Indeed, the odds of an individual trusting the national government and being undecided and indifferent are 1.2 times as large as the odds of an individual not trusting his national government and displaying an indifferent and undecided attitude. The indifferent and undecided respondents are also more inclined to trust the EU ($e^b = 2.944$, $p<0.001$). Moreover, the odds that those who feel proud to be European present ambivalent and indifferent attitudes are 1.68 times greater than those who do not share this sentiment.

Individuals associating European integration with a loss of national identity are both less likely to support the EU ($e^b = 0.320$, $p<0.001$) and to be undecided and indifferent ($e^b = 0.694$, $p<0.001$) about it when compared to their eurosceptic counterparts. Similarly, expecting negative changes in the household's financial situation is negatively associated with support ($e^b = 0.655$, $p<0.001$) and with indifference and ambivalence ($e^b = 0.606$, $p<0.001$). Expecting positive changes

Table 2.9: Effects of individual-level variables on index of support towards the EU: multinomial logistic regression

Independent variables	Dependent variable: Index recoded in 3 positions (2004) (ref. category: 1 opponents' attitudes)	
	Supporters' attitudes	Undecided and indifferent attitude
Constant		
Sex: Male	**1.206****	**0.902***
Younger people (15–24 years old)	**1.297***	**1.520****
Older people (55 years old and over)	1.083	1.076
Managers	**2.089****	**1.365****
White collars	**1.599****	**1.350****
Workers	**1.230***	1.071
Inactives	**1.426***	1.116
Education : low	0.892	0.910
Education : high	**1.622****	1.005
Political scale : Right (7–10)	0.960	**0.821****
Political scale : Left (1–4)	**1.309****	0.960
Satisfied with the life they lead	**1.726****	**1.256****
Financial situation : better	**1.190****	0.961
Financial situation : worse	**0.655****	**0.606****
Tend to trust national government	**1.635****	**1.248****
Tend to trust European Union	**9.013****	**2.944****
EU subjective knowledge (Scale 6–10)	**0.831****	**0.505****
Understand how EU works	**1.416****	1.152
Leadership opinion index : low	**0.862****	1.123
Leadership opinion index : high	0.991	**0.869***
Proud to be national	**0.573****	1.132
Proud to be European	**6.617****	**1.684****
Loss of national identity	**0.320****	**0.694****
N	22 896	
N (reference category)	3887	
Nagelkerke R²	0.478	

Source: Standard Eurobarometer 62.0; Author's own computation based on data from Mannhein Eurobarometer Trend File (1973–2002)

Note: The figures reported are odds ratios (e^b); * $p < 0.1$ - ** $p < 0.05$ - *** $p < 0.001$. Country dummies were included in the model but the respective odds ratios are not shown.

in the household's financial situation is not a predictor of indifferent and undecided attitude, whereas it is a predictor for support (e^b = 1.190, $p<0.05$). This is also true for national pride, as the odds that individuals who are proud of their nationality support European integration are 0.573, less than individuals who do not express national pride – but this has no impact on indifferent and ambivalent attitudes. Following this, placing oneself on the right of the political scale is negatively associated with indifferent and undecided attitudes (e^b = 0.821, $p<0.05$) whereas placing oneself on the left is positively associated with support towards the EU (e^b = 1.309, $p<0.001$).

Furthermore, it is important to stress the key role played by politicisation, sophistication and cognitive mobilisation variables. Individuals who are more knowledgeable about the EU are less likely to support the EU ($e^b = 0.831, p<0.001$) and also less likely to adopt indifferent and undecided attitudes towards the EU (e^b = 0.505, $p<0.001$). These results lend support to the thesis that higher levels of information exposure, political awareness and sophistication may lead to increased critical attitudes (Ehin 2008). On the other hand, if understanding how the EU works has a positive effect on support (e^b = 1.420, $p<0.001$), it is not a significant predicator of indifferent and undecided positions. The role of politicisation is also present in terms of gender, given that being a man has a statistically significant negative effect on undecided attitudes (e^b = 0.902, $p<0.1$). In other words, women are more likely to adopt an indifferent and ambivalent position than men, whilst the latter are more likely to support the EU. Politicisation and knowledge variables thus have mixed effects, because better informed and more politicised citizens are more likely both to support and to reject the EU.

These results need to be further analysed, given that these regression analyses were only intended to be exploratory. However, it seems that it is not certain that the permissive attitude has evaporated. Indeed, citizens who are undecided and indifferent are more supportive of their national governments and have greater trust in the EU. At the same time, they are also more proud of being European than their eurosceptic counterparts, but they declare that they know less about the EU. Thus it seems quite clear that citizens with indifferent and undecided attitudes cannot be simply equated with opponents of European integration. They also distinguish themselves from the more supportive citizens, in particular on the measures of politicisation and cognitive mobilisation. As a result, one cannot consider that a decline in explicit support should be taken as a sign of an increase in euroscepticism, nor that the indifferent and undecided attitudes can be equated with the more supportive opinions. Borbála Göncz in her recent chapter, narrowing my own research on the East countries, arrives at a very similar conclusion, underlining that 'according to the results of the regression models it seems that the same drivers are determining whether one holds a positive or neutral opinion as opposed to negative ones'(Göncz 2013: 206).

Recent evolutions: using the 'neither/nor' category as a proxy

As the index was only available until 2004, and in order to get a better view of recent evolution, I now include the percentages by modalities for the classic and often-used membership item (for the EU) until 2011. By doing so, I propose to use the 'neither-nor' category as a proxy for indifferent *and* undecided attitudes. Indeed, as Table 2.10 shows, the two questions are closely linked and the relationship between them grows over time until 2002. This seems to suggest that ambivalence and indifference are more and more linked to each other. This relationship and the content of the 'neither-nor' category will be further characterised using qualitative data (*see* Chapter Five). These analyses will confirm the fact that the 'neither-nor' category can refer to both ambivalence and indifference.

Figure 2.6 displayed the distribution of data for the index of support towards the EU for eight long-term member-states during the period 1973–2004. In the early 1980s, just over 30 per cent of the citizens of the eight member-states included displayed strong support and 22.3 per cent affirmed moderate support. Throughout the 1980s, moderate and strong support for European integration rose steadily and peaked in 1991 with a combined percentage of 74.3 per cent. According to the classic membership question, the two modalities of moderate and strong support then slumped and stayed at a lower level after Maastricht, with some annual fluctuations. After 2006 and the failure of the ratification process, the measure of support (EU integration is a good thing) oscillated around 50 per cent whereas the category of opposition (EU integration is a bad thing) grew slowly from 15 per cent in 2006, to 18 per cent in 2010.

Confirming the results presented in the previous sections, one can note that the percentage of undecided and indifferent citizens grew steadily, from 15.3 per cent in 1992 to 23.8 per cent in 2002, whereas the categories of opposition (strong and moderate) rose from 16.7 per cent to 17.5 per cent for the same period. Although the percentages of respondents evaluating their country membership as 'neither good nor bad' are systematically higher that the percentages recorded for the undecided and indifferent attitude, they follow a similar trend. More importantly, they continue to increase slightly after 2002. Indeed, despite the fact that it decreased a little between 2006 and 2007, following the failed Constitutional Treaty ratification process, the 'neither-nor' category still represents 31 per cent of Europeans in 2011, the last available Eurobarometer data. Note that if the percentage answering 'neither-nor' lowers before major events of European integration with high amounts of media coverage, such as the Treaty of Maastricht in 1991, the introduction of the euro in 2002, the ratification process of the TCE in 2005 and the Treaty of Lisbon in 2009, it systematically goes up after each of these events of high politicisation. This is also true when considering evolution after the economic and financial crises of 2008. In this regard, because the curve of opposition towards the EU ('bad thing') – so to say the evolution of euroscepticism – follows a very similar pattern, we can hypothesise that the grow in the neither-nor category – used as a proxy for indifference and indecision – is a side-effect of growing macro politicisation.

Figure 2.6: Public support for European integration (1973–2011, %, EU8 and EU)

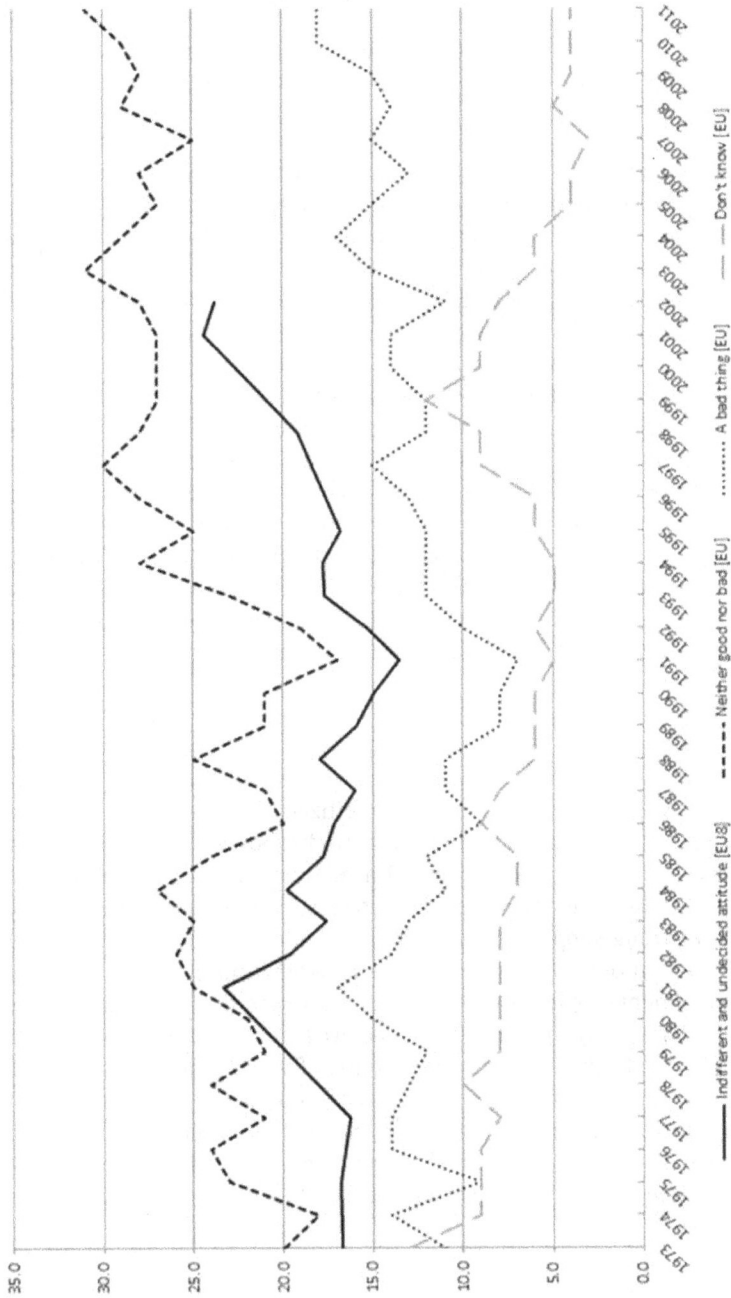

Source: Mannheim Eurobarometer Trend File (1973–2002); European Union, 1973–2011; Author's own computation based on data from Mannhein Eurobarometer Trend File (1973–2002)

Table 2.10: Pearson's correlations between the membership and regret questions

	1991	1992	1993	1994	1995	1998	2001	2002
Pearson's correlations	.604**	.658**	.647**	.674**	.675**	.669**	.674**	.689**

At the same time, as noted by Pieter De Wilde and Michael Zürn, one can see a decline in the percentage of respondents answering they 'don't know' (De Wilde and Zürn 2012: 148–9). The percentage 'not knowing' whether membership is a good thing or not declines from 13 per cent in 1973 to 4 per cent in 2011.[27] This decline in the 'don't know' category, coupled with the uptrend of the 'neither-nor' category, underlines the fact that Europeans are indeed more aware of the EU and are more able to position themselves. However this awareness is not a synonym of the salience of the European matters. Nor is it of polarisation. Citizens are more aware of and, probably, knowledgeable about the EU and its policies but this doesn't mean that they are more polarised. Indeed, the distribution in recent years is characterised by a non-polarisation of attitudes, because the 'neither/ nor' modality is higher and much larger that the opposition category and is still growing in recent years. Indeed, considering the similar pattern of evolution of the category 'neither good nor bad' and the indifferent and undecided attitude of my index, I argue that, in the post-Maastricht era and also since the eurozone crisis, one cannot assume that European citizens' attitudes have become polarised.

Conclusion

Empirically, this chapter has enabled me to shed light on a significant but previously understudied phenomenon: citizens' indifference *and* indecision regarding European integration. In the period following the difficult ratification of the Maastricht Treaty, we observed a reinforcement of the median category, made up of indifferent and undecided citizens, particularly at the expense of the category of strong support. As a result, it is no longer possible to summarise the current situation only by the thesis of a breakdown in the permissive consensus in European public opinion (in the countries where this consensus existed); nor can we conclude only that there was a polarisation of opinion in any of the eight countries studied here. My analysis in terms of variance and kurtosis enables me to demonstrate that a decrease in opinion favourable to the integration process has been accompanied by an increase in the number of undecided and indifferent citizens and, to a lesser extent, of eurosceptic citizens. This has led to a flattening of the distribution of citizens' opinions and attitudes.

---

27. The other trend questions concerning benefits (from 23 per cent in 1983 to 11 per cent in 2011), unification (26 per cent in 1973 to 9 per cent in 1995) and scrapping the EU (13 per cent in 1973 to 5 per cent in 2004) show declines as well (De Wilde and Zürn 2012: 148–49).

Indeed the proportion of the population falling in the opposition categories (strong and moderate opposition combined), for the eight countries, has increased from 16.7 per cent in 1992 to 17.5 per cent in 2002. The proportion falling into the intermediate category, those who are indifferent and undecided, has increased from 15.3 per cent to 23.8 per cent for all of the eight countries for this period. If one uses the 'neither/nor' category as a proxy for indifference, the percentage grows from 20 per cent in 1973 to 31 per cent in 2011. In the same period of time, the percentage declaring that membership is a 'bad thing' grows from 11 per cent to 18 per cent whereas the percentage considering membership as a 'good thing' declines from 56 per cent to 47 per cent.

Thus it seems clear that the drop in the strong support category has occurred to the benefit of the indifferent and undecided category – clearly on the increase since Maastricht. Consequently, the lack of attention paid to this category in the Eurobarometer data in the post Maastricht period is problematic. In order to observe this evolution I performed a re-analysis of the survey data over the long term, using the measures of variance and kurtosis. On a methodological level, I have demonstrated that the constraints of the data in terms of temporal periods and the choice of measurement instruments and indicators also have a role to play in the relative blindness of European scholars regarding this evolution occurring before their very eyes. As a result, I argue that the study of this absent figure of citizens' attitudes is essential, and it has profound theoretical implications (*see* Chapter Six). As Bernhard Wessels points out, neither dissatisfaction nor scepticism are the exact opposites of support because 'non-support' can also include indifference (Wessels 2007: 290). Here I have demonstrated that 'non-support' – as 'non-rejection' – can also include indifference and indecision.

In proposing to re-analyse the survey data in terms of distribution and dispersal of support, this chapter also aimed to pave the way for some new paths of reflection in the study of citizens' attitudes towards European integration, in the context of a broader reflection on the legitimacy of the process underway. The goal was to provoke new research questions and hypotheses that might provide jumping-off points for further exploration of the survey data and further, more detailed empirical validation with other quantitative but also qualitative data from focus groups.

Chapter Three

Focus Groups as a Microscope

> The lesson to be drawn for other social sciences is the need for more systematic data-rich comparative projects that combine qualitative and quantitative methods and do not hesitate to answer macro questions with a microscope (Guiraudon 2006: 5).

The remainder of this book aims to contribute to the questions raised in the two previous chapters by offering a complementary perspective, based on the analysis of 24 collective interviews conducted in (francophone) Belgium, France and Great Britain in December 2005 and June 2006. Although complementary – qualitative – data is unfortunately not available for periods prior to this, one additional qualitative data was collected following a moment of exceptionally intense public debate on European integration: the failed EU Constitution (Schrag Sternberg 2013: 160–96). This chapter presents the research design used here, the object of which was to reveal all the aspects of the problem of acceptance of the new political order and, by extension, the politicisation of the European space. This chapter will thus be dedicated to the methodological and epistemological choices that led to the writing of this book.

My approach is – at least in part – situated in what has come to be known as the sociological approach to European integration (Saurugger 2008), or a sociology of the EU (Favell and Guiraudon 2011). It is also part of the CITAE research project, which chose to innovate by using focus groups in its methodology (Duchesne, Frazer, Haegel and Van Ingelgom 2013). The first section of this chapter will present the justification for the use of focus groups as a microscope through which to study ordinary reactions towards European integration and provide a detailed presentation of this methodology, still relatively rarely used within European studies.[1] Then I will move on to the justification of how this methodology is articulated with the Eurobarometers and the advantages of combining these two types of data in understanding the research object in all its complexity. In so doing, this book takes a mixed-methods perspective, defined here as 'an approach to knowledge (theory and practice) that attempts to consider multiple viewpoints, perspectives, positions, and standpoints (always including the standpoints of qualitative and quantitative)' (Johnson, Onwuegbuzie and Turner 2007: 113).

---

1. Among the studies having mobilised focus groups, to various degrees, within European studies. (*See*: Bruter 2005; Gaxie, Hubé and Rowell 2011; Hurrelmann and Schneider 2013; White 2011 3)

The second part of this chapter shows how the focus groups were constructed and conducted in order to enable a comparison on several levels. Considering the amount of existing literature, both normative and empirical (*see* Chapter One), it would have been difficult for the research design to attempt to be totally inductive. Essential advances in this research field could not go unobserved. It appeared to me that certain results could be considered as a scientific 'given'. This book thus takes on the thesis of scientific cumulativity; but cumulative does not necessarily mean repetitive. The research design used here was constructed on the basis of a series of postulates and hypotheses. The wide variety of literature has demonstrated the importance of social cleavages and national differences in attitudes towards Europe; these two variables thus served to structure the population (Duchesne *et al.* 2013). The comparison between (francophone) Belgium, France and Great Britain enables me to shed light on substantial national differences in the ways in which this new political order has been and is perceived (Haegel 2013). From the perspective of social comparison, the typification of the population into three categories – 'workers and those in temporary employment', 'employees' and 'managers'[2] – reflects the sociological cleavages in place (Duchesne 2013).

In the third and final section of this chapter I will outline the protocol for conducting the focus groups and the mechanisms enabling the emergence of the debate. I will come back to the rationale of political diversification that accompanied the recruitment of participants as well as to the scenario for the discussion and, finally, to the particular methods for running the groups. This section will enable me to demonstrate to what extent the framework was in fact a real experimentation of politicisation (Duchesne and Haegel 2009: 46–7).

By way of conclusion I will emphasise the importance of the 'complementarity of approaches' (Abélès 1997) in the context of a broader reflection concerning the place of this book in mixed-method research.

The focus group as a research tool

The objective of the previous chapters has been to provide an in-depth analysis of citizens' attitudes towards European integration in the long run, using survey data. A specific and innovative method of study was chosen to complete the survey data analysed in Chapter Two. This section presents the focus-group method, more broadly referred to as group interviews, as a research tool. It deals with the question of how this method is specific in its contributions to the study of citizens' reactions to European integration and, in particular in this book, to the absence of these reactions. The image of this method that I draw here is necessarily selective and centred on the choices that guided the CITAE research project.[3] I

---

2. The terms chosen to name the group categories are purely descriptive and should not be seen as conveying value judgements of any kind.

3. The book by Sophie Duchesne and Florence Haegel (2004a) is the key reference in the francophone literature but there are many studies and textbooks on focus groups in the Anglo-Saxon tradition (*see*, for example, Barbour 2007; Morgan 1996, 1997; Wilkinson 2004).

will begin by presenting certain fundamental points of this methodology, which are indispensable for the presentation of the research design that is to follow.

What is a focus group?

The definitions and uses of the method are varied and diverse, as one can see by the many related terms. 'Collective interviews', 'group interviews', 'discussion groups', or 'focus groups' all refer to interviews conducted with several respondents at the same time. In order to define more precisely what is meant by this term, I will begin with the three-point definition provided by David L. Morgan, an author who was essential in developing this method for use in social sciences. He defines a focus group 'as a research technique that collects data through group interaction on a topic determined by the researcher' (Morgan 1997: 130). Three elements stand out in this relatively inclusive definition. First, the focus group is a research method designed to collect data. It is thus intended for research interests, in other words, collecting discursive data destined for analysis; data provoked and collected by a researcher on themes that she or he has chosen (Duchesne and Haegel 2004a: 42). Second, in the focus group the source of data lies in the interaction within the discussion group; the social relations that characterise them are not reduced to the relationship between the interviewer and interviewee but require the interactions of a collective discussion to be taken into account. Third, and finally, the focus group supposes the active intervention of the researcher in the creation of the group discussion in order to collect data.

This definition enables us to exclude a series of configurations similar to focus groups, such as collective interviews used outside a research context, for example, for marketing or training purposes. It also enables us to distinguish this method from other procedures that included multiple participants but which do not allow the emergence of interactive discussions between them, such as group experiments aimed to record actions rather than discourse. This definition also excludes direct observation of naturally occurring discussions that cannot be described as interviews in so far as the researcher does not intervene in the creation of data. Collective interviews therefore cannot be assimilated to ordinary conversation, such as might occur in everyday life. The framing of the discussion is always made clear by the presence of a moderator, who imposes the subject on the participants and makes sure – in a more or less direct manner – the discussion is kept alive. The focus group thus differs on these different points from the citizen conferences initiated by the EU as a way of including citizens in the political decision-making process and reinforcing deliberation and public debate (for example, Boussaguet and Dehousse 2008; Kies and Nanz 2013).

The choice of focus groups as a research tool

Beyond the actual definition of the focus group, the scientific uses of the method are also quite diverse. Indeed, focus groups can be used in very different epistemological frameworks, which I will not review here. Like any method, the success of the focus group is in part due to its appropriateness for the question posed by the research and the place accorded it in the research protocol. So before I go into the detail of the research framework and its practical dispositions, it is important to justify the use of focus groups and their appropriateness for the object of this study.

Firstly, the choice of focus groups as a research tool is based on the conviction that individual attitudes are not given but result from a process of construction that occurs through the use of speech in a collective and sometimes even contradictory context (Duchesne *et al.* 2013; Duchesne and Haegel 2004a). At the heart of the method is thus the analysis of shared meanings and disagreements, thanks to the visibility of social interactions that come through in the discussion. It enables us to access the common sense and cultural models that are shared by a particular group. Indeed, the few studies that have systematically compared the results obtained by collective interviews and individual interviews have confirmed that the former tend to reinforce shared elements of a group through a sort of mechanical effect (Banks 1979; Wight 1994). Indeed, the construction of common sense is at the heart of the research question addressed here, to the extent that the EU is not a fixed object but a constantly evolving construction. As such, it has been described by Ronald Inglehart as a *floating referent* (Inglehart 1970a, 1970b) and by Jacques Delors as an *unidentified political object* (cited in Schmitter 1996). As a result, it is essential to know what citizens hear and understand when they talk about European integration, Europe or the EU. The ability to observe the construction of common sense, shared meaning is thus a fundamental advantage of this method.

A second justification, intrinsically linked to the first, is that the collective interview facilitates individual expression. One knows from previous studies – qualitative and quantitative – that European integration is a subject that is far removed from everyday experience for most individuals and which can be perceived as complex, overly institutional or technical; this affirmation being all the more potent at the lower levels of the social hierarchy (*see* Chapter One). Through the group dynamic that it unleashes, the focus group facilitates participation for certain interviewees, in particular on sensitive or complex subjects. This method thus helps to reduce individual inhibitions through a 'copycat effect' (Barbour 2007).

The use of focus groups also reveals a related advantage in that it has been applied in situations where there was a substantial difference in perspective between researchers and those they were studying (Barbour 2007; Morgan 1996: 133). This argument has been developed in the context of studies on the risks of HIV within the male homosexual and bisexual community (Joseph *et al.* 1984) and it seems that it can be usefully applied to my research object. Indeed, a minimum of reflexivity is required regarding the profile of European specialists and their generally very specialised and europhile perspective, which calls into question their ability to consider the EU in terms that correspond to the reality of more working-class social groups, in particular when these are eurosceptic or euro-indifferent. Moreover, the idea of giving the floor to more marginalised groups can easily apply to the attitudes of lower social categories towards the European integration process (Barbour 2007: 19–22). The first chapter showed for how long the ordinary citizen was ignored by European studies. One also knows that lower social categories often eschew participation in surveys. Yet, everything was done to reach those populations who escape this kind of study, generally because of their feeling of incompetence for anything connected to political issues. This led to the choice, which I will come back to below, to construct artificial groups, concealing the subject of the study from the participants and remunerating them for their participation.

Finally, given that these groups were constructed in order to harmonise their social composition and diversify their political composition, the use of focus groups enables us to determine with reasonable precision the main cleavages that structured (or not) reactions to European integration. Not only do collective interviews allow the observation of opinions in the context in which they are uttered but the participants can also more easily be encouraged to express them over a long period of time, which means that tensions, ambiguities and even changes can be observed. The attitudes of ordinary people to Europe and beliefs in the legitimacy of the EU can thus be considered as social constructs in all their complexity. Taking into account the ambivalences and tensions appears essential, given the quantitative results (*see* Chapter Two), but also given the results of the qualitative turn recently taken in European studies that has underlined the low salience of European integration for ordinary citizens (*see* Chapter One).

The place of focus groups in the research design

The third element to be addressed in this first section is the place of the focus groups within my research design. Although combining methods has become a very fashionable phenomenon, four is based on very important methodological decisions that must be justified by their connection to the research objective. In particular, focus groups have been widely used alongside other methods. In the context of a survey of contributions using focus groups, David L. Morgan cited more than 60 per cent as the number of empirical publications using focus groups along with another method (Morgan 1996: 130). As a result, the combination of methods has been the object of close attention in manuals on focus groups, methodological reflections anchored more broadly in a concern for triangulation (Barbour 2007: 46–7).

Most often, collective interviews are used alongside individual interviews or quantitative surveys (Morgan 1996: 133–4). Studies using both focus groups and opinion surveys, drawing on qualitative and quantitative data, are thus very common. Yet this brings its own forms of complexity, given that these two methods produce very different kinds of data, the articulation of which is not always straightforward (Haegel and Garcia 2011). David L. Morgan also pursued this reflection in depth, proposing a conceptual framework that identified four different ways of combining qualitative and quantitative methods – and collective interviews and opinion surveys in particular (Morgan 1993; 1996: 134–6).

The first combination, which is also the most widely used traditionally, means conducting collective interviews in an exploratory phase of the research before establishing a questionnaire. As with any other qualitative method, the advantage of focus groups is here to refine the research hypotheses and provide elements that are useful for the formulation of questions. This might include the terms of the discussion itself and the words and expressions used and shared by participants in order to facilitate the writing and administering of the questionnaire.

In the second combination, it is the survey data that constitutes the preliminary phase, used to guide the collective interviews, which, consequently, constitute the primary methodology. Typically, studies taking this epistemological position use the data provided by surveys or quantitative studies in order to select populations and constitute the focus groups. In this instance, the idea is that the survey data allow for the segmentation of the population into different categories relevant to the subject under study.

The third combination uses quantitative data as the primary method and focus groups as a tool for improved interpretation of the data produced by them. The standard way of proceeding is to re-contact the respondents of a study in order to conduct a more detailed and illustrative analysis, either with individual or collective interviews.

More interesting on a methodological level are efforts made to clarify results that remain difficult to interpret with the simple analysis of the survey data (Morgan 1996: 135). The fourth and final combination inverses the order of the previous one, using survey data as a tool for the confirmation of results observed in focus groups. There is a certain resistance to this combination, however, among researchers who use focus groups (and qualitative researchers more generally). This is because they seek to avoid encouraging the implication that quantitative data is necessary for 'verifying' the results of qualitative analyses.

The research design used in this book draws on the second, third and fourth of these epistemological positions. As suggested by the second approach, the constitution of the groups was based upon the results of quantitative studies, providing a comparison in both national and social terms (*see* the next section; Duchesne *et al.* 2013). It also uses quantitative data to confirm that the interpretative analysis of the groups did not produce abnormal results, as suggested by the fourth position. The reader will find the results of this return to quantitative data in Chapter Two. As is often the case, the presentation of this book does not necessarily follow the development and the chronology of the research process. But the primary use of focus groups in the context of this book above all reflects the third combination of methods. Here, focus groups serve to explain what existing survey data does not allow us to grasp fully, that is, the acceptance of a political order, with its active and passive components. Thus, the idea is to combine qualitative and quantitative methods in ways that ostensibly bridge their differences, in the service of addressing a research question. In particular, this allows me to emphasise the question of indifference and indecision regarding the European integration project. The analysis of the focus groups conducted here serves to formulate new hypotheses and to develop a theory that works towards the reconceptualisation of the problem of the acceptance of a political order, using a sociological approach to European integration.

Constructing a qualitative comparison

Although I have justified the choice to use focus groups in this study and specified their place in the research framework, it is still necessary to outline the decisions that guided the way the focus groups were conducted, in order to construct the comparison. Setting up collective interviews involves a series of choices linked to procedures of recruitment and organisation of the discussion. To the extent that the researcher is particularly active in the construction of the research framework, a high degree of reflexivity is necessary, at least in retrospect. Here I return to the particular way in which the CITAE project conducted the focus groups used in this book, by underlining how this allows me to analyse indifference and indecision in three different national contexts.

The findings of numerous quantitative studies have shown that citizens' attitudes towards European integration are profoundly diverse and divided along national and social lines (*see* Chapter One). In light of this, groups were set up in such a way as to enable the discussions to be compared on these two dimensions.[4] The CITAE study was designed to be calibrated around the social segmentation of the national populations. Although the national comparison was self-evident, the social comparison required a significant amount of work in recruitment and a meticulous selection of participants. The solution to operationalising this methodological framework consisted in identifying classes and groups for each country according to a simplified model of social stratification; indeed, comparison implies a crucial operation in the reduction of complexity. The groups were constructed around ideal-type categories 'workers and temporary workers', 'employees', and 'managers'. Ideal-types provide 'a useful basis for a comparative approach, because of [their] selective nature', providing 'an intelligent principle for the illustration of contrasts' (Coenen-Huther 2003). The decision was also made to introduce the participants' degree of specialisation or involvement with politics and, more precisely, with Europe, by distinguishing these three categories from those of militants or party activists. Four categories were thus constructed, with the latter group – the activists – acting as the control group. Moreover, in order not to put the research entirely at the mercy of group dynamics, the number of groups conducted was doubled for each one of these categories. Between December 2005 and June 2006, therefore, we conducted eight focus groups per country, a total of 24 groups. Each group contained between four and seven participants: a total of 133 participants (*see* Appendix Three).

---

4. There is no doubt that other dimensions could have been taken into account. The rural–urban cleavage or the professional occupation of participants spring to mind, for example; one could have brought together farmers, Eurostar managers, etc. However, material constraints forced us to make choices since adding an extra dimension systematically increased the number of groups to conduct and analyse.

The national comparison

Since the beginning of the new millennium, a qualitative shift has occurred in European studies, in order to respond to the limits of survey analysis and, specifically, of the Eurobarometers. This quantitative data dominated the study of European citizens' attitudes for a long time. The first chapter enabled me to shed light on the difficulties encountered in European studies in understanding national differences and particularly in deconstructing citizens' frames of perception and understanding of the European integration process. The need to systematically collect qualitative information makes the comparative approach an appropriate compromise between case studies and quantitative analysis dealing with a large number, or even all, member-states (Diez Medrano 2003: 8). This book is part of the qualitative shift but remains in continuity with – rather than a departure from – the results of prior quantitative work.

In order to allow an international comparison, the CITAE study was conducted in three countries – or, more specifically, three cities in three different countries: Paris, Brussels and Oxford.[5] The choice of a comparison between (francophone) Belgium, France and Great Britain was determined, in addition to pragmatic reasons,[6] by the diversity of their positions within the EU and their specific characteristics. These are dissimilar countries in terms of their history within European integration. Indeed, on face value, the differences between these three countries are clear: Belgium, a small founding member housing the main European institutions and the elites that have always been broadly supportive of its development (Pilet and Van Haute 2007); France, a stronghold of European construction since the beginning but torn by its desire for sovereignty, the ambivalence of which marks its relations to the EU (Lacroix 2007; Rozenberg 2007); and Great Britain, on the periphery of the continent, a latecomer to the integration process and characterised by its euroscepticism (Harmsen 2007; Spiering 2004).

At the time the focus groups were conducted, immediate attitudes to the EU were also very different in the three countries. In France, a referendum on the Constitutional Treaty had just been held in May 2005, some six months before the groups were conducted. In Belgium, the Treaty was ratified by the parliament, though the French debate and vote was widely followed. In Britain, the debate on the Constitutional Treaty did not lead to any ratification procedure. In the three cases, this momentary politicisation was very real at the time the collective interviews were conducted, although it is likely that this politicisation was different and of different degrees in the three cases. Indeed, the three national

---

5.　It is clear that London would have represented a better field site – more immediately comparable with Paris and Brussels, at least in terms of its status as a European capital – but logistical constraints pushed us to choose Oxford. The study of Juan Diez Medrano, conducted in two towns per country, enabled him to demonstrate that the regional specificity is not relevant as far as attitudes towards EU are concerned. The exception is Germany, where Eastern Germans differ from Western Germans in the way they frame Europe; whereas English and Scots on one hand, and Spaniards and Catalans, on the other, frame Europe largely in the same way. This finding leads us to think that Paris, Brussels and Oxford will reveal relevant elements as to the way the French, French-speaking Belgians and the British frame Europe, even though we are aware that local specificity and, especially, the urban context impact on the way Europe is perceived.

6.　I have clearly benefited from the research project within which my own doctoral research took place and, in particular, from the professional networks that preceded it.

cases considered here are also very different from an institutional standpoint. The groups are drawn from one consensual and two majoritarian political systems. As Table 4.1 shows, the three country cases can be considered as 'most different' from this point of view as well.

If we now turn to the classic indicator of support for one's country belonging to the EU in 2006, the year the focus groups were conducted, and in 2011, the differences between the three countries are also clearly apparent.

The different levels of support in these three countries are indeed significant, as one can see in Table 4.2. Belgium is among the countries most favourable to European integration, which, historically, have also included the Benelux countries and Ireland, joined afterwards by Spain. In this first group of countries, in 2006, around 70 per cent of citizens declare that their country's membership of the Union is a good thing and levels of rejection are very low (around 10 per cent in 2006). France is part of a second group of countries, including Germany, Denmark, Portugal, Greece and Italy, in which a small majority of citizens support membership of the EU. This second group is also characterised by a more marked opposition to the European project, with the negative category attracting between 12 and 19 per cent of respondents. The European mean is situated in this second group. Finally Great Britain is part of a third group of countries in which one also finds Finland, Sweden and Austria. Citizens of this group prove to be both less inclined to support their country's membership of the EU (between 34 and 49 per cent) and much more likely to oppose it, with a quarter to a third of the population declaring membership is a 'bad thing'. These three different groups emerge regardless of the measurement instruments used and the period considered;[7] one of the cases studied here is found in each of them.

Yet in spite of the notable differences one has just observed, the three cases show an evolution over the long term that cannot be fully explained by the thesis of a polarisation of the European citizen space (De Wilde and Zürn 2012; Hooghe and Marks 2008). In the post-Maastricht period, in all three of these countries, we can witness a reinforcement of indecision and indifference. If I refer to the support index constructed in Chapter Two, one can see a linear evolution of the percentage of individuals in the indifferent and undecided position. In France, in Belgium and in the United Kingdom, these percentages passed from 15.5 per cent, 16 per cent and 17.3 per cent respectively in 1991 to 28.7 per cent, 28.8 per cent and 27.2 per cent in 2002.

If we examine the curves for the evolution of the 'neither/nor' category, we can see a similar evolution up until 2002, with a strong increase in this category, moving beyond the 30 per cent mark in all three countries in 2002. One can then observe that this category drops off in France and in Belgium in 2004. This year is preceding the ratification of the Constitutional Treaty and it was marked by the many debates surrounding it. In 2005, the 'neither-nor' category saw a new increase in France and Belgium before dropping off again in 2006. In the United Kingdom there was also a slight decrease in this modality between 2004 and 2006. From 2007, we can see an increase in the median category in all three cases. In 2011, after more than three years of economic crisis, 23 per cent of

---

7.   At the very most one can observe certain slippages over the long term. For example, Denmark was closer to the Eurosceptic group in the past, whereas the French were more favourable in the past than they are now (Belot and Cautrès 2006: 86).

Table 3.1: EU member countries consensus-majoritarianism dimension score

Country	Consensus-majoritarianism score
Belgium	**4.22**
Finland	3.71
Italy	3.70
Denmark	1.10
The Netherlands	0.99
Sweden	-0.29
France	**-0.50**
Germany	-0.64
Austria	-2.64
Ireland	-3.55
Luxembourg	-4.28
United Kingdom	**-10.41**

Source: Mair 1994: 120, cited in Beetham and Lord 1998: 88.

Table 3.2: Indicator of support for one's country belonging to the EU (EU-15) in 2006 and 2011[1]

Country	Good thing	Neither good nor bad	Bad thing	Don't know
Ireland	78% (↓63%)	12% (↑18%)	7% (↑12%)	3% (↑7%)
Luxembourg	74% (↓72%)	16% (↓13%)	9% (↑13%)	1% (↑2%)
The Netherlands	72% (↓68%)	15% (↑19%)	12% (=12%)	1% (=1%)
Belgium	**69% (↓65%)**	**21% (↑23%)**	**10% (↑11%)**	**0% (↑1%)**
Spain	62% (↓55%)	19% (↑22%)	9% (↑17%)	10% (↓6%)
Denmark	61% (↓55%)	24% (↑28%)	14% (↑16%)	2% (↓1%)
Germany	58% (↓54%)	26% (=26%)	14% (↑16%)	3% (↑4%)
Greece	57% (↓38%)	31% (↓28%)	12% (↑33%)	0% (↑1%)
Total UE	**53% (↓47%)**	**27% (↑31%)**	**16% (↑18%)**	**4% (=4%)**
Italy	52% (↓41%)	29% (↑36%)	14% (↑17%)	5% (↑6%)
Portugal	50% (↓39%)	28% (↑30%)	18% (↑26%)	4% (↑5%)
France	**50% (↓46%)**	**30% (↑33%)**	**19% (=19%)**	**1% (↑2%)**
Sweden	49% (↑56%)	25% (=25%)	26% (↓17%)	1% (↑2%)
Finland	39% (↑47%)	38% (↓33%)	23% (↓19%)	1% (=1%)
Austria	36% (↑37%)	37% (↓36%)	23% (↑25%)	5% (↓2%)
United Kingdom	**34% (↓26%)**	**28% (↑37%)**	**34% (↓32%)**	**7% (↓5%)**

Source: Eurobarometer 66.1 (autumn 2006); Eurobarometer 75.1 (spring 2011)

---

1. In brackets, one finds the percentages for 2011

Figure 3.1: Evolution of indifferent and undecided positions between 1990 and 2002 and the 'neither-nor' category between 1990 and 2011 (France, Belgium and United Kingdom)

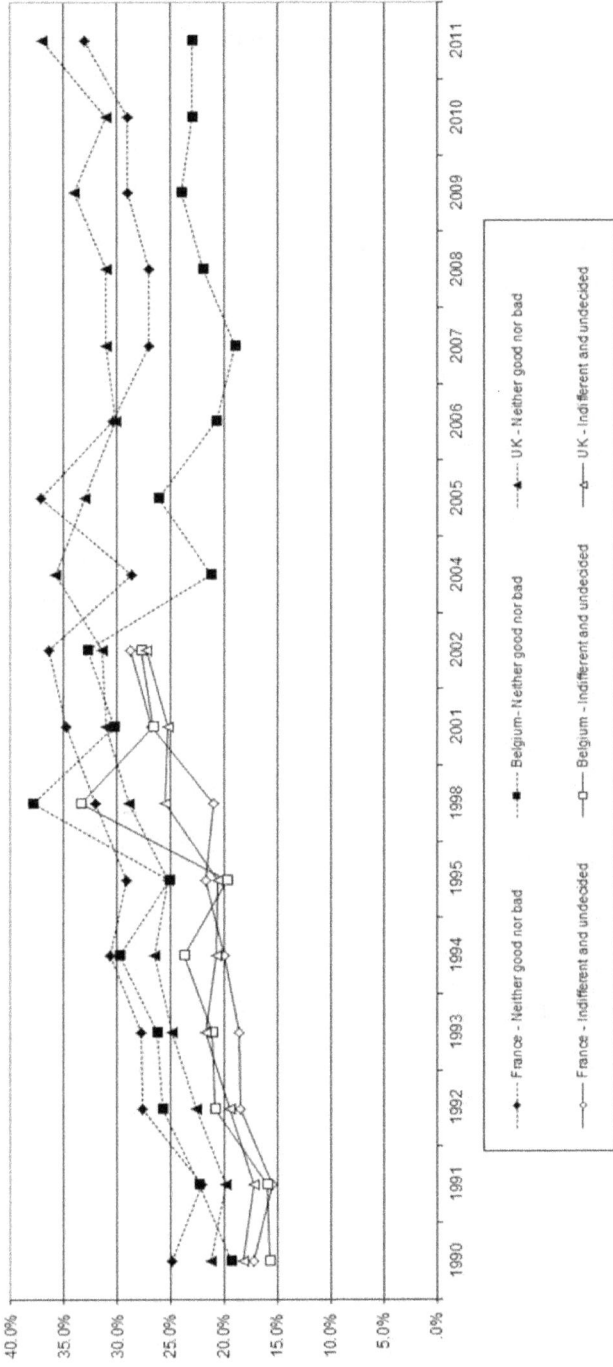

Source: Author's own calculations; Mannheim Eurobarometer Trend File (1990–2002); Eurobarometer Interactive Search System (1990–2011)

Belgian respondents, 33 per cent of French respondents and 37 per cent of British respondents report that their country's membership of the EU is neither a good nor a bad thing. These results cannot be explained by the thesis of a constraining dissensus and the increased politicisation of European integration such as it is currently formulated. The three countries, selected for their similarities and their differences, present prime conditions for a rich international comparison.

Social comparison: between critical variable and methodological necessity[8]

Although the national comparison was relatively straightforward, comparison between the different social categories was more difficult because it required a meticulous recruitment and a thoughtful selection of participants. In practical terms, participants were selected following the administration of a questionnaire, which was relatively short and structured around a series of questions about their socio-professional characteristics and their political opinions (*see* Appendix Four). In order to form the three categories, 'workers', 'employees' and 'managers', the recruitment and selection of the participants was at the heart of the research framework. We were very careful in this selection in order to ensure complete comparability of the corpus and thus the generalisability of the results. The recruitment of activists and party militants was conducted differently from that of the other three categories – by contacting political parties directly – because the principal selection criterion here was political membership rather than socio-political characteristics. I will therefore not discuss it further in this section of the chapter (Duchesne *et al.* 2013: 180–1).

Recruiting ordinary citizens from all walks of life

In order to have maximum control over the selection process, we chose to construct groups that were lacking any kind of pre-existing sociability, in other words, groups in which the participants were anonymous to each other as well as to the researcher. Yet friendship groups or social groups represent the most common form of basis for collective interviews. The interviewer secures the participation of one respondent, who is then responsible for bringing together other people of his or her acquaintance. This is notably the case in William Gamson's classic study (Gamson 1992). This author observes that the participant tends to bring together relatively competent people, chosen amongst the most competent that they know. Interpersonal recruitment thus does not allow a choice of all participants, which was essential for this study. Artificial groups, differentiated according to a typological base, were preferred for this reason. We sought to preserve both the social homogeneity and the political, ethnic and gender diversity of each group. We also wanted to reach a population that is most often excluded (or self-excluded) in opinion surveys.

---

8. This section of the chapter contains elements that have already been published in an article with Guillaume Garcia (*see* Garcia and Van Ingelgom 2010). I would like to thank him very warmly for his comments during the writing of that article, from which this section is largely taken. The arguments presented here are influenced by this collaboration but I alone bear responsibility for them.

Thereafter, one of the objectives was to enlarge recruitment beyond the circle of groups that spontaneously agree to participate in this kind of study, that is, to reach those whose feeling of competence – particularly political competence – is low, predisposing them to avoid this kind of participation. Consequently a financial incentive in order to attract those who are generally missing was considered indispensable from the very beginning. Having to speak publicly in front of strangers on potentially controversial political subjects whilst being filmed for three hours is clearly a particularly unusual and potentially harrowing experience and might have discouraged certain potential respondents. Many participants confided that this was the case when contacted by telephone, as well as on the day of the interview. In order to get beyond this reticence, we could do no less than promise remuneration at least equivalent to the daily minimum wage in each country. The level of remuneration was thus calculated on the basis of an amount of 50€ in Paris and Brussels and £40 in Oxford (*see* Appendix Five). For the same reasons, the subject of the discussion was not communicated to the potential participants, in order not to discourage citizens not interested in (or even repelled by) European issues from participating.

Although collective interviews are not more complicated than individual interviews in terms of recruitment, they are in terms of their implementation. For example, if a casting error occurs in an individual interview, the interview in question can always be set aside in a later phase of analysis. This is not the case for collective interviews. Such an error may hinder, or even compromise, the group discussion and the interpretation of the overall results for that group. Given the human and material costs of the organisation of each group, this kind of error must be avoided. It is clear that the group dynamic is at the heart of the methodological problem. Of course, the interactions that take place in the context of these collective interviews always involve a certain 'social alchemy' and are, as a result, at least partly unpredictable. However, the recruitment should enable the researchers to anticipate and control what will take place as much as possible, notably by controlling the social homogeneity of each group. Reflecting the deliberative ideal, we considered that a good discussion dynamic would be one that enabled each participant to express themselves and thus to understand others and be understood. This means that participants must speak the same language and that each was able to identify and 'gauge' their co-protagonists as quickly as possible after meeting them, and to situate themselves in relation to the other participants. From this perspective, the recruitment aimed to avoid bringing together people that were too far removed from each other socially, in order to facilitate discussion between strangers. Thus, by selecting typical individuals (in other words situated roughly at the same level in the social hierarchy), based on their similar professions, level of education or similar family origins, we were counting on a 'class' identity emerging through shared social or cultural references. These parameters do not encompass, in any respect, the social status of participants, which is also associated with factors such as assets and revenue, for example. Belonging to a social milieu remains an extremely complex phenomenon. Its full and entire identification cannot be reduced to a single type of relationship, for example to professional occupation, level of education or social origin (as it was in our case). Other kinds of relationships could have been used here, for example, age or the effect of generation, or of religious and cultural practices and so on. However, using a questionnaire administered by telephone, as well as the impossibility of combining too many selection criteria, obliged us to make choices among these parameters. Individuals considered too deviant, that is visibly – i.e. 'physically' (in terms of dress style, body language and so on) or audibly (in terms of accent, registers of language or cultural references) – above or below other respondents in social terms are strongly susceptible to complicating group function. It is for this reason that we aimed to avoid them in recruiting and bringing together the participants.

Selecting participants: searching for social homogeneity

Far from being self-evident, the construction of this kind of social typology – and thus the selection of candidates – actually produced a number of obstacles. The research team thus had to face the difficulty of harmonising professions and qualifications into more general categories that made sense in the three countries (Kieffer, Oberti and Preteceille 2002). The comparison between these variables was even more delicate because of the heterogeneity of the categories typically mobilised in each country in order to classify social position and level of qualification.

The approach adopted by the CITAE project consisted in choosing those respondents who were the most coherent in terms of their professional situation and level of qualification, neutralising as much as possible – but not entirely – the effects of social mobility. Along the lines of the method used by Alain Desrosières and Laurent Thévenot, it was thus important here to *select* the 'good examples' (in the sense of the most coherent cases) through a process of *typification* of social categories (Desrosières and Théuenot 1996: 57–9). It is important to note that this *typification* was initially conducted essentially based on the French case, which was the first field trial conducted. The models of typical relations were subsequently amended according to the particularities of the two other sites.

In order to provide proof of the efficiency of this operation, we chose to present the results in the form of a multiple correspondence analysis. This allowed us to visualise the layout of the categories of groups based on the intersection between the first and second factorial axes (*see* Figure 3.2).[9] To simplify this presentation, only the modalities that were decisive for these two axes are shown here, that is, those for which the contribution for each axis was above average.

In Figure 3.2 it appears that the first axis, the horizontal one, is structured around an opposition between the modalities on the left (corresponding to the negative sign), 'higher prof. manager',[10] 'lower prof. manager', 'father manager', 'higher education', and on the other hand, on the right (the positive co-ordinates) the modalities of 'working class', 'father working class', 'secondary education'. We are thus dealing with several extremes of the scales mobilised to construct the typologies. One can note that this opposition is particularly skewed by the

---

9.   The analysis was conducted using the computer programme SPAD.

10. These modalities correspond to the responses to the questions posed in the questionnaire used to select the participants and is reproduced in the Appendix Four.

Figure 3.2: Multiple Correspondence Analysis – active modalities and classes constructed

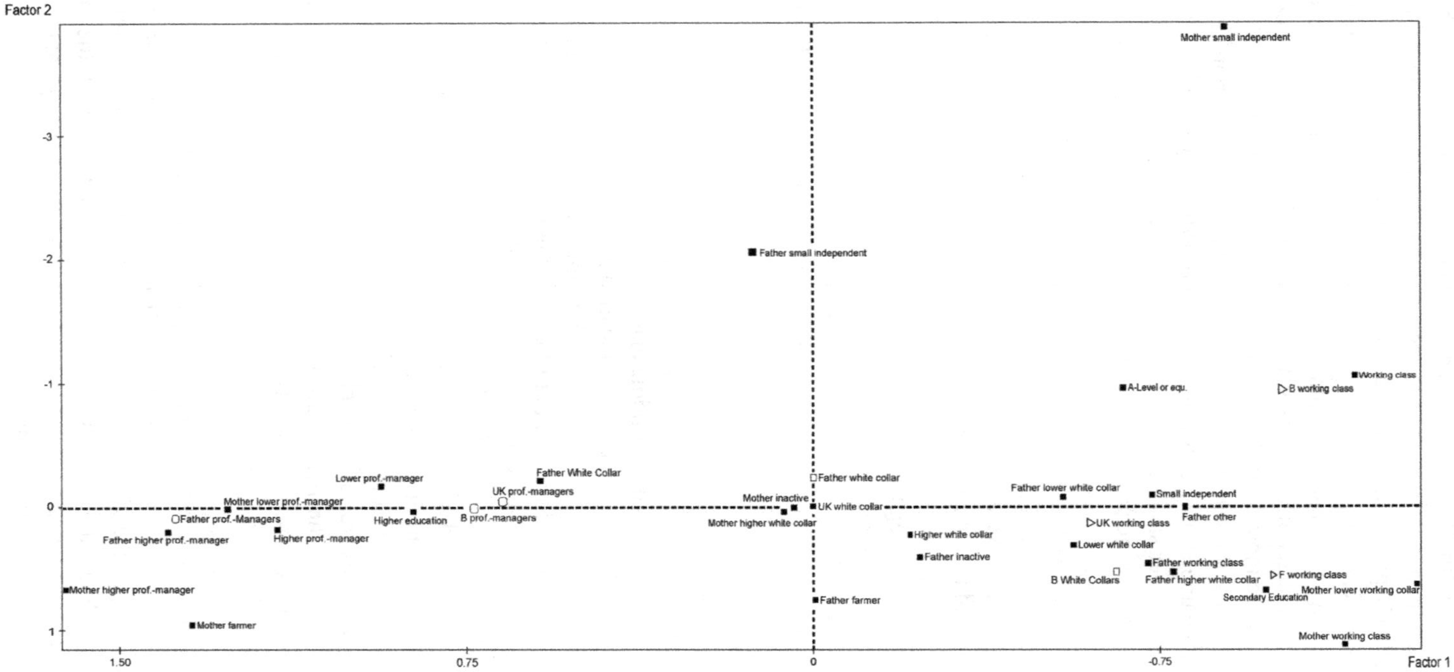

* *Notes*: The active modalities marked by a black square refer to individual characteristics. Illustrative variables are marked by an empty circle for the managers, an empty square for the employees and an empty triangle for the workers groups. These empty shapes thus refer to the groups in which the individuals were placed during the selection process.

rare modalities of 'mother's profession'. Unlike most studies of mobility, the CITAE project did not restrict itself to recording the father's profession but also took the mother's profession into account – when this indicator was available. Although there were many inactive mothers and this information was logically less comprehensive than that of the father's profession, the (quite rare) occurrences of mothers in managerial positions was far from insignificant. This enables the identification of the most typical individuals in the modelling process.

The second axis, the vertical one, presents a secondary opposition between the modalities in the upper quadrants (the positive co-ordinates), such as 'father small independent', 'mother small independent', 'A-level equivalent', and those in the lower quadrants (the negative co-ordinates), such as 'working class', 'mother white collar', 'secondary education'. Here, one finds an opposition between 'small independent' social backgrounds and the working classes. Between them, these two axes form the factorial plane presented in Figure 4.2. The projection of classes of groups into illustrative modalities enables us to extend the interpretation of the factorial plane and to confirm that the model based around these three ideal types has functioned correctly.

The groups of 'managers' (the empty circles) are all situated close to those modalities that make up the universe of higher-level socio-professional categories, which is indicative of the strong coherence of the classes we have reconstructed. With little to distinguish them on the vertical axis, they are more differentiated on the horizontal plane because of variations in family background amongst individuals in this category. The French participants, situated at the extreme left of the figure, appear to have the highest profile on this measure. The Belgian participants and, especially, the British, are situated closer to the centre of the figure, closer to the world of the middle class.

The 'employees' groups (the empty squares) appear at the centre of the figure surrounded by the elements that make up intermediary social worlds and which are generally less homogenous on both axes. At the centre of the factorial plane, the French and British groups are very close on the horizontal axis but slightly more separated on the vertical axis. The Belgian groups, close to the British on the vertical axis, are situated much more to the right on the first axis, on the limit of the area corresponding to the working class world.

Finally, although the 'working-class' groups (empty triangles), situated at the extreme right of the figure, are quite close to each other, they can be distinguished both on the first axis (the British groups are slightly closer to the 'employees' groups) and on the second axis (the Belgian groups are situated higher, closer to the 'mother working class', 'A-levels equivalent', 'lower white collar' or 'small independent' modalities).

Overall, the three classes of French groups can be characterised by a significant distance on the factorial level, which means that they are very different from each other and that the typification process functioned well. The interval between the classes of the Belgian and English groups is less marked, although the hierarchy between the social categories is respected. In the Belgian case it is, above all, the separation between employees and workers that is less clear, with the managers quite distinct from the rest. The configuration is a little different in the case of the British groups; the gap between the three classes is clear but it occurs on a lesser scale, with the three groups closer together. This seems to suggest that, in the last two cases, the typification functioned but less dramatically than it did in Paris. On this point, the fact that the Parisian fieldwork was conducted first undoubtedly influenced the two other field sites.

The limits of social homogeneity: between will and constraint

The model constructed thus appears to be solid overall. Ultimately, only a dozen or so cases (out of 9,911), presented a distinctly atypical profile. There were several factors that meant we were limited in our choice of typical participants and thus in our ability to provide a perfectly homogenous corpus in this respect.

Firstly we were limited by the unequal structure of recruitment areas.[12] Dealing with local contexts to construct the three samples of candidates represented a serious problem. We had to take 'social geography' into account, that is to say, the characteristics that vary from one field site to another. Conditions of enrolment also differed between field sites both because of unequal availability or efficiency in the solicitation procedure, as in the influence of the time factor on recruitment. Indeed, even if one leaves aside the obstacles linked to the lack of equivalence between the indicators used by the various national statistics, each field site, without necessarily being idiosyncratic, presents particularities that cannot be overlooked. These had an impact on our range of action, in particular, to do with the choice of appropriate candidates. In this respect, from the very beginning of the study we were very conscious of the particular characteristics of the population living in the Oxford area (given the relative importance of the University and its public in this town).

The constraints of recruitment, typical in any comparative research process, also influenced the final result (Duchesne et al. 2013; Garcia and Van Ingelgom 2010). These constraints emerged acutely because of our choice to construct 'artificial groups'. The size of the recruitment areas, particularly given the amount of ground to be covered, also played an important role here. But there was another practical problem: that of the constraints imposed by the duration and the cost of the stay necessary to conduct the different field sites of a comparative research project. Similarly the choice of the paths for recruitment (internet, free newspapers, flyers, posters, etc.) also had an influence on the profile of the candidates. Finally the major inconvenience of this research tool lies in having to bring the people selected together at the same time and place. The availability of participants is a genuine constraint on this. Although it might seem obvious, we thus had to make

---

11. Remembering that the recruitment of party militants or activists was conducted using other methods. As a result, these participants do not figure in this analysis. For more details on the recruitment process, *see* the methodological chapter of *Overlooking Europe* (Duchesne *et al.* 2013).

12. For more details on the influence of 'social geography' on the recruitment of the participants, *see* the article I co-wrote with Guillaume Garcia (Garcia and Van Ingelgom 2010).

do with the respondents who were available. Although the impact of this factor on the homogeneity of the corpus extends beyond this study, it was strongly felt here, given that each group had to be formed on the basis of six people on average. The difficulty in finding a time that suited several people at once, in a seasonal context that was often unhelpful, thus limited our choice and, as a result, the possibility of conducting the groups as they were ideally laid out on paper. The anticipation of the risk of drop-outs sometimes led us to 'upgrade' or 'downgrade' available respondents when faced with a dearth of a particular profile for a particular time. We wanted to ensure a minimum of coherence between the properties of the groups actually conducted and the specificities of the French, English and Belgian social structures, by avoiding, for example, the effects of social mobility.

Other factors, more directly linked to the logics imposed by the study tool itself, also contributed to limiting the operationalisation of a socially homogenous composition of the groups; we will see this in the next section, in which I will outline the methodological framework in detail.

Focus groups as an experience of politicisation

Overall, the CITAE research project was not concerned with naturally occurring conversations, quite the contrary. The research design was therefore more akin to an experiment, in the sense of a test of politicisation (Duchesne and Haegel 2009). There are two main reasons for this choice.

Firstly, as has been widely documented in the literature, opinion surveys do not always measure opinions that are well founded: above all, they measure answers to questions, without any indication as to the salience of the opinions expressed. Salience is, however, at the heart of my investigation into the politicisation (or lack thereof) of the European political order. As far as European integration is concerned, a real debate exists on the question of whether the opinions expressed are structured or not. The use of collective interviews provides the possibility of measuring the salience of these opinions and gauging their consistency, which is far from negligible when dealing with a question that is as complex and removed from the daily experience of most citizens. The risk of producing artefact, that is, directing non-attitudes, is therefore reduced and the possibility of studying ambivalences is reinforced.

Like any other method, the use of focus groups can only be understood in connection with the research strategy of which it is a part; in other words, in relation to a research question within a scientific debate and associated with a particular field site upon which the empirical material is based. Given that one knows that, socially, the tendency is to avoid conflict, the focus groups were constructed to allow politicisation. According to David L. Morgan himself, under certain conditions, this method enables us to document more extreme positions than in an individual interview because it is a good method for creating polarisation – polarisation that is, as we have seen, at the heart of this research (Morgan 1997: 15). In particular, the specific way of conducting the focus groups, resulting from research by Sophie Duchesne and Florence Haegel, is based on the idea of using conflict and contestation as an indicator of the salience of opinions expressed about European integration (Duchesne and Haegel 2004a). In fact, work by the interactionists has demonstrated how much the ordinary frame of interactions is unfavourable to the expression of discord. This defiance in the face of conflicts provoked by the confrontation of different perspectives has been confirmed by studies in other research traditions as well (Conover, Searing and Crewe 2002; Noelle-Neumann 1984). People 'naturally' resist entering into conflict in a public discussion. The appearance of such politicisation, here considered in terms of 'for and against' (pro and anti), presupposed certain conditions and an explicit incitation. A series of experimental mechanisms (discussion scenarios, rules of the discussion, mediation and so on) were thus implemented, in order to facilitate the emergence of discord and debate. I will now focus on these mechanisms in more detail.

In search of the polarisation of attitudes

As mentioned, the CITAE project chose to bring together people who did not know each other beforehand, in order to make the emergence of debate and conflict possible. Indeed participants may have otherwise been reticent to publicly expose their disagreements with those they know, especially when being recorded. Moreover, when conducting collective interviews, the construction of the research framework can only be directed by the search for social homogeneity. Yet the overall sampling protocol must also seek an appropriate diversification, taking into account other criteria that are considered relevant depending on the objectives of the study. The goal is to guarantee that the participants are basically representative, not in order to produce a miniature vision of society but rather to include diverse and contrasted situations in the themes of the discussion (Duchesne and Haegel 2004a: 48). But the diversification of perspectives also aims to encourage the development of group dynamics that are favourable to debate and thus to the politicisation of the discussions.

The notion of representativeness does not carry the same significance in studies based on interviews as it does for quantitative studies for two reasons, one practical and the other theoretical. First, it is impossible to take into account all the socio-demographic characteristics of participants, especially in constructing small groups (four to seven participants). Secondly the objective is not to reproduce the structure of the parent population in miniature but rather to obtain a maximum diversification in order to optimise the comparison between situations that are (hypothesised to be) the most contrasted and which typically reproduce socio-political groups of which the characteristics have an incidence on the phenomenon under observation (Duchesne and Haegel 2004a: 48). In concrete terms, we planned to generate a potential for minimal confrontation in these discussions, in order to control (as much as was possible) the probability of the emergence and activation of a certain number of cleavages considered to be fundamental to attitudes towards European construction.

In order to do this we chose to create the conditions for the emergence of a political opposition within each group. During the administration of the selection questionnaire, we asked respondents to indicate their ideological orientation, their vote at the last general national elections and their position on the European Constitutional Treaty (*see* Appendices Three and Four).

To the extent that it was important to create the conditions for polarisation and not to produce a strict equivalence between the cleavages thus established, the equivalence of the ideological scales in the three countries was not overly important. Based on these samples, which were quite skewed to the left, we rebalanced them to create clearer left–right oppositions by reducing the relative importance of those leaning to the left and the extreme left (to end up with roughly equivalent levels in all three countries), in favour of those leaning right and extreme right.

Still seeking to activate cleavages and provoke politicisation, the choice was made to confront people whose opinions on Europe diverged (at least on paper). Thus the questionnaires included two items used to judge citizens' attitudes to the European integration process. The first question asked respondents about their vote (or hypothetical vote) on the Constitutional Treaty.[13] Although this question referred to a real situation in France, because of the referendum that had taken place little more than six months prior, it took on different meanings in Belgium (where the Treaty had simply been ratified by a vote in parliament) and, above all, in England (where the ratification of the Treaty was hardly even a source of debate after the French refusal). In the second questionnaire, administered only to participants, a second question was asked, used to evaluate attitudes concerning the membership of one's country in the EU.

As Table 3.4 shows, although the majority of group participants gave a positive evaluation of European integration on paper, we also included in the corpus a significant number of Eurosceptic participants, as well as undecided and indifferent ones. We were, however, dependent on a category combining the undecided and the individuals who refused to respond. Given the research question here, this category was obviously of particular importance. Overall, out of a total of 133 participants, 51 individuals fell into these two last categories of responses. Similarly, 83 respondents out of 133 declared that they didn't or wouldn't have voted, or didn't know what they would have voted. The objective of splitting the groups on the European question is thus also present in the distribution presented in Table 3.4.

Alongside this, wherever possible we operated with a rationale of ethnic and gendered diversification of each group (or at least each class of groups). The choice to include a diversification along ethnic lines also explains part of the alterations to the social homogeneity of the groups. In addition to the 'injunctions' introduced by the prompts (one of the questions in the interview protocol proposed a debate on the possible entry of Turkey into the EU), we hoped that this would stimulate the emergence of 'ethnic' cleavages that would be difficult to express

---

13. 'If you were able to vote in a referendum regarding the Treaty establishing a Constitution for Europe, would you: vote, not vote? If you would vote, would you vote: yes, no, don't know, won't answer?'

Table 3.3: Auto positioning on left–right scale: (respondents to the ad) and selected participants

Left-right scale	Paris	Brussels	Oxford
Extreme left	(9.5%) 5.6%	(9.7%) 6.7 %	(5 %) 6.1%
Left	(29.2 %) 25.0%	(31.2%) 30.0%	(38.7%) 21.2%
Centre	(16.8%) 16.7%	(23.7 %) 20.0 %	(26%) 33.3%
Right	(21.2 %) 25.0%	(24.7%) 33.3%	(17.1%) 30.3%
Extreme right	(1.5%) 2.8%	(2.2%) 3.3%	(0.6%) 3.0%
Don't know	(21.9%) 25.0%	(3.2%) 0%	(12.7%) 6.1%
Refuse to answer	(0%) 0%	(5.4%) 6.7%	(0%) 0%

Table 3.4: Vote or hypothetical vote in European Constitutional Treaty referendum and country membership (respondents to ad) and selected participants

	Paris	Brussels	Oxford
Vote or hypothetical vote in referendum			
Yes	(21.9%) 39.2%	(41.9%) 26.6%	(33.1%) 32.6%
No	(34.7%) 41.5%	(24.7 %) 42.6%	(25.4%) 27.9%
DNA / Did not / would not have voted	(43.3%) 19.3%	(33.3%) 31.2%	(41.5%) 39.5%
Country membership*			
Good thing	53.1%	85.4%	48.8%
Neither good, nor bad	26.5%	9.8%	37.2%
Bad thing	20.4%	4.8%	14.0%

* The membership question was only directed to participants and not to all the respondents to the advert.

in a normal context. This was the justification for including Mina in a group of workers. A service-sector employee with A-level qualifications, this 48-year-old woman of Indian origin was more middle class (her parents were a superintendent at British Railways and a dressmaker respectively), but she participated in a group of workers. She was thus 'downgraded' in order to better resist against the possible hostility of the other four participants, all British but of more modest backgrounds, or to at least be able to defend herself against them in the conversation. The choice of candidates was also inseparable from concerns regarding the gender of the potential participants. It was imperative to take into account the fact that women have a propensity to adopt passive positions in collective discussions when groups are mixed (Crawford 1995; Monnet 1998). As a result, on several occasions, we selected female respondents whose socio-cultural profile was slightly higher than that of the men in the same discussion group.

The introduction of these criteria into the selection process explains part of the particularities we observed (twelve out of 99). The case of Justine encapsulates in itself the complexification of the initial framework that led to these heterogenisation factors. Given the large proportion of individuals who were both working class and members of cultural minorities within the Belgian pool, the choice was made to construct homogenous groups mainly made up of these two factors (with two men and two women). Due to one female candidate dropping out the day before the meeting, a last-minute replacement was found in Justine. This candidate had been slightly socially 'downgraded' compared to the other participants; she was an unemployed accountant, with A-level qualifications and whose parents were an engineer and a housewife respectively. Her profile had the advantage of satisfying both diversification criteria previously mentioned. From a political point of view she declared herself close to the CDH (Humanist Democratic Centre, formerly the Christian Social Party (PSC)), a rare attribute in working-class areas and consequently in the pool of participants. Her presence also rebalanced the group; without her, it would have been skewed to the left. Of Congolese nationality she also increased its diversity from an ethnic point of view. Finally, the participation of a second woman, who was slightly older (38 years old) than the group average (32), was necessary because this group already included four men.

An experimental research framework

In order to foster the emergence of political discussions, a scenario made up of five questions – outlined in Table 3.5 – was constructed and tested in a pilot group in each country. This scenario, although it enabled a genuine flexibility in the comments of the participants (*see* Chapters Four and Five), also had to regularly reintroduce the question on Europe into the debates. It also had to enable conflict to emerge during the discussions, which generally lasted around three hours. The first question 'What does it meant to be European?' was used as a warm-up for the participants. The question 'How should we distribute power in Europe?' was intentionally designed to be complex, in order to study how citizens approach complexity in politics. During the first session, the participants had the opportunity to discover, or to detect, each other's opinions and were thus supposed to be able to identify the participants that they agreed or disagreed with on European questions. Indeed, to the extent that contestation results from the formation of alliances, we wanted to give the participants time to identify the positions of their fellow group-members so that alliances might be formed when a more controversial issue was raised (Duchesne and Haegel 2004b, 2007). The second session, following the break, included two questions that were supposed to provoke conflict or at least debate: 'Who profits from Europe?' and 'For or against Turkey joining the European Union?'

The moderation technique also included elements that aimed to facilitate the politicisation of the discussion and the polarisation of opinions expressed in it. Developed by Sophie Duchesne and Florence Haegel in their previous research on the politicisation of discussions, this moderation technique was adapted from the method developed by a German consulting company Metaplan (Duchesne and Haegel 2004b: 882). The moderation was based on posting the groups' comments on large boards that face the participants. In order to illustrate this description, a diagram of the typical layout of one of our interview rooms is produced in Figure 3.3.

As previously mentioned, the objective here was not to reproduce the conditions for a natural discussion but, on the contrary, to create those of a public debate, through an experimental approach. The participants were spread out in a semi-circle facing the boards and the moderator. The camera was also most often facing the participants. The experimental nature was thus entirely explicit and intentional. The moderator put the elements of the discussion up on the boards as they were raised, which made not only the arguments and opinions but also the disagreements and misunderstandings apparent. Thus the participants could follow the evolution of the discussion on the boards and the cards written by the moderator. Figure 3.4 shows what a table typically looked like. This table responds to the question 'Who profits from Europe?'

Moreover, this method of conducting the groups (called 'flash') includes an important rule introduced by the moderator at the beginning of the collective interview. When participants manifest their disagreement, or don't completely understand, or want to comment on the comments on the board, the moderator draws a 'lightning bolt' next to the card, indicating to the participants that the discussion would come back to this point. The lightning bolt was clearly presented in a positive light by the moderator and thus represented a clear encouragement to express disagreement. This method is based on a clear structuring of the participants by the moderator, who takes a central role in encouraging the expression of disagreement.

Given this encouragement, conflict was at the heart of the interpretative analysis of the groups. The idea is that the participants, even if they generally prefer to avoid conflict, were in a position here to oppose each other on issues that

Figure 3.3: Diagram of Room Layout (Brussels)

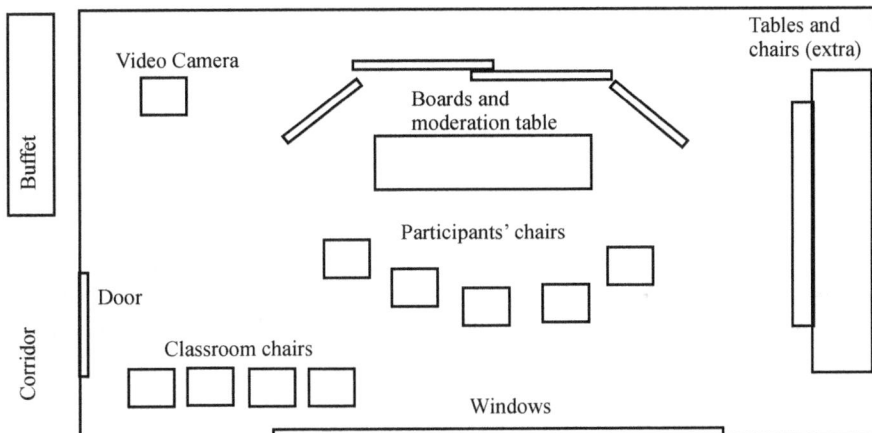

Table 3.5: Discussion scenario

Question 1: What does it mean to be European?
Duration: 30 minutes
The participants discuss the question while the moderator writes what is said on cards that are stuck up on the board, so that the participants are faced with comments made in the discussion.

Question 2: How should we distribute power in Europe?
Duration: 45 minutes
The two boards on which the question is posed are divided into four segments. In each one is a source of power: the nation, MPs, experts, the market. The participants are invited to discuss the advantages and disadvantages of giving power to each of these bodies. Finally the participants each receive six stickers and are asked to vote on the distribution of power between these four sources.

Break
Duration: 30 minutes

Question 3: Who profits from Europe?
Duration: 30 minutes
The participants work in pairs (or groups of three). They write their answers to the questions on cards (one response per card). The cards are then collected by the moderator and mixed up before being each discussed in turn by the group as a whole.

Question 4A: In favour or not of Turkey's entry in the EU?
Duration: 30 minutes
The participants are encouraged to vote using a sticker, for or against the entry of Turkey into the EU. Then the group as a whole is encouraged to find arguments for and against, beginning with the least popular arguments.

Question 4B: Amongst these political parties, who is for or against the entry of Turkey into the European Union? (followed by a list of political parties)
Duration: 15 minutes
Participants are invited to mention the parties that they want to talk about themselves. A card with the logo and the photo of the party leader is available for each national party. The participants decide on where they would like to situate a party on the board, in relation to the 'for' and 'against' poles, with an explanation as to their placement.

Figure 3.4: Example of board with cards for question: 'Who profits from Europe?'

Note: The darker cards were written by the participants themselves, in their response to the question. The lighter cards were those added by the moderator following the comments of the participants. The flash mark is encircled.

counted for them. In the way the discussions were conducted, the moderators left the participants free to evolve in the exchanges towards the subjects that were of interest to them. We will see in the next chapter, in fact, they often used this as *the opportunity to abandon the area of European questions altogether* (*see* Chapter Four). In other words, the framework enabled us to observe on which subjects the participants took the risk of engaging in conflict and to note which of these conflicts actually dealt with European issues (Duchesne *et al.* 2010).

Towards complementary approaches

The evolution described in Chapter Two, that is, the increase in the undecided *and* indifferent category of citizens, opens up a considerable research area, because of the breadth of the questions that it raises. It also encourages the renewal of methods of observing citizens' attitudes towards European integration. This chapter aimed to present the epistemological and methodological choices that guided the collection of qualitative data in conducting 24 focus groups. Each methodological choice and its place in the research design were justified and the chapter ended with a presentation of the way the comparison chosen by the CITAE project was constructed.

In practical terms, the CITAE project chose a comparative qualitative methodology, based on the organisation of focus groups in France, Belgium and in Great Britain. The analysis presented in Chapters Four and Five covers 24 groups of four to seven people, conducted between December 2005 and June 2006. The main characteristics of these groups were discussed in this chapter. Given that we decided not to work with pre-existing social networks, the search for social homogeneity governed the selection of participants, although for other criteria (gender, political orientation, attitudes to European integration, ethnic origin) heterogeneity was preferred. This is why the importance of the recruitment and selection of participants was thoroughly emphasised in this chapter.

Moreover, as this chapter has demonstrated, the CITAE research is part of the qualitative turn in European studies and the sociological approach to European integration. The penury and incompatibility of existing theories that aim to reflect national differences in terms of citizens' support for European integration, as well as the symptomatic lack of attention to the increase in indifferent and undecided attitudes, all contribute to the justification of the inductive approach used in part here. However, from my perspective, these choices in no way mean ignoring the existing data or research, which are principally quantitative, by opting for a purely qualitative and inductive approach.

In this chapter, I have argued for a complementarity of approaches and, by that, a complementarity of methods. This complementarity is part of the broader mixed-methods paradigm. At the heart of this research framework is the concept of triangulation, which refers to the idea that the more than one method is used in the process of empirical validation, thus ensuring that the variance explained is the result of the phenomenon observed and not an effect of the method (qualitative or quantitative) (Johnson *et al.* 2007: 113–14). The convergence of results obtained by using several different methods increases the chance that the results are valid and not the result of methodological artefact. The combination of methods and data aims to confirm, or corroborate by triangulation, previously obtained results. But this combination must also, perhaps above all, enable the development of the analysis by providing the researcher with new perspectives through the iteration of one research logic to another. Beyond this, the complementarity of approaches should allow us to develop new ways of perceiving European integration. Indeed, convergence, inconsistency or contradiction in the results obtained throws light on citizens' acceptance (or not) of the European political order. This occurs both by bringing to light the modes by which the European Union is appropriated by citizens but also through the connection of this problem question with that of the polarisation of the European political order and its possible politicisation.

Thus, in spite of the criticisms that might be levelled at it (Gaxie *et al.* 2011), my approach is based on the conviction that survey data remains a precious tool for European studies, if it is correctly understood and complemented by other data – qualitative in this case. Through the use and analysis of focus groups and a return to the Eurobarometers, the objective of this research has been to obtain an improved understanding of the problem of the acceptance of a political order, considered in the specific context of an emerging political system. When used in this perspective of triangulation, collective interviews are highly complementary to the survey data that is typically used.

Chapter Four

Revisiting 'Framing Europe'

Therefore some aspects of the European Union and European integration are perceived similarly everywhere, whereas other aspects acquire more salience in some countries or regions than others (Diez Medrano 2003: 249).

Today, the questions raised by the process of legitimating European integration, whether by academics (for example, Schrag Sternberg 2013: 220–33) or in European political discourse, come down to an interrogation of the possibility, and for some the desirability, of its politicisation.[1] In a context marked by the increasing involvement of political and social actors (political parties, social movements, interest groups) in public debate about the content and objectives of European integration, the stakes are likely to become clearer for European citizens, as these same debates are relayed in national media. Euroscepticism, and resistance to European integration more broadly, have been interpreted as the product of a heightened polarisation of European issues, in other words as the result of their increased political salience.

As a result, for those who wish to study the politicisation of the European political order at the individual level, the most important question is whether or not the debates relating to what 'Brussels' decides (at the macro level) are known to the general public (at the micro level). Indeed any interrogation of the possible politicisation of European integration and, in particular, discussions about Europe, supposes that ordinary citizens are familiar with European issues, that they have appropriated them as political issues for them and that they do indeed identify the European level of policy-making. In very concrete terms, this chapter will not aim to determine the actual and relative place of European issues in public discourse but instead to gauge what citizens – in particular those participating in these focus groups – make of these issues and how they mobilise them. This chapter will

---

1. As underlined in the first chapter of this book, 'politicisation' has recently become a 'buzzword' in European studies. This view is also noted by Claudia Schrag Sternberg, who stresses, in her very recent book, 'the literature around politicisation comprises and often combines, two types of approaches. Part of it is concerned with establishing the occurrence, analysing the nature, and explaining the causes of this development. Another perspective argues that this process should be encouraged and emphasised, for instrumental and/or normative reasons' (Schrag Sternberg 2013: 221). Following Pieter De Wilde and on a basis of a review of the growing literature around politicisation of EU politics, I would define the process of politicisation of European integration 'as an increase in polarisation of opinions, interests or values [concerning EU institutions, decision-making processes, as well as issues] and the extent to which they are publicly advanced towards the process of policy formulation within the EU' (De Wilde 2011: 559).

therefore investigate the assumption that actual knowledge of European political issues stems from the European level and explore the actual salience of these issues for Europeans. In this, my point of departure mirrors that of John Zaller, when he argues, in a very different context:

> the impact of people's value predispositions always depends on whether citizens possess the contextual information needed to translate their values into support for particular policies or candidates, and the possession of such information can […] never be taken for granted (Zaller 1992: 25).

The CITAE project provides a specific angle from which to observe this question; by studying the way in which participants talk about Europe. Through collective interviews conducted in three countries, this project aimed to encourage participants to express themselves on questions relating to European integration, a subject that, on face value, might seem likely to be unfamiliar to many of them. Reproducing a public discussion aims to enable us to observe how ordinary citizens talk about Europe. The analysis of discourses of legitimation in the public space – in the media, parliaments, academic journals or, as we are interested in here, in conversations between citizens – offer researchers a view of the complex and multidimensional nature of beliefs about the legitimacy of a public order. The discussions within these focus groups can be used to sketch the structure of discourses of (de) legitimation, the arguments used to support citizens' beliefs and demands for legitimacy, the normative references, the criteria of acceptability that they propose and the way they understand the interpretations and evaluations of this political order, in the sense of *framing* (Hurrelmann 2008: 190–211).

The notion of *frame* is used here following on from Diez Medrano's work. It constitutes a powerful analytical tool for studying attitudes towards European integration to the extent that 'frames mediate the effect of micro and macro sociological factors on people's attitudes toward European integration' (Diez Medrano 2003: 6). James D. Druckman contributes a further analytic distinction to this concept, which is particularly useful and relevant to this chapter. He distinguishes between 'frames in communication' and 'frames in thought' (Druckman 2001: 227–8). The former refer to frames that are produced in elite discourse, understood in a broad sense and communicated by these elites (essentially, via the media). The latter refer to the frames of the individual, that is, the individual representations that result from the reception of the 'framing messages' transmitted by the elites (Fuchs 2011: 46). This chapter mobilises the latter of these two perspectives. Specifically, it focuses on the way the positive and negative representations of the European order are cognitively constructed by citizens in the three countries studied here. Furthermore it seeks to determine from which debates these representations have sprung. In other words, it asks which representations citizens mobilise to justify their positive or negative evaluation of European integration.

In the context of the CITAE project, we conducted a series of 24 focus groups in Britain, France and (francophone) Belgium in 2006. This chapter begins by presenting the data collected in these focus groups, in order to see how this data enables us to understand on what ground ordinary citizens (de-)legitimise the European regional project. The material collected is particularly substantial, representing some 2000 pages of transcriptions and close to 52 hours of discussion.[2] Concretely, the chapter questions the salience of European issues for ordinary citizens, analysing the arguments put forward by the participants as a way of evaluating the process of European integration. Firmly part of the *qualitative turn* recently taken by European studies, this approach will enable us to present the content of these discussions and also, by extension, to present what we did not find.

The analysis proposed here is intentionally and explicitly influenced by that developed by Juan Diez Medrano in his remarkable book *Framing Europe* (Diez Medrano 2003). Indirect comparative analysis (I did not have access to Diez Medrano's data directly) using the theoretical framework of Diez Medrano enables me to produce a diachronic comparison using two sets of qualitative data (interviews and focus-groups collected at ten years distance (mid 1990 and 2006) in different national contexts.[3] By means of this indirect diachronic comparison with *Framing Europe,* the re-analysis of the data collected in the focus groups held in 2006 enables me to distinguish the common frames of (de-)legitimation recorded in Western public spheres. Enlarging the temporal and spatial scopes reduces the influence of the countries chosen and of the temporal context as much as possible. In doing this diachronic comparison, I hope also to contribute to qualitative research on European regional integration.

Concretely, the chapter begins with a detailed presentation of the systematic analysis techniques used for the groups, putting forward an identification of European issues within the discussions, and the evaluation of these issues (*see* the next section). The systematic coding conducted brings us back to the principal frames used by the participants in their understandings and evaluations of the European integration process. Above all, the process of coding caused me to evaluate and nuance the (sometimes confused and confusing) contributions of the participants that specifically dealt with European issues. The difficulty that the participants had in actually discussing Europe, and even more so European integration, is clearly evident here. Beyond the importance of this observation in itself, the analysis enables us to better understand how ordinary citizens understand and construct Europe on a cognitive level; and how they evaluate it. The subsequent section helps identify the shared frames of perception and evaluation used by citizens in the three countries, across all socio-demographic

---

2.   The number of pages of the transcriptions varies considerably from one group to another, from 53 pages for one of the groups of workers in Oxford, to 230 pages for a group of activists in Paris. Although the scenario of the focus groups is the same, the length of the discussions varies considerably, from one hour and 51 minutes from a group of activists in Oxford to three hours for certain groups in France and Belgium. The length of discussion did not exceed three hours because that was the length of time the participants were engaged and paid for.

3.   Spain, the United Kingdom and Germany for Juan Diez Medrano; Belgium, France and the United Kingdom for the CITAE project.

categories. The final section of this chapter forces us to explicitly question the perception of uniformity of attitudes towards the European Union. The analysis conducted here underlines the plurality of perceptions, which differ from one country to another, as other studies have demonstrated in other national cases (Belot 2000; Diez Medrano 2003; Gaxie, Hubé and Rowell 2011). In conclusion, I will argue that citizens do have representations of European integration but these representations, and the acceptance (or not) of the European political order that results from them, are still seen through the prism of the nation. In other words, the EU is still perceived and evaluated through the national frame. Although certain arguments may have changed since the publication of Diez Medrano's study, the mechanisms demonstrated by the author remain decisive in understanding the attitudes of European citizens in 2006 and, hypothetically, nowadays.

Specifically, this chapter will focus on what is similar in Western democracies, by analysing comparative data collected in 2006 through focus groups and by mobilising the categories of (de-)legitimation discourses constructed at a different times and in different countries using different kinds of data. These convergences guarantee the solidity of the results and, by replication, contribute to the cumulativity of qualitative research on European regional integration. Identifying what is common will enable future research to focus more precisely on other aspects that have acquired more salience in some countries than others. Finally, it will open up the possibility of a diachronic comparative analysis in order, for example, to understand what have been the impacts and consequences of the current crisis in terms of (de-)legitimation discourses of ordinary citizens. To this end, the data collected in the past are far from being outdated. Archiving qualitative data and mobilising secondary analysis (as developed in this chapter in an indirect way) will facilitate the comparative research that is necessary. Hence, qualitative data archiving will help individual scholars make comparisons of many types – across space (countries, cities, and so on); across time; across policy areas; across groups, and so on – that could otherwise require additional research resources or assembling a research team (Elman, Kapiszewski and Vinuela 2010: 24). Investigating empirical legitimacy and assessing politicisation at the individual level requires these comparisons. From the point of view of this book, we need first to study the common content and structures of (de-)legitimation discourses. This is the first step if we want to compare the (de-)legitimation discourses of Europeans after the crisis.

Identifying European issues

This chapter favours a renewal of the methods used in observing and analysing the subjective or empirical legitimacy of the European integration process (Bellamy and Castiglione 2003). Opinion surveys necessarily focus the respondent's attention on the research subject in question and thus have a tendency to exaggerate the levels of salience associated with it.[4] On the other hand, although the subject of

---

4. I will be taking a critical stance concerning the emergence and importance of certain themes within the discussions, unmistakably linked to the scenario of the discussion itself. For example, the subject of Turkey's membership of the EU was only coded if it appeared outside of the

Europe was imposed as a topic in the focus groups,[5] the questions remained very open and allowed for a certain freedom in the discussions; they revealed the issues which took on particular importance within the three populations studied. The effect of engagement in the dynamic of the discussions encouraged the participants to produce a discourse that was easily distinguished from the problems imposed by the researcher. The objective of this the next section is to determine to what extent citizens are conscious of European issues and even more how (or indeed whether) they take these issues on as their own. The first stage of the analysis therefore aims to respond to this twofold question: what are the European issues that are evoked in the discussions? And in what terms are they discussed?

Systematic coding of European themes

Coding is the most common method of systematically analysing a corpus of data, especially if it is made up of transcriptions. However it is important to emphasise that the coding of these group interviews was preceded by a long period of deciphering and interpreting the range of arguments and ideas mobilised by the participants. This interpretation was based on the construction of syntheses of each group, including a summary of the discussion and an intuitive analysis of the group and its dynamic. This period of interpretation constitutes the first phase of the researcher's internalisation and appropriation of the data, which is fundamental to the analytic process. Indeed, comments made by the participants are only meaningful in the context of what was said in the discussion, rendering any analysis of a de-contextualised extract virtually impossible. A holistic knowledge of the discussion in detail is a vital preliminary to the codification process. It supposes the mobilisation of all available material, first and foremost the video recordings and transcripts. However, it is difficult to describe this phase of interpretation, which is why I focus here on a presentation of the data along with the detailed explanation of the coding protocol.

Coding those parts of the discussions that specifically deal with an aspect of European integration allow for the falsification of the analysis by, in theory, making it possible to verify each code. At the heart of the analysis of these transcriptions is the identification of each segment of discussion, in order to be able to trace its interpretation and its role in the conclusions reached. In this respect, coding requires the researcher to conduct a systematic exploration of the corpus in its entirety. The systematisation of this procedure means fighting against the tendency to over-reliance on those elements of the corpus best suited to the demonstration and which conform best to the initial hypotheses (Duchesne and Haegel 2004: 98).

---

question specifically targeting this issue. As a reminder, because of its specificities, particularly concerning the group dynamic, I have preferred to exclude question four from the analysis.

5. The CITAE study is very different from those directed by Diez Medrano. Unlike him, we did not directly pose the Eurobarometer questions in the group interviews. As a result it is particularly difficult to distinguish the arguments intended to justify their positions relating to the European integration process. The CITAE study is also different from White's study, because that author preferred to adopt a research design that did not directly lead to the subject of Europe in the interviews; and he also observed the low salience of European issues (White 2011).

Moreover, the systematic coding of group interviews enables the researcher to link different elements of the corpus to each other. These linkages appear throughout this chapter. Indeed, as the reader will see in the rest of this chapter, the systematic coding of European themes and their evaluation in positive or negative terms could be used in two very different ways – qualitatively or quantitatively. The objective of the coding is thus to provide the means to describe the content of the focus-group discussions but also to understand how the different categories of codes work together.

A CAQDAS (Computer Aided Qualitative Data Analysis Software) programme, Atlas.ti, was used to identify the different cognitive frames and arguments of (de-)legitimation of European regional integration. Empirically, given that the principal advantage of focus groups as a research tool lies in the interactions between the participants, it is essential that the dynamic of the discussion forms the basis of the data analysis. In this chapter, the analysis is conducted at group level rather than at individual level, although individual characteristics were also coded. The qualitative coding consists in identifying the points of convergence and divergence in the European themes evoked by the participants in the corpus. It is worth noting that the unit of code and analysis used here is a segment of text, which has been coded in terms of a European theme. I have not opted for a predefined unit of code based on a given convention (words, phrases, paragraphs and so on), as would be the case in statistical content analysis (with the programme ALCESTE, for example). The coding led me to distinguish different sequences of interview of varying length. The codes relating to European themes refer to passages involving several participants but are also non-exclusive categories. One segment of text may thus be simultaneously coded in many ways and the codes may only partially overlap. This type of coding is particularly well adapted to rendering the particular discussion dynamic of group interviews and also to revealing the polysemy of discourse that is characteristic of them (Duchesne and Haegel 2004: 100).

The methodological difficulties related to taking into account the positive or negative nature of a sequence are significant. Indeed, even for those who do not hesitate to invest in methodological innovation, the systematic treatment of these evaluations poses substantial difficulties. Coding themes and knowledge presupposes taking the time required and remaining consistent in the codes throughout; but coding evaluations raises specific problems to do with the tension between principles of interpretation. Coding necessarily requires a certain amount of de-contextualisation because it requires applying a code to a specific sequence – preferably quite short – and referring to an object that is as clearly identified as possible. However, the interviews show that, in general, exchanges between participants are complex and often correspond to substantial segments that cover portions of text that vary greatly in length. The coded evaluation corresponds to a real exchange between participants, in which several themes and arguments are intertwined. It is therefore doubly difficult to code an evaluation without taking into account the context of the interaction in which it occurred and in isolating a particular relation to a single object. Similarly, it isn't always easy to evaluate the positive or negative associations of these objects or to distinguish them from a general emotional engagement that characterises a particular segment of text.

In spite of these difficulties, I have systematically applied a positive/negative code to all segments evoking a European theme, distinguishing between the emotional tone of the sequence and the argument mobilised. Looking back at the quotations once they have been coded, it is often tempting to revise certain codes: coding becomes a form of permanent negotiation. However, this trait – the necessarily debatable nature of the coding – is one of the advantages of the method from the point of view of 'grounded theory'. According to this theory, the codes and their relationships are the means by which concepts are constructed; they are not objects in themselves and therefore their finality is not in the objective description of a corpus but instead in theory-building.

Coding categories as the first result

In order to determine the importance of European issues, understood broadly, both in sector-specific and institutional terms, it was important to begin by identifying the moments of the discussion in which the participants talk about European integration, as well as the arguments they use to justify or oppose the process underway. In this, one can implicitly observe the representations and conceptions (in other words the frames) that are at the heart of this coding. Concretely, the indicators chosen refer to European issues in a broad sense and the positive or negative evaluations of these issues.

As already discussed in Chapter One, the process of coding is firmly and deliberately based in the tradition of Diez Medrano's work *Framing Europe* (Diez Medrano 2003: 21). In the hope of engaging with this fundamental author, I have, as far as possible, ensured that my coding categories correspond to his. This decision aims to underline the evolution that can be observed between these two studies conducted a decade apart. On this point, my epistemological position may appear in contradiction with the grounded-theory approach to sociology but, in practice, this is not necessarily the case. Following Udo Kelle, it appears that the unfeasibility of a purely inductive research strategy, which would require the researcher to be a blank slate as opposed to just having an open mind, can not only be demonstrated on epistemological grounds but also seen in research practices (Kelle 2005). The founders of grounded theory also emphasised this:

> of course, the researcher does not approach reality as a tabula rasa. He must have a perspective that will help him see relevant data and abstract significant categories from his scrutiny of the data (Glaser and Strauss 1967: 3).

By putting 'theoretical sensitivity', understood as the researcher's aptitude to 'see the relevant data', before any kind of inductive purism, I constructed a coding system initially similar to that developed by Diez Medrano. As coding progressed, the initial categories were honed and focused and new categories emerged. This evolution over the course of the analysis eventually led to seventeen different codes, nine of which are found in *Framing Europe* (Diez Medrano 2003: 27–8).

Table 4.1: Coding protocol for the group interviews

Codes from *Framing Europe* (Diez Medrano 2003: 68)

* Comprehension: contributes to better understanding between peoples and cultures and to unity.
* Democratic deficit: European institutions suffer from a democratic deficit.
* Governance: the governance of European institutions is poor, complicated, bad, unsatisfying, weighed down by supplementary norms.
* States too small: states are too small to face economic or military challenges.
* Free movement and competition: free movement of workers will mean competition from foreign workers.
* Single market: the single market is economically beneficial.
* Peace: will contribute to peace.
* Sovereignty and identity: membership in the European Union has or will have a negative effect on national sovereignty and identity.
* Removal of barriers: the removal of barriers to the movement of people is a good thing (mobility, travels).

New codes

Benefits for future generations: European construction is a good thing for future generations, our grandchildren.
Offshoring: businesses are offshored to Eastern Europe, or outside Europe.
Discord between countries: member-countries often disagree (Iraq, CAP, VAT).
Enlargement: enlargement to 25 happened too quickly and stretched too far.[6]
Immigrationw: European construction increases immigration (into Europe and/or into one's own country).
Inflation: the single currency has led to or will lead to an increase in prices and a loss of purchasing power.
Solidarity: European integration benefits solidarity between rich and poor countries.
Utopia: European integration is a utopia, a concept; it doesn't exist.

The new codes principally reflect a negative evaluation of the integration process, in codes such as 'Offshoring', 'Discord between countries', 'Inflation', 'Immigration', and 'Utopia', but also, to a lesser extent, positive themes such as 'Benefit future generations' and 'Solidarity'; the latter mobilises issues to do with regional and structural funds. Other codes used by Diez Medrano appeared, in a less extensive way, within the collective interviews of the CITAE project. This is particularly the case for the following codes: 'CAP: the Common Agricultural Policy is a bad policy'; 'Against isolation: membership of this country is necessary to break the country's isolation, isolation is disadvantageous for the country';

---

6. References to the possible membership of Turkey in the EU have not been coded in this category because the last question of the interview protocol deals specifically with this problem. As a result, coding segments of discussion linked to Turkey would have introduced an error, in the sense that this category of code would have been artificially inflated by the interview protocol itself.

'Voice: the country's voice is not taken into account within European institutions';
'Modernisation: the country will modernise as a member of European institutions.'

The suppression of certain categories and the emergence of others in fact constitute a first level of results in the qualitative analysis. This evolution reflects the content of the group interviews, both on a conceptual and a descriptive level. As this chapter seeks to demonstrate, the analysis of these different national cases makes us realise the multiplicity of cognitive frames and thus to adjust the categories used by Diez Medrano. Given this, it is logical that the frames that characterise perception in the German or Spanish cases, are not, or not as, significant in the focus groups conducted in Britain, in (francophone) Belgium and in France. This is particularly true for the 'Lessons of World War II', 'Isolation', and 'Modernisation' codes; the first is characteristic of the German case, whilst the second two refer more specifically to the Spanish case. Adding two new national cases (Belgium and France) necessarily bring out specific categories. For example, and as a taste of what is to come at the end of this chapter, the code 'Benefits future generations' is particularly characteristic of the Belgian participants, whereas the French evaluate the integration process by evoking questions of daily subsistence such as inflation as a result of the single currency.

Beyond these few differences the categories developed by Diez Medrano have shown themselves to be a precious tool, well adapted to the analysis of the group interviews. Amongst all the European themes raised by the participants, 917 segments of text were coded and associated with a positive or negative evaluation. Although a great variety of arguments, justifications and explanations are mobilised in the discussions of Europe, the respondents do tend to converge towards a more coherent group of themes, presented in Table 4.2.

The four major frames of perception distinguished in *Framing Europe* can also be distinguished in my corpus: the benefits of the single market; the small size of member-states; the removal of borders; and governance (Diez Medrano 2003: 26–33). Within the 917 occurrences of these thematic and evaluative codes, 645 come from these four major frames identified by Diez Medrano; 322 in the Belgian corpus, 335 in the French corpus and 260 in the British corpus. I will come back to the content and distribution of these different coding categories in the different groups in more detail in the next section of this chapter. However, one can already see how relevant these four categories developed by Diez Medrano are in exploring the content of the discussions specifically relating to the European integration process and its evaluation. They are key frames for comprehending the (de-)legitimation discourses of ordinary citizens, both in the nineties and in 2006, after the referendum on the Constitution. Overall, the participants' comments reflect different kinds of argumentation that are broadly similar to those described by Diez Medrano in his study of individual interviews (Diez Medrano 2003: 22–6). Thus, despite the fact that these two studies are separated by more than a decade and use different research tools, the discourses observed converge on many points, both in their forms of expression and in their content. This in itself validates the two research protocols. The next section will present the content of each of these four coding categories in detail.

Table 4.2: Themes mobilised in justifying or rejecting the European integration process, by group (N=917)

Codes	Workers			Employees			Managers			Activists			Total
	B	F	UK	B	F	UK	B	F	UK	B	F	UK	
COMMON MARKET													**203**
Benefits of common market (+)	3/1	6/1	2/2	3/3	1/2	3/5	1/2	1/2	5/1	4/1	3/1	5/4	62
Free circulation and competition (-)	4/4	0/4	4/1	2/4	3/3	2/2	0/4	2/1	2/0	1/4	5/3	0/2	57
Offshoring (-)	4/2	1/1	0/1	1/1	1/2	0/2	1/3	1/1	0/0	3/1	2/3	1/1	34
Immigration (-)	1/0	0/2	5/2	2/3	2/0	2/2	0/1	2/2	2/0	0/1	0/0	0/1	30
Inflation (Euro) (-)	2/0	3/1	1/0	1/2	2/1	0/0	0/0	1/3	0/0	0/0	1/1	0/1	20
STATES ARE TOO SMALL													**148**
Countries too small (+)	3/2	2/5	3/8	5/1	9/6	4/5	4/8	2/3	1/4	4/7	8/7	2/6	108
Discord between countries (-)	4/1	4/3	3/2	0/0	1/0	1/1	1/2	3/0	3/3	4/0	1/2	0/1	40
REMOVAL OF BORDERS													**108**
Easier mobility (+)	6/6	5/2	1/2	4/4	2/1	6/2	6/4	5/3	5/1	5/3	4/2	4/3	86
Understanding and unity (+)	1/2	2/0	0/3	1/2	1/4	0/0	0/0	1/0	0/0	3/0	2/0	0/0	22
GOVERNANCE													**186**
Governance (-)	4/1	9/5	2/3	2/1	0/1	4/4	2/9	4/6	5/5	9/9	10/6	1/2	104
Democratic deficit (-)	3/3	3/0	3/0	3/1	1/2	3/3	3/4	2/7	4/2	6/7	12/7	3/0	82
OTHER THEMES													**272**
Peace (+)	0/0	0/0	1/0	0/0	0/0	0/1	1/1	2/1	1/1	3/3	7/3	2/0	27
Future generations (+)	5/0	1/0	0/1	8/0	0/1	0/1	2/2	1/0	2/0	0/0	0/3	1/0	28
Solidarity (+)	3/1	3/0	2/1	4/2	3/3	3/2	3/2	3/1	2/0	2/2	5/2	2/3	54
Sovereignty, identity (-)	4/2	2/0	7/4	2/5	1/5	11/1	2/3	2/4	8/4	2/4	7/5	4/3	92
Enlargement (-)	2/2	4/3	1/0	1/1	3/2	1/0	1/5	1/4	1/1	2/2	3/1	1/2	44
Utopia, doesn't exist (-)	2/2	1/0	0/0	1/1	0/4	1/0	0/1	3/1	2/0	1/0	2/2	2/1	27
Total	80	73	65	71	67	72	78	75	65	93	120	58	917

Key: Two group interviews were conducted per category for each country so the frequency of each code is given for each particular group. The first number refers to set 1 and the second to set 2.

Talking about Europe: a difficult exercise

Even before presenting the analysis of the group interviews in detail, the identification of European themes and their evaluations enables us to underline several important results. Firstly, the presence of coded arguments leads me to think that, although the majority of the population pays little attention to European issues, repetition nevertheless has an impact – because citizens have, over time, accumulated a certain amount of latent knowledge about the EU (Diez Medrano 2003: 22). The participants thus took the exercise seriously, including the participants from the workers' and temporary workers' groups, who might have regarded their participation as a paid service. Some participants even remarked that they hadn't thought they knew as much as they did about this issue. The dynamic of the discussion thus revealed its full potential here and even allowed us to confirm our decision to use focus groups. As can be seen from Extract 4.1, taken from the discussion of a group of workers in Oxford, Robert and then Brenda humorously acknowledge their ignorance about European integration:

Extract 4.1: Set 1, Oxford, workers

Robert: If you went out on the street and you ask ten people, six or seven people they wouldn't be able to tell you that much of what the EU's about. You know what I mean? I don't know much about it but I've learnt more about the European Union since I came here tonight than what I've knew before. (*General laughter*)

Brenda: Same as me. I thought that Switzerland was part of it as well. (*Laughs*)

Robert: I'm being honest, it's true.

However, the focus on European issues in the discussion extracts presented in this chapter should not lead the reader to suppose that talking about European integration is particularly stimulating for all the participants. Although European issues were clearly present in these discussions, their presence and salience (Duchesne, Frazer, Haegel and Van Ingelgom 2013) should not be exaggerated. Indeed although all the participants expressed their opinions on European integration at times, their discussions on the subject were more or less extensive and revealed more or less familiarity with the issue. Although it is clear that the participants in the workers' and the employees' groups made an effort to apply themselves to this subject as directed (a subject which, participants often admitted, was far removed from their everyday concerns), the discussions often moved out of the frame that was imposed on them. In order to illustrate this point, Table 4.3 presents the relative amount of each discussion that was coded. European themes only represented a fifth to a quarter of the subjects discussed in these focus groups. Significant national and social differences can be observed in this. From the point of view of international comparison it is important to signal the specificity of the Belgian corpus, where the participants were more inclined to talk about European integration: 25.44 per cent of this corpus is made of discussions on European issues. From the point of view of social comparison, in spite of a few minor differences, the participants from lower social groups tended to talk about the EU less than the activists and executives.

This initial count enables us to put into perspective the amount of discussion dedicated to the EU within our focus groups, even though the subject of discussion was Europe. It also sheds light on the structuration of these discussions, which were differentiated in both social and national terms. Like all the results presented in this chapter, this count is corroborated by our interpretative analysis of the groups, which enabled us to distinguish the groups of workers and the disadvantaged respondents and, to a lesser extent, the groups of executives and activists: the first being ultimately not very concerned and not very familiar with the subject, whereas the latter were significantly more engaged in the discussion and appropriated European terms and the issues to a greater extent (Duchesne 2013).

The analysis continued with the identification of a vocabulary specifically linked to the European Union and to Europe, as a second indicator of the presence of Europe and European integration in the discussions. An automated search allowed the location of all the terms related to the EU, to its institutions, or to their corresponding adjectives. The detail of the occurrences of the words 'Euro', 'Europe', and 'European' within each of the categories, for each group and per country, is presented in Table 4.4.

In all three countries, the groups of workers and employees make fewer explicit references to Europe and also talk less about European integration. The groups made up of workers use nearly half as many terms linked to Europe as do participants in the executives' or activists' groups. Although they do speak less overall, as we can see by the total number of words spoken, the vocabulary linked to Europe is nonetheless significantly smaller in these groups. Thus, when these lower-social-class categories talk about European integration, they do so in more abstract, not specifically European, terms.

In terms of the national comparison, the study of the frequency of the words 'Euro', 'Europe' and 'European' again reveals a notable difference between the three countries studied. The Belgian respondents used more European vocabulary than their French and English counterparts and this was true at all levels of social comparison. The Belgian groups were much more familiar with the European integration process in talking about the European Union than their French or English counterparts. An interpretative analysis of the Brussels group shows that they appear to be the most competent (Duchesne *et al.* 2013). They know the history and institutional mechanisms of the EU and refer to a certain number of public policies, such as the agricultural, education, competition or health policies. By way of revealing this level of competence, all the explicit references to the EU, its institutions in a broad sense, its policies or its history have been coded within the collective interviews. Thus references to the European Commission were coded as a marker of competence, as were references to the Common Agricultural Policy or any mention of a European political figure such as Jean Monnet, or any reference to a treaty. Indeed, if the number of total references is not noticeably

Table 4.3: Distribution of European themes coded within the collective interviews

	Workers	Employees	Executives	Activists	Total
Brussels					
Codes (words)	10271	22233	14013	23336	69853
Total (words)	61134	74171	69809	69425	274539
%	16.80	29.97	20.07[*]	33.61	25.44
Oxford					
Codes (words)	8811	9819	11782	8835	39247
Total (words)	45259	42467	50355	46483	184564
%	19.46	23.12	23.39	19.00[**]	21.26
Paris					
Codes (words)	15758	11878	15510	29321	72467
Total (words)	90943	79485	80270	113526	364224
%	17.32	14.94	19.32	25.82	19.89

[*]   One of the two groups of activists in Oxford turned out to be quite dysfunctional, which explains the low percentage for the British activist groups.

[**]   The second group of managers conducted in Brussels turned out to have a quite particular character. One of the participants in this group, Gaston, an extreme-right sympathiser, had a strong personality and led the discussion to focus on particularly polemical issues. He often launched into grand tirades and life stories, in which the connection to Europe was not always clear. Moreover, his unusual personality and his often-extreme opinions meant that the dynamic of the discussion was concentrated around him. This reminds us of the importance of the recruitment process (or the variability of recruitment).

Table 4.4: Distribution of the occurrences of the words 'Euro', 'Europe', and 'European', per total words spoken

	Workers	Employees	Executives	Activists	Total
Brussels					
Euro- (words)	267	391	571	662	1891
Total (words)	61134	74171	69809	69425	274539
%	0.0069	0.0053	0.0082	0.0095	0.0069
Oxford					
Euro- (words)	143	243	436	366	1188
Total (words)	45259	42467	50355	46483	184564
%	0.0032	0.0057	0.0087	0.0079	0.0064
Paris					
Euro- (words)	282	183	417	559	1441
Total (words)	90943	79485	80270	113526	364224
%	0.0031	0.0023	0.0052	0.0049	0.0040

different between the French (N=173) and Belgian groups (N=175), that is because of the French activist groups that very dramatically increase the score recorded by the Parisian groups (N=95). The French activist groups essentially replayed the debate on the Constitutional Treaty. If one leaves them out of the equation, the superior expertise of the Brussels groups emerges clearly, with 117 explicit references compared with just 78 for the Parisian groups and 68 for the Oxford groups. As might be expected, the British groups were by far the least competent. The singularity of the Belgian corpus compared to the other two was measured by combining an interpretive analysis with an automatic analysis using the programme ALCESTE, conducted by Sophie Duchesne and interpreted by Florence Haegel (Haegel 2013). Indeed, from a purely arithmetical perspective, the ALCESTE analysis enabled the construction of six classes (or six semantic spheres) from the Belgian corpus, whereas only four were constructed for the two other corpuses. Moreover, the Belgian corpus is not only semantically richer; it is also more closely linked to Europe and European integration. Inversely, and as one might expect, the English participants appeared to be the least likely to use these same words (in quantitative terms). However, given that the British participants were also the least talkative all round, although they didn't speak much, they did speak about Europe using a European vocabulary. On the other hand, the French participants did not talk much about integration, although they were by far the most talkative generally. The results of the CITAE study enabled me to emphasise this specificity of the French participants (Duchesne *et al.* 2013). Briefly, I can conclude that the Belgian participants spoke a lot, and lots about European integration; the English did not speak much but when they did so they talked, as requested, about European integration; and, finally, the French participants spoke a lot but ultimately did not talk much about European integration.

More specifically, the Belgian participants demonstrated particularly sophisticated reasoning concerning the European Union. This Belgian expertise can be explained by the clear schooling they have received (the European Union appears to have been taught in the school system), through their experience and the proximity they have to the European system as inhabitants of the Brussels area. Whatever the cause may be, the European expertise of the Brussels groups is also and above all due to the fact that the Belgians are able to integrate the European political system into their political understanding through a mechanism of analogy with their own national system. In this respect we follow the analysis of Vivien Schmidt, when she argues that, for the macro level, 'the addition of a highly complex European system destabilises all the national regimes and increases the complexity of national systems but this impact is much more intense in simple systems than in complex ones' (Schmidt 2008). The same mechanism appears also to affect individuals. The familiarity of the Belgian participants with multi-level systems and complex political structures clearly facilitates their understanding of the EU. It also means that they can adapt more easily to the new international system that is emerging at the European level (Frazer and Van Ingelgom 2013).

In conclusion, even though they were interviewed about European integration and they attempted to construct their discussions around this theme – a goal reinforced by their remuneration – the participants actually spoke fairly little of European integration. Beyond this observation, the social and national differences are striking. The more working-class groups appear to have had the most difficulty appropriating the terms of the discussion and occasionally lost the topic entirely. They also demonstrated a lack of familiarity, even a perceptible remoteness, from this theme. Although this is not surprising, it is nonetheless interesting regarding the need to make clear the actual relative importance of Europe in these discussions, particularly in the two more working-class categories of respondents.

It is essential to begin by drawing the attention of the reader to this point in order to avoid conveying a false image of the groups and, in particular, to avoid assimilating the *presence* of European issues to the *salience* of these issues. The relatively small amount of discussion concerned with European issues has to be linked to our interpretative analysis of the groups, which enables us to affirm that the European-integration process does not result in (or only rarely results in) a sense of personal implication and personal engagement in contestation for the participants. This is unlike other subjects of conversation spontaneously discussed by the participants (particularly immigration, colonisation, unemployment, education and so on), particularly in the groups of employees and workers (Duchesne *et al.* 2013). The results of this systematic analysis thus converge with the results of a range of qualitative studies looking at attitudes towards integration that have observed the low salience of European integration.

One final observation remains to be made. The presence of positive and negative arguments within each of the groups is partly linked to our desire, theoretical and methodological, to create a cleavage between the participants on the question of Europe, with the aim of generating discussion (Duchesne *et al.* 2013). If the 'pro' and 'anti' arguments are indeed present in the interviews, their presence is partially artificial, linked to the research protocol itself.

In conclusion, this observation of low salience of European issues at the level of citizens should encourage researchers to interrogate the logic of de-politicisation linked to European integration; this is, however, beyond the scope and the aim of this text.

Common views of European integration

In this section, the comments have been organised according to the four major frames of perception identified by Juan Diez Medrano. These are: the benefits of the single market; the small size of member-states; the removal of borders; and governance. As a reminder, these four frames were very prevalent within the 24 focus group interviews, representing 645 occurrences out of a total 917 segments of text coded. These four frames are presented each in turn, underlining the evaluations that are made of them and the evolutions observed since the publication of *Framing Europe*. By doing so, this section sets the stage for the analyses presented in the rest of this book.

The single market: between benefits and critics

On the side of those who argue in favour of European integration, the most frequently mentioned theme in Diez Medrano's work concerned the characteristics and the expectations of benefits linked to the realisation of the common market (Diez Medrano 2003: 27). This type of commentary is based on the belief that the single market will have a directly positive impact on wellbeing and economic growth. Although this theme was often present in the groups conducted as part of the CITAE project, it was not the most commonly discussed theme. Of the 917 occurrences of codes attributed in the corpus, 62 relate to the benefits of the single market. It thus arrives in sixth place in terms of importance and is the third most important advantage put forward by the participants in justifying the European integration process.

Generally, comments refer to the benefits of removing barriers to commerce by creating a larger market. Almost systematically, in response to the question 'who benefits from Europe?', we see the word 'businesses' on the cards written by the participants; and this regardless of the category or the country of the group considered.[7] This is, for example, the case in Extract 4.2, in which this aspect is emphasised by André and Farouk, participants in a group conducted among workers in Brussels.

Extract 4.2: Set 2, Brussels, workers

Moderator: (*Who benefits from Europe?*) Businesses.

André: Yes, because now with the free market; the last fifteen years, the increase of profits to business, it's more than twenty or thirty per cent per year. We're talking about billions of euros for each European business with this free market.

Moderator: Ok, increasing profits in the market. Did I hear 'management'?

Farouk: Businesses, too.

André: Yeah it's the same thing.

Thus, the argument that the realisation of the single market benefits businesses was very widespread in these groups (to differing degrees). Here, behind the businesses it is indeed the management that is targeted and not the employees or the workers in these businesses.

The participants broadly recognise that the completion of the market and the free circulation of goods have opened new markets for big business. But there are other types of benefits linked to the single market. Access to all types of goods is also perceived as a linked advantage. In Extract 4.3, in response to the question of

---

7. For a systematic analysis of the distribution of cards created by participants, *see* the chapter by Sophie Duchesne in *Overlooking Europe* (Duchesne *et al.* 2013).

what it means to be European, Kamal underlines having more choice of products commercially available. He gives the example of food and wine, an example that provokes laughter among the other participants in this group (conducted with employees in Oxford); but, according to him, the list is endless.

Extract 4.3: Set 1, Oxford, employees

Kamal: More choice.

Moderator: More choice.

Kamal: In terms of everything: trade, goods, food, wine.

Moderator: Food and wine. (All laugh)

Kamal: The list is endless.

The mobility of factors of production, as well as the possibility of working overseas and employing overseas labour, are also seen as advantages resulting from the single market. From a discussion among a group of workers conducted in Oxford (Set 2), Bridget evokes some of these benefits of the single market, again for businesses: 'I think from being European, they're pooling together. There's more scope for them to grow and advance, to have more people working for them, which would obviously help them to grow and obviously profit financially.'

As Juan Diez Medrano has pointed out, and however much one might expect this result, it is nonetheless important to emphasise just how much the EU has managed – at least up until recently – to popularise the idea that a larger market with increased competition is good on an economic level (Diez Medrano 2003: 26). Popular support and approval regarding the single market are based on beliefs at least as much as they are on rational judgment or on an actual knowledge of the European economic situation.

However, and even two years before the 2008 economic and financial crisis, it seems that the situation described by the participants in the CITAE project groups is clearly different, in that it is less positive, from that described in *Framing Europe*. As a reminder, the author observed that, in his interviews, a kind of unanimous belief as to the benefits of economic liberalism reigned (Diez Medrano 2003: 26). On the contrary, a substantial part of the focus groups' discussions dealing directly with the economic aspects of European integration mobilises an often quite biting critique of the free market and the accomplishments of the single market (merchandise, work and capital).

Of the 202 arguments referring to an aspect of the single market, 62 have been coded as positive and 140 as negative. The ratio between the positive and negative evaluations linked to the single market is 0.44, which underlines the significance of the critiques levelled at the single market. In spite of the shared faith of many of the participants regarding the benefits of the single market and its economic advantages, this optimistic approach towards European integration is heavily counterbalanced by a tangible anxiety concerning its harmful effects, resulting from differences between salaries and social benefits. This social anxiety has already been noted elsewhere, particularly from survey data focused on the French case (Dehousse 2006: 154; Sauger, Brouard and Grossman 2007: 89–98). Without drawing any conclusions too hastily, one can nevertheless note the evolution that has occurred over the past ten years, compared with Diez Medrano's depiction. In Great Britain, as well as in Belgium and in France, the liberalisation of the European market no longer fuels only arguments in support of integration. Thus, well before the 2008 crisis, citizens in francophone Belgium, in France and in Great Britain were already widely denouncing the harmful impacts of economic liberalism.

The critiques levelled at the single market emerge principally as part of a discourse condemning intra-European competition on the labour market. This critique, although it was already present in the German interviews conducted as part of *Framing Europe,* can be found very strongly in the three populations studied here – including in the British case, although it is less clear. The 'free circulation and competition' code was assigned 47 times in these collective interviews. Once again, this code refers to the negative aspects related to the freedom of circulation and competition. In Extract 4.4, taken from a group of employees in Brussels, Tina suggests that liberalisation of the markets in terms of competition and lowering prices could be advantageous; Pierre, however, is very critical of this integration and links it to the question of competition between businesses, using an analogy between workers and athletes.

Extract 4.4: Set 2, Brussels, employees

Tina: It's true that on the level of the labour market we're a bit worse off, but on an individual level, when I can get a reduction on my telephone every month and have unlimited calls to landlines, I'm not saying no.

Pierre: Liberalisation often goes along with competition. We talk about the winners, right? (*Jonathon agrees.*) I might come back to this problem a lot, there are a lot of people who are more affected by all that. My example is this. In my town, at one stage we had eleven football teams, seven basketball teams, but we all just played for fun. Then they introduced competition, they wanted to set up a division. Now there's no more basketball at all. The neighbouring town took all the best footballers. There is competition, the best found a place for themselves, the five best players got places in the next team but there are 70 or 90 young kids who don't play anymore. It's a bit the same in the economy. In competition between businesses, we only talk about the winners, for the winners it's good.

Michèle: Yes, but it's true that there are perhaps companies that will lose out.

This criticism of the single market in terms of competition is often connected to the more specific disapproval as to the negative effects of the market in terms of immigration. Immigration is thus presented as one of the main negative effects of the single market (30 instances) as Extract 4.5, among a group of workers in Oxford, illustrates. From the beginning of the interview, immigration and, by extension, the illegal work of Poles and Croats are condemned as being the major negative aspect of European integration. Unemployment is explicitly attributed to open borders and the mobility of workers, which sets up an opposition between the British and Irish on one hand and those from eastern-European countries on the other. The arrival of a cheap workforce is seen here as the heart of the problem of immigration and unemployment, but also the problem of the minimum wage.

Extract 4.5: Set 1, Oxford, workers

Robert: Obviously the other bad side of it is the people coming away from poor countries. A lot of people say they're taking the place of people who are British people, English people and who want employment. If you go to building sites, nowadays I mean, I worked on building sites and like over 50 per cent of the building site would be people from like eastern European countries like Poland.

Moderator: Right.

Mary: Poland, yeah.

Robert: Used to be like ten years ago if you went onto a site there'd always be like Irish labourers like this you got there and bricklayers.

Brenda: It's all sorts now.

Ron: Now it's Croatian.

Robert: Yeah, Croatian.

Brenda: Some of them are illegal so now they're coming here to work and they're illegal and as soon as they have an accident or as soon as they seem to do anything wrong, nothing is done about it.

Robert: What it is a lot of them are working for the reason? Why a lot of the foreigners and eastern European ones are getting the labour jobs on building sites? Because they're working for agencies and they're working for less money, for £5 an hour whereas someone English over here wouldn't do a labouring job for £5 an hour. But someone from Poland would do it for £5 an hour because it's a lot more money than they'd get back home.

Mary: Yeah.

Brenda: But it isn't helping the minimum wage working people for less because that means we'll always be working for less.

The inequality in salaries and social benefits between European countries is thus condemned in itself, but also because it is the source of offshoring practices (33 instances). In Extract 4.6, the benefits of the single market for French companies who move offshore are opposed to the wellbeing of French workers. The participants in this group of French employees, although they disagree on many points throughout the discussion, finally end up agreeing in their condemnation of the negative effects of economic liberalism.

Extract 4.6: Set 2, Paris, employees

Martin: Well, me, I don't agree because I've the impression that there are lots of companies. I'm not talking about people but companies, who go offshore, and who go offshore precisely to the new countries in the Community, because there is a practical advantage, (*Pablo attempts to interrupt*), financial of course, salaries and all that.

Pablo: That's the expression I was thinking of.

Martin: However, it's true that on a more personal level it's less clear. I'm saying companies, the companies benefit from this European openness.

Paul: Yeah, they have more of an interest to come here than for us to go there.

Samira: Yeah, there you go.

Pablo: For the moment they're offshoring with all their strength.

Martin isn't questioning the fact that European integration benefits companies, particularly because they find economic advantages in moving within Europe, but he condemns the impact of these moves on French people when stressing that 'the average wage over there was 100 euros a month. So even workers earning the minimum wage here in France wouldn't even agree to the principle.'

Inevitably, those who are seen as responsible in both extracts are mainly the new member-countries. The vocabulary may vary between groups: some use the famous 'Polish plumber' expression, where others prefer the more technical references to the Bolkenstein directive. Either way, it is the same phenomenon that is denounced: the increase in competition on the labour market within Europe, in particular following enlargement to eastern European countries[8]. The inequalities between European countries are accused of being the cause of offshoring towards these countries where salaries and social benefits are lower, particularly the new member-countries. Pushed to its extreme, the argument leads to the condemnation of a race to the bottom in terms of social benefits, as Brenda points out at the end of Extract 4.5, when she talks about the minimum wage. Fabienne, a member of a

---

8.   The question of enlargement is found throughout the major frames of perception. As a result, I have preferred to include it in the 'other themes' category of the overall table.

group of employees in Paris, in Extract 4.7 criticises the Bolkenstein directive as being 'the worst thing possible' because it puts European employees in competition with each other.

Extract 4.7: Set 2, Paris, managers

Fabienne: I'm just reacting to what you said about the market. We won't agree again (*smiles laughs, Gabriel pouts*), but still, I think that most of the power is given to the market. There is always something, there's a social reality that we can see in France, and we see elsewhere. Since the beginning of the discussion about the market, we still haven't spoken about the Bolkenstein directive (*smiles*), which is the worst thing possible.

Serge: Yes I did mention it.

Fabienne: What's more, it forces employees in different countries to be in competition with each other (*Toufik agrees*), and uses the poverty of certain countries, Poland for example, to attract employees.

Finally, although the participants acknowledge the advantages of the shared currency, particularly in terms of ease of circulation because of the lack of currency exchanges (*see* next sections) the euro is also a synonym of inflation (20 instances). Behind this denunciation of inflation linked to the adoption of the shared currency, which is seen as negative, is the loss of citizens' purchasing power – as we can see in Extract 4.8, from a group of employees in Belgium. In this group, Michèle puts forward the arguments in support of European integration based on a positive evaluation of the benefits of the single market. She attempts to extol the virtues of a strong euro against the dollar, particularly for companies. By way of response, Tina, a participant who is pro-European but in an unstable financial situation at the time of the interview, closes the discussion by linking the question to the problem of employees' purchasing power, a problem that is closer to home for all of them.

Extract 4.8: Set 2, Brussels, employees

Michèle: From a financial perspective, Europe does enable exchanges between companies. Well companies are better off. It seems to me, or maybe I'm wrong. Since for example, we buy in the United States, dollars cost less now than they did when we had the Belgian franc. So it's linked, if companies know how to buy cheaper, then automatically salaries will follow. And companies will make a bit of profit.

Tina: Yes but the cost of living goes up too, not just salaries. So I don't think it can help much.

Thus, two new important and cross-cutting themes appear in these focus groups; themes that couldn't very well appear in *Framing Europe*: the euro and increasing prices, as well as the enlargement of the Union. The participants link them directly to criticism of the single market. These two themes can also be found in relation to labour mobility and the euro and themes to do with power and governance in enlargement. It is important to note that instances linked to the adoption of the single currency are divided into the positive category of 'Removing borders' and the negative category of 'Inflation', whereas those relating to enlargement are partly coded in the criticisms of the market ('Competition', 'Immigration' and 'Offshoring') and in the category labelled 'Enlargement'. The latter refers specifically to the idea that enlargement occurred too fast and that it led to a loss of power and problems of governance, as illustrated below. This point, and the last extract that it is based on, open the way for a second category of arguments described by Juan Diez Medrano, which refers to the question of power.

States are too small

Directly related to the theme of the single market is the idea that European integration is justified by the fact that in a globalised world, European states have become too small. This argument is both geopolitical and economic, and was already prominent in Juan Diez Medrano's study: half of his respondents mentioned this aspect at one point or other, particularly in reference to the famous motto 'Unity is Strength'. This argument is also widely present in the CITAE study, among all nationalities and socio-professional categories; in fact it is the theme that is most frequently mobilised by the participants, with 109 coded occurrences.

Behind this theme lie a series of ideas that are significantly distinct, even though the underlying phenomenon they all describe is the view that, in this age of globalisation, states have become too small and that unity has thus become indispensable at the economic and military levels. Running through this we observe the themes of power and the weight that Europe can and/or should have in the world, both on an economic level and as a model of society. In the first five minutes of the discussion, seen in Extract 4.9, the group of employees from Brussels introduces the issue of power to define what being European means. Maria even cites the motto 'Unity is Strength.'

Extract 4.9: Set 2, Brussels, employees

Tina: Well, what I understand, and what I think, is that before we were Belgian and now we've become European. Like before that when you were from your neighbourhood, or your town or whatever. But European, that's because now we're obliged to counter-attack, regarding what happens overseas.

Maria: Other powers and other countries.

Tina: Yes because Belgium alone, France alone, Germany alone, against all those powers like the United States, what's that?

Michèle: Yes, that's what Europe is.

Tina: Because, we were already European underneath. Underneath, we didn't even question it.

Jonathan: I think that everything that happens at the European level for the moment, it's above all, political and technical and economic. The feeling of belonging to a neighbourhood, or the desire to go and see somewhere else, to meet other people, you know, we didn't wait for Europe to do all that. So these great debates there are now about Europe, I think that it is all just to set Europe apart from the United States or Asia. It is happening with the good and bad things that that means at the local level, in each country.

Maria: Yes, I totally agree. But it's true that in the beginning I think that Europe was created in those areas that are still dominant. Economic, political domains and so forth. 'Unity is Strength', that's kind of to counteract, to position Europe in relation to other major powers.

In the British case, the need to be a part of the single market is more frequently cited than the idea that otherwise Britain would become isolated, which it cannot allow in this increasingly interdependent world. Another version of this argument invokes the idea that European states have become too interdependent and can no longer develop alone, particularly on an economic level. In Extract 4.10, this argument is defended, with difficulty, by Sundai, a young and particularly Europhile manager.

Extract 4.10: Set 1, Oxford, managers

Sundai: When you look at it from an economic point of view, it is necessary to belong to the European market.

Alexander: Why is it a necessity?

Sundai: It becomes very necessary.

Alexander: But why? We traded well before, didn't we?

Sundai: We did but, what I'm saying, now because of the number of countries which are coming together to become part of European Union, you have Britain standing by itself.

Alexander: Well we were beside ourselves before, we had the pound. Then we have the pound now, we are more within Europe now. Ok? So what's different?

Sundai: In terms of international trade, you can't stay by yourself. You need integration with other countries.

Some participants share the perception that the European states can only counter international competition by forming an economic bloc. The European states, when considered individually, are no longer powerful enough to counteract the superpowers. Jeremy, a participant in the English employees' group (Set 2), summarises this argument very well, saying 'well, yes, but it's still a question of competing against America and other major nations such as Japan and China.'

This perception of economic interdependence in the international trade scene also corresponds with a view of the globalisation of the problems that are affecting humanity. Among the most commonly cited of these problems is, as might be expected, the environment, (particularly global warming), but also disasters or diseases that could cross national borders. A group of Belgian managers (Set 1) discuss the then current issue of avian flu. In this regard, Valérie argues that 'crises show that Europe is necessary', emphasising that, 'For example, for the bird flu, it wouldn't be much use for Belgium to close its borders because it would come in anyway, from other countries. So we have to take general measures. If we don't unify the measures that are taken, it's not very useful. I was only talking about Europe but in fact it has to be at the international level.'

Although the 'Unity is Strength' argument seems to find support in each group, the unity upon which European power – be it economic, political or military – is supposed to be based appears to be fragile in the eyes of the respondents. Indeed, when the question of European unity was raised, criticism of the disagreements between European countries often also appeared. In light of this, member-states are perceived as being too different from each other and, as a result, agreement is seen as impossible to obtain. However, even if the criticism was clearly present in almost all the interviews, it was in the minority. Arguments in favour of the integration process linked to the need for unity far outweigh negative arguments linked to disagreements between countries. Of the 149 instances coded, 109 refer to the positive argument, according to which states have become too small, and 40 refer to the negative argument, which is to do with discord among European countries. The ratio of positive to negative arguments is inverse in relation to that of the single market and is 2.72 for the whole corpus.

More specifically, the example of the war in Iraq or Afghanistan was often raised to support this critique of the disagreement between European countries. In Extract 4.11, these issues were raised by Claire and described as a missed opportunity to act as a genuine European Nation, with clear and firm positions. Like Franck, Claire regrets the fact that the nations were not able to see past their own interest.

Extract 4.11: Set 1, Brussels, managers

Moderator: So is it good or not to give power to the nations?

Alban: Well, it worked well up until now.

Valérie: Humpf (*sceptical*).

Franck: I don't know. If the objective is to make Europe, the European Union, then no. Because each nation will want to have its own piece of pie, do things that are in its own interests.

Claire: I think that in the conflict in Afghanistan and in Iraq we were not a European nation, with firm clear decisions (*Franck agrees*). Each country had its own idea, and that's where we could have been European. And that was where we didn't really have a European policy.

Other sensitive issues were also raised in the condemnation of the discords that undermine European unity. There were also current issues of the time: to do with 'mad-cow' disease, between France and Great Britain; concerning contribution to and distribution of the European budget (already!), particularly in relation to the Common Agricultural Policy; or the question of lowering VAT in France. In this respect, Extract 4.12, from a group of workers in France, is particularly enlightening. Just as Jean-Marie tries to present the argument for the unity of European people – of which he is himself not entirely convinced, it has to be said – the other participants denounce misunderstandings between European countries, visible every day according to them. One can see in this extract that, although Jean-Marie is familiar with arguments in favour of the European-integration process, he is not always convinced by them (*see* Chapter Five for a detailed explanation of this ambivalence).

Extract 4.12: Set 1, Paris, workers

Jean-Marie: And there's another thing I wanted to say, that being European is wanting to unite the needs of different peoples. That's to say that being European is having an energy policy, a food policy or whatever that is shared between the countries, between the states. But that's not the case (*he shakes his head*). It was what the countries wanted at the start.

Cédric: For me, there is not understanding between countries. We see it every day.

Margot: They're not even capable of agreeing on VAT (*joking tone*).

Jean-Marie: No, but at the beginning that's what they wanted. When they started, at the beginning there was France and Germany and then England. But now there are so many countries that being European doesn't mean anything anymore.

As the end of Extract 4.12 suggests, EU enlargement to 25 countries is also inevitably part of the critique. The question of enlargement is clearly linked here to that of European governance, a criticism I will return to later, and which is most often formulated as 'we already had trouble getting along at 15, how will we manage at 25?' The unity upon which Europe ought to have built its power is continually threatened by discords between European countries, which only increase as the number of states and the differences between them increase. Patrice, an employee in Paris (Set 1), clearly expresses this idea, saying: 'We won't be a force at all in the end, I think. Maybe we opened ourselves up too much. Personally I think so, because the original idea was to become a force.'

The question of the power of states in a globalised world takes on a specific importance within the frames of perception mobilised by the participants to justify the European integration process. There is no doubt that, at a time when Greece seems capable of capsizing the European ship all by itself, these frames of perception and evaluation will be reinforced, as economic and financial interdependence become increasingly visible and unpopular. The latest European summits and the thorny question of the European budget and the financial framework for 2014–20 appear to be yet another illustration of this discord, as perceived by the participants of these discussion groups. Despite the fact that these interviews were conducted in 2006, the comments of the participants resonate strongly in the issues of Europe today; just as between the CITAE project and *Framing Europe,* the examples changed or multiplied but the frames of perception and evaluation remained the same.

The elimination of borders

The third positive attribute that is widely present in the participants' cognitive construction of the EU is of a non-economic nature. It is to do with the possibility of moving freely throughout Europe, without obstacles, a mobility facilitated by passports, the single currency (already mentioned) and the absence of border controls. The lack of borders and the single market that enable this mobility indeed constitute key arguments in the justification of the European integration process. Both the image of the tourist who moves easily and without formalities – and without having to change money – and the image of the student, who can study more easily overseas, through programmes like Erasmus, are used to illustrate this heightened mobility. Ultimately, for many of the participants, the eradication of borders should reinforce understanding between European peoples, as argued by transnationalism (Deutsch 1953; Kuhn 2011).

Extract 4.13 is taken from a group of activists in Brussels (Set 1). It clearly illustrates how the erosion of borders should and does allow people to approach each other, to build a European 'we'. Thus at two distinct moments, quite far apart in the discussion, Aurélien comes back this point on understandings between peoples. The first time is in response to the first question 'what does it mean to be European?' and the second much later in the discussion on the question 'who profits from Europe?'

Extract 4.13: Set 1, Brussels, activists

Aurélien: Now, we can go to Spain. I remember when I was little, I went to Spain and there were customs officers who were searching. Now I think there is a certain cohesion. Thanks to Erasmus, there is a certain cohesion that is formed, a certain freedom of movement. It has never been so easy to go shopping in Cologne or in Lille, it is really an opportunity to go towards other people. [...]

Moderator: Tourists [profit from Europe].

Simon: That's a bit the same idea as the consumer. It's a form of consumption.

Clément: No customs, no exchange rates.

Aurélien: No customs, no change rates, no passports either. Now it's extended to other countries than Europe but still.

Stéphane: It's good.

Simon: No formalities.

Aurélien: None of the various formalities, I'd even go further, no prejudice. From the moment that you're European and you travel in Spain or elsewhere, the fact of being European means that, and I've experienced this, means that it's easier to make conversation. We're at home.

Although certain respondents, like Aurélien, stress that removing borders reinforces or could reinforce their feeling of belonging to the EU, there are others, on the other hand, who see in this a particularly negative aspect of integration. Loss of identity and sovereignty are unavoidably part of this critique: they clearly characterise the English corpus. We will come back to this in the next point in dealing with the persistence of national frames of perception and evaluation.

As was the case for the argument linked to the EU as a means of power, positive arguments related to open borders, particularly to ease of mobility and understanding between peoples, far outweigh negative arguments in the group interviews on this question. Of the 158 coded passages related to this theme, 108 were positively coded, and 50 negatively, bringing the ratio of positive to negative to 2.1 for this cognitive category. One has to begin by noting that the ratio of the Brussels' groups is particularly positive. I will come back to this aspect when I discuss the specific frames of perception and evaluation. Two negative aspects linked to the removal of borders, specifically immigration and inflation, have been evoked above in Extracts 4.5 and 4.8. Although the adoption of the single currency is intrinsically linked to the theme of mobility in its positive aspects, it is also often a synonym of increased prices. Paul (Set 2, Paris, employees) demonstrates this ambivalent evaluation linked to the adoption of the single currency in saying: 'I take the example of the currency. I think everyone has realised that, since we have the euro, it's good to go to other countries and you don't need to change money. But I've noticed that prices in France have gone up by 30 per cent.' This negative aspect is also emphasised by Ali, a worker in Belgium, who says he tries to be positive but admits that Europe doesn't bring him much on a daily basis. The argument to do with mobility made easy by the single currency is well known and acknowledged but the price he has to pay every day appears to him much more important 'I heard what you just said, and I try and be positive about Europe. In my everyday life, I admit I try. Yes it's true that I can use the euro when I go to Spain this summer. But, I mean, between what I think it costs us on a daily basis, and what it's cost us over the years, I don't know, who profits from Europe?' (*Saïd agrees and slaps his thigh.*)

The participants in these discussion groups regularly put forward the argument of easy mobility and increased understanding between peoples, thanks to the removal of borders. But they are also perfectly aware that this mobility scarcely concerns them at all. In the words of Adrian Favell, they see themselves as *stayers*, for whom mobility is not that important, compared to the others, the *movers* (Favell 2008: IX). Pierre, an employee in Belgium (Set 2) formulates this argument particularly well in distinguishing 'the frontrunners, who charge on and who can travel' from 'the rest who stay behind'; the participants of this group placing clearly themselves among the latter.

Extract 4.14: Set 2, Brussels, employees

Michèle: So there are two levels in Europe. There is the political Europe and there is the Europe at the level of the people.

Maria: Social, in inverted commas. Well of course (*she spreads her arms*), we all agree, one over there (*indicating her right*) and one over here (*indicating her left*).

Michèle: Yeah that's it.

Maria: Europe should change that.

Pierre: And especially, I don't think that we can make Europe without people. Actually, lots of people are asking where we're going, and if we're going in the direction of the people.

Maria: Yes.

Pierre: Because there's the frontrunners who charge on, and who can travel, who can do everything, and the rest who stay behind, who can't keep up for long.

What is important here is that, in the context of a reflection on the frames of perception, the removal of borders constitutes an essential element in the way individuals comprehend European integration, either in terms of legitimation or delegitimation. Indeed, a substantial number of comments raise this issue and it remains fundamental in understanding how citizens conceive of and evaluate Europe.

Governance and the democratic deficit

These evaluations of a Europe without borders are complemented by a near-universal negative evaluation of governance and democracy at the European level. In Diez Medrano's study, nearly half of the respondents expressed an aversion to the administrative and non-democratic institutions of the Union. This criticism is also present in these groups. With 104 recorded occurrences, it is, in fact, the primary criticism that participants levelled at the EU. The importance of these arguments relating to *input legitimacy* contradicts a purely functionalist vision of the European process (Ehin 2008). In these discussions, when the dimensions of *input legitimacy* are mobilised to perceive and evaluate European integration, they are formulated in exclusively negative terms. However, we cannot ignore the fact that the relative importance of this theme is partly due to the research protocol. On this point, the participants' question of 'how should power be distributed?' introduces the issue of representatives, particularly European representatives, and experts. Keeping this in mind, it seems that the criticisms levelled at European governance and democracy are still important, given that they also appear outside the framework of this question. Finally another element leads me to think that the theme of democracy is particularly resonant in these groups. Almost systematically, the participants ask the moderator to add a category of actors, in the form of a card saying 'ours' or 'to citizens', in the reading of the question of the distribution of power in Europe (Frazer and Van Ingelgom 2013). This was particularly the case in Extract 4.15. In this group of employees in Oxford, Kamal interrupts just as the moderator finished explaining the question and suggested beginning with the category they choose.

Extract 4.15: Set 1, Oxford, employees

Kamal: What about power to the people? (*Nina smiles*)

Mike (*smiling*): That is better.

Pat (*smiling*): I can see me there.

Moderator: Where on the board should I put that power to the people?

Kamal (*pointing at board*): Over the question.

Thus, in these collective interviews the question of European governance is particularly prominent and the EU is depicted as opaque, remote, inefficient, ill-adapted, as well as paralysed by national egos, eroded by corruption and obsessed with the most minute details of regulation. National egos and discord have already been signalled as the principal hindrance to European unity and thus to the construction of a powerful Europe. As one might expect, the distance between European institutions and citizens is also widely condemned (*see* Chapter Five for more details on distance). The European representative, in particular, is at the heart of this critique, as the following passage shows. Taken from a group of managers in Paris, Extract 4.16 comes just as they begin to discuss the question of representatives as a possible source of power in Europe.

Extract 4.16: Set 2, Paris, managers

François: A European MP, that seems like someone pretty far away from us.

Stanislas: Well we elect them don't we?

François: Oh yeah, that's true.

Stanislas: There you go.

Louis: Well I think that most French people wouldn't even be able to give the name of a European MP.

Stanislas: Or their region.

This inability to name one's European MP often appears in the group discussions, including among managers and militants. Moreover, the opacity of the European political system is also criticised. Generally, this criticism occurs when the question of experts is raised. Thus, lobbies are often denounced as being those who really have the power at the European level, submitting the construction of Europe to the supremacy of the market economy. Extract 4.17 is from the same group of managers in Paris as that above, and here the participants pinpoint experts as being the bad players of the European political system.

Extract 4.17: Set 2, Paris, managers

Patrick: But in fact it is perhaps them who have the real power.

Louis: Well yes, that's what I was saying before.

Jean-Paul: The experts?

Patrick: Yes.

Francois: That's the dark side of Europe (*laughs*).

Jean-Paul: The experts, you think of a puppet master, but that's all. It's all very obscure and obtuse.

The degree and the nature of the dissatisfaction linked to European governance may be expressed differently in the three countries. The British stand out, in particular, because of repeated denunciations of the European trend towards harmonisation and standardisation. This question of over-regulation is perceived as a violation of British sovereignty (Belot 2000; Diez Medrano 2003; Van Ingelgom 2011). Rebecca, a participant in the group of managers in Oxford (Set 2), evoked both the single currency and also the example of the standardised size of bananas (an example that came back several times in these discussions), when asking 'Why am I supposed to change my pounds? You hear all these things, quibbles, you know. Why have we got to change as well? Why can't we have different size of bananas? Why can't we do this? Why have we got to have that? Whereas you wonder how much influence Britain has on the way its affected French way of life and Italian way of life.'

Intrinsically linked to the question of European governance are the comments on the democratic deficit from which the integration process suffers. These two questions are very often tangled together in the arguments put forward by the participants, so much so that it is not always easy to tell them apart. The impact that this debate – initially academic and political – has had in the three populations is significant. As proof of this actual perception, it is important to emphasise that the expression 'democratic deficit' is used as such by the participants in the focus groups. Mike, an British employee (Set 1), condemns this deficit at the European level in precisely these terms: 'With that point is of course that the European Parliament doesn't actually earn the same power or doesn't actually produce the legislation at the bottom end. There is only a certain number of fields open to the European Parliament to vote on. Through, I think, the co-decision procedure, I can't remember. There is sort of a democratic deficit in as much the European Parliament doesn't actually have a power to oversee all the legislation that actually comes out of Brussels. [...] I think that's a growing issue. It's not as democratic an institution as it could be'. The limited powers accorded to the European Parliament are also lamented by Bertrand, a participant in a group of activists in Paris (Set 2), who even describes the role of this European institution as 'a simple rubber-stamp.'

There is a marked tendency to evoke these negative comments linked to European governance among the groups of managers and activists. In fact, of 186 occurrences, only 61 were found among the more working-class categories. One observes a similar configuration for the argument justifying the European integration process in terms of peace among European peoples. Of the 27 coded occurrences, only two were recorded among the more working-class groups. However, the democratic criticisms addressed to the EU do not only come from the activists. Linked to the democratic question, the Belgian groups, in particular, lamented the fact that they were not consulted, as were their neighbours, the French. In a group of workers and short-term employees, conducted in Brussels (Set 1), the participants came back several times to the fact that they would also have liked to express themselves by referendum on the pursuit of European integration. Participating in this group, Ali declares 'With Europe, I have the impression that there is, in Belgium anyway, a democratic deficit in the sense that this constitution was imposed on us, whereas in certain other countries that didn't happen or it happened with a referendum. In Belgium, they talk about Europe, democracy, when we've just been imposed a treaty, that treaty, without people necessarily agreeing. I think we talk a lot about Europe but we don't ask often ask what people think about it.'

Although the question of the democratic deficit was particularly characteristic of the German corpus in Juan Diez Medrano's study, one can see it broadly in the three cases studied here and, in particular, amongst the groups of managers and activists who have widely accepted this criticism of European integration (Diez Medrano 2003: 34–43). Democracy and governance play an important role in the – nonetheless exclusively negative – perceptions and evaluations of European integration. From this point of view, the referendum on the Constitutional Treaty is generally perceived in a negative light by the group participants in France and Belgium; the former because their 'no' was not respected and the latter because they weren't consulted at all.

By way of a conclusion to this section, it is important to note that, beyond the few differences outlined in a general way, the arguments identified within the participants' arguments echo those described by Diez Medrano. Indeed, the single market, globalisation, the erosion of borders and governance all continue to constitute the principal frames of perception mobilised by these citizens when they come to evaluate the European integration process. The four themes identified are particularly common in the three cases studied in the CITAE project. But certain contrasts have also been observed in the ways that they have been dealt with in the different countries. Beyond these shared frames of perception and following the work of Diez Medrano, we know that the nation-state still functions as the principal agent of political socialisation and thus plays a fundamental role in frames of perception and evaluation. In other words, (de-)legitimation of the European order passes through the prism of the nation. The next section analyses these national differences in and of themselves, as well as trying to understand the different ways of (de-)legitimating European regional integration in the different national contexts.

National images

Acceptance of the European order passes through the prism of the nation. While the analysis here also aims to understand how ordinary citizens construct Europe on a cognitive level, and how they evaluate it, it also specifically questions the uniformity of reactions towards the EU. An analysis that emphasises the plurality of these reactions, differing from one country to the next is, of course, preferable here. Previous sections have in fact already sketched certain national differences in the way of apprehending and evaluating European integration.

National differences in common views

In this section, I would now like to come back to this question of national differences more systematically, as they relate to the four themes we have already dealt with: the single market, small states, erosion of borders and the democratic deficit. The specific themes that characterise each of these national cases are discussed in detail in the next section.

First, behind the overall importance of the frames of perception and evaluation linked to the single market lie significant national differences. Indeed, systematic analysis of the groups combined with an interpretative analysis of them shows, first and foremost, the higher propensity of British participants to support European integration by referring to the potential benefits of the single market.

Out of the 62 positive comments coded as fitting into this frame of perception, 27 come from the British focus groups. This latter also appear to be less critical towards the market economy, only recording 32 negative comments relating to the establishment of the market, compared to 52 and 54 for the Belgian and French groups respectively. The ratio between the positive and negative groups is thus 0.79 for the groups conducted in Oxford, compared to an average ratio of 0.44 for the groups overall. The groups conducted in Brussels and Paris registered ratios of 0.34 and 0.31 respectively. This relative predisposition to support the accomplishments of the single market is all the more interesting given that it cannot be attributed to a stronger presence of positive attitudes towards the European integration process among the British participants. Instead, it is explained by the lesser presence of negative themes linked to European integration. In particular, concerning the theme of offshoring, only five references were recorded among the British focus groups, out of 33 references overall.

On the other hand, the British participants appeared to be more ready to critique the integration process in terms of immigration. Out of 30 references coded for this theme, 14 came from the Oxford groups. More specifically, the opening of European borders is problematic in their eyes, presenting a security problem in the form of drug-trafficking, illegal immigration and other forms of crime. Certain participants even declare the Channel Tunnel to be a weak link, a gap by which the evils of Europe creep into their island nation. Thus, for them, illegal immigrants do not stop in France, preferring Britain instead, and the country is seen as being far too welcoming. Taken from a group of workers in Oxford, Extract 4.18 clearly illustrates this point.

Extract 4.18: Set 1, Oxford, workers

Brenda: European, but you also get people coming now from Africa or further every day. It just seems to be, England is just like too welcoming. Sorry.

Mary: Yeah, no you're right there.

Robert: No, of course it is. It must be the most welcoming country in the world.

Mary: But it's not very big is it, like you've got France. France is absolutely massive but they just turn people away and they come here.

Robert: But everybody seems to want to come to England.

Brenda: Yeah I know we're too soft. Do you think we're too soft a country?

Ron: Definitely.

Brenda: Do you think we're too soft a country or do you think we're just very welcoming?

Ron: Too many illegal immigrants in this country. [...]

Brenda: The ones that just come over from France.

Ron: Hide in lorries and all that.

Brenda: But they're bringing lots of diseases and stuff that comes with these people. That isn't being horrible about anybody by the way.

Robert: No, no, see health wise. Illegal immigrants coming over on the back of lorries, the male ones coming over and some of them might have HIV and could be sleeping with girls.

The French and Belgian groups by comparison focus on condemning the negative effects of intra-European competition on the labour market (out of 57 occurrences, 23 are from Brussels groups, 21 from Paris groups and only 13 from Oxford groups), offshoring (of 33 occurrences, 16 are Belgian, 12 French and only 5 English), and inflation. On the issue of inflation, the French participants are the most critical: for them alone, 13 occurrences were recorded out of 20 overall that were coded in relation to the increase in prices following the adoption of the single currency.

The two following extracts, from the same group of Parisian managers, provide very explicit illustrations of denunciation of the problem of inflation – the fault being explicitly attributed to the EU and, more specifically, the introduction of the euro. Extract 4.19 comes from the first five minutes of the discussion, when the participants are trying to respond to the question 'What does it mean to be European?' François gives a definition that is surprising, and which reveals a French frame of perception that is anchored in daily life and its economic difficulties.

Extract 4.19: Set 2, Paris, managers

Francois: For me it's above all: 6.55 957. Exponential inflation. But that was just stupidity, total stupidity. It mucked everything up. It's a euro-ineptness. No pun intended.

Extract 4.20 comes much later in the discussion (the second part of the group interview) and once again involves François, now with Stanislas as an ally on the economic question. The participants are discussing what each country, old and new, gets out of Europe. This passage comes in the context of the question 'Who profits from Europe?'

Table 4.5: Themes to do with the single market, by country

	Brussels				Paris				Oxford				
	W	E	M	A	W	E	M	A	W	E	M	A	Total
Benefits	3/1	3/3	1/2	4/1	6/1	1/2	1/2	3/1	2/2	3/5	5/1	5/4	
	4	6	3	5	7	3	3	4	4	8	6	9	62
Total (+)		18				17				27			
Competition	4/4	2/4	0/4	1/4	0/4	3/3	2/1	5/3	4/1	2/2	2/0	0/2	57
Offshoring	4/2	1/1	1/3	3/1	1/1	1/2	1/1	2/3	0/1	0/2	0/0	1/1	33
Immigration	1/0	2/3	0/1	0/1	0/2	2/0	2/2	0/0	5/2	2/2	2/0	0/1	30
Inflation	2/0	1/2	0/0	0/0	3/1	2/1	1/3	1/1	1/0	0/0	0/0	0/1	20
	17	16	9	10	12	14	13	15	14	10	4	6	
Total (-)		52				54				34			140
Ratio +/-		0.34				0.31				0.79			0.44

Extract 4.20: Set 2, Paris, managers

Patrick: No, I mean, each one can get something out of it, the old countries too.

Jean-Paul: Yeah, yeah.

Patrick: It opens up new markets. [...]

Moderator: So everyone is getting something out of it? (*Laughs*)

Louis: Everyone is getting something.

Francois: So who says that?

Jean-Paul: It's them over there.

Louis: But who says that? (*Towards Michel and Patrick*) It's them again.

François: Ah, but that's because you're getting something out of it for you?

Louis: They're (*the new countries*) changing sides.

Stanislas: Have you had a raise since the euro? (*Laughs*)

Although the discussion was focused on the economic benefits for the new member-states and older member-states in terms of access to new markets, it is brought back to daily concerns related to the lack of wage-indexation since the adoption of the euro. Thus, more broadly, when the French participants talk about economic aspects of European integration, they evoke questions of daily subsistence, purchasing power and inequalities to do with housing or employment linked to immigration (for more details, *see* Haegel 2013). On the contrary, and quite logically, the increase in prices to do with the introduction of the single currency is only mentioned twice in the British groups.

In terms of these themes to do with the issue of European unity as a site of power in a globalised world and discord between European countries, there are no notable differences between the three countries, as we can see in Table 4.6.

Considering the ratio between the positive and negative evaluations or the occurrences recorded for each category of this theme, the three countries reflect almost perfect similarities, thus reinforcing the weight of this theme as the substrate of a shared vision of European integration. But the critiques are equally as intense in all three countries and the context of the economic and financial crisis can only reinforce the vision of increased discord between European member states.

If we turn now to the theme of erosion of borders, we can see the emergence of a particular characteristic of the Belgian corpus. Indeed, as we can see in Table 4.7, where the evaluation ratios are 1.61 and 1.68 respectively for the French and British groups, this ratio is doubled for the Belgian groups (3.61). This underlines the advantages in terms of mobility and comprehension between peoples that are perceived by the participants in Brussels. The francophone Belgians appear to have developed a frame of perception that is more positive in regard to the erosion of borders than their French and English counterparts.

The British participants mention the eradication of borders as a frame of perception – either positive or negative – the least often of all the participants. Although Europe has removed its borders, it can never remove the physical border that is the Channel. In particular, the argument linked to a greater understanding between peoples is absent from the British groups, with the exception of one group of workers. This reflects the lack of a representation of cultural ties between British people and other European peoples.

Although the ratio in the British corpus – positive but relatively low compared to the Belgian one – is not surprising given the country's insularity, the low French ratio is worth questioning. While negative aspects linked to the removal of borders are also present to a lesser extent in the Belgian and British groups, they are particularly characteristic of the Parisian groups and, particularly, the groups of French managers. In this regard, when a French participant raises the issue of mobility and exchange as the main foundation of a positive appreciation of Europe on a non-economic level, someone almost always retorts that mobility only benefits a minority. This argument linked to inflation also appears in the Belgian and British corpuses but the French case is particular in that this argument emerges in both groups of militants and managers and thus is independent of the social category of the group itself. Extract 4.21 is taken from a group of Parisian activists and this aspect is once again emphasised by Emmanuelle, who argues that the average citizen probably doesn't have the means to travel, given the average wage.

Extract 4.21: Set 2, Paris, activists

Emmanuelle: To just come back to the subject of Europe. Well we're in it anyway. The economic situation is very important. No one in France, well the average French person, as they might be defined, say a man and a woman, two individuals who earn roughly 2000 euros. I think it's 2200 the average net financial income. I'm not sure that Europe is very concrete, for them, because they don't travel very much. Because when you earn 2200 euros a month it's tough to save. They might not be travelling at all that's for sure. Well, I've had more chance than some to travel, to see what the countries of Central Europe look like, Eastern Europe, see what happens on the other side of the Mediterranean. So they (*average citizens*) have a different vision of things. So do we live better or less well now than we did before in Europe?

This passage enables us once again to underline the specificity of the French discussions, which often bring the European question back to daily economic difficulties (Duchesne *et al.* 2013; Duchesne *et al.* 2010). When the French participants talk about European integration, they do so in relation to the degree of proximity and raise questions relating to daily subsistence. Also within the Parisian groups, when the example of Erasmus is raised to illustrate the advantages of the European construction in terms of mobility, the argument is generally quickly countered. These student exchanges are seen being more like holidays than real university training and only really involving students who are financially well off. Once again, mobility is dependent on the economic resources of citizens and the decline in purchasing power is constantly condemned. In Extract 4.22, Fabienne, who is still a student completing her PhD, intervenes violently on the subject of Erasmus programmes, which she sees as reserved for minority that 'have the means.'

Extract 4.22: Set 1, Paris, managers

Inès: In terms of education, for example, with all the Erasmus programmes and things (*Toufik agrees*). It's a step forward. Afterwards, I don't know what it's worth in real terms, in reality, but there's a way of going towards something else.

Céline: In reality, the concrete equivalence of degrees is difficult.

Fabienne: And in concrete terms, it is severely restricted to the people who are able to pay for accommodation for their children. Erasmus, for me, is a vast fraud (*smiles*). It's once again a selection based on money, i.e. it's only those who are able to pay for accommodation for their children and a decent life overseas that can do it.

Inès: Well it's not up to scratch, but it's the start of something.

Finally, if we consider the critiques linked to governance and democracy at the European level (Table 4.8), we can see the slightly lower level of occurrences in the British case. It is the British activists, in particular, who are the least talkative on the question of governance and democratic deficit in comparison with their French and Belgian counterparts, who discuss these subjects at length. However, in all three cases, the criticisms relating to European governance outweigh those relating to the democratic deficit, which suggests once again that there is apparently a critical consensus between the three populations on this issue.

Specific national images

Beyond these differences linked to the shared frameworks and principles of perception and evaluation of European integration, a series of arguments that are specific to one or other of the three cases studied here has emerged through the systematic analysis of the themes covered in these collective interviews.

First of all, the Belgian groups can be distinguished from the French and British groups to the extent that they have developed a national frame that particularly emphasises the advantages of European integration for future generations. Indeed of the 28 occurrences of this theme, 17 are from Belgian groups. On this point, the participants in the Brussels groups hope that it will be their children who will profit from the system that they pay for today. Extract 4.23, from a group of employees, clearly illustrates this. Although the participants in this group are themselves young (less than 30), they think that Europe will benefit future generations more than their own. It is interesting to note that the participants in this group of employees even consider that they benefit from it without realising. With a certain degree of poetry and lots of humour, the members of this group defend the idea that all this will be even more normal for the generations to come.

Extract 4.23: Set 1, Brussels, employees

Moderator: Europe will benefit future generations.

Victor: Nice that, very poetic (*laughs*). I fully approve. […]

Faissal: No no, but it's true. It's for us. We won't get the benefit so much. We already benefit a bit just with the euro. You can see it with the freedom of circulation in European countries, but more than that concretely.

David: We benefit without knowing it. That's the thing, but we don't really realise it.

Victor: That's what I think too.

Faissal: It's true that it's for future generations.

David: We don't have the barriers to deal with, and it's normal.

Faissal: Yes, it's true, and it will be even more normal for our children.

Table 4.6: Themes linked to the view that states have become too small, by country

	Brussels				Paris				Oxford				Total
	W	E	M	A	W	E	M	A	W	E	M	A	
States too small (+)	3/2	5/1	4/8	4/7	2/5	9/6	2/3	8/7	3/8	4/5	1/4	2/6	
	5	6	12	11	7	15	5	15	11	9	5	8	
Total (+)		34				42				33			109
Discord (-)	4/1	0/0	1/2	4/0	4/3	1/0	3/0	1/2	3/2	1/1	3/3	0/1	
	5	0	3	4	7	1	3	3	5	2	6	1	
Total (-)		12				14				14			40
Ratio +/-		2.75				3				2.35			2.72

Table 4.7: Themes to do with the eradication of borders, by country

	Brussels				Paris				Oxford				Total
	W	E	M	A	W	E	M	A	W	E	M	A	
Mobility	6/6	4/4	6/4	5/3	5/2	2/1	5/3	4/2	1/2	6/2	5/1	4/3	86
Under-standing	1/2	1/2	0/0	3/0	2/0	¼	1/0	2/0	0/3	0/0	0/0	0/0	22
	15	11	10	11	9	8	9	8	6	8	6	7	
Total (+)		47				34				27			108
Immigration	1/0	2/3	0/1	0/1	0/2	2/0	2/2	0/0	5/2	2/2	2/0	0/1	30
Inflation	2/0	1/2	0/0	0/0	3/1	2/1	1/3	1/1	1/0	0/0	0/0	0/1	20
	3	8	1	1	6	5	8	2	8	4	2	2	
Total (-)		13				21				16			50
Ratio +/-		3.61				1.61				1.68			2.1

For these participants, the future benefits justify the present state of European integration, which underlies the importance of temporality in explaining the attitudes of European citizens and in particular national differences (Belot and Van Ingelgom 2012).

The participants in the British groups appear to be more preoccupied with the question of national sovereignty and the loss of national identity. Of the 92 occurrences coded for this theme, 42 are from the groups conducted in Oxford. This result corroborates analyses conducted by Diez Medrano and Belot, in particular (Belot 2000; Diez Medrano 2003). From their different studies of the British case, these authors have also emphasised the importance of these two major themes in explaining the positions of British citizens in regard to European integration. Extract 4.24, taken from a group of workers in Oxford, clearly shows the importance of sovereignty and identity regarding a possible decision made by 'Brussels' and the loss of the pound sterling.

Extract 4.24: Set 1, Oxford, workers

Robert: Yeah, well if Britain, if it does become part of the EU, it will obviously have to like to go over to the euro or something so. It's just one of those things we don't have any […] It's just one of the things if you want to be part of the EU. […]

Mina: Yeah keep it same as before. What's wrong? Why we doing all these changes?

Brenda: That means everybody in Europe is telling us what we're doing, which I don't agree with.

Robert: If Britain was part of the EU, who rules it? Who makes the decisions for each country? Who's making the decisions? Who's pulling the strings? I suppose you'd have it in the votes instead of voting in England, you'd be voting in the European election.

Moderator: Instead of voting in England?

Robert: If England was part of the EU

Brenda: There wouldn't be […] You think the government would be different? It would be run from Brussels, is that what you're saying?

Robert: Yeah.

Brenda: And we wouldn't have our own government, is that what you're saying?

Robert: Well no. You would have […] You'd still be England and you'd still have an England parliament.

Brenda: Well not necessarily, if you're European.

Robert: At the end of the day, if you're in the EU, there'll be some decisions made from Brussels or wherever. You know what I mean?

In this extract, the issue of the possible loss of the pound sterling is linked to the question of identity and sovereignty. Mina's comments also reveal how keeping things 'same as before' is essential for many English participants. Brenda and Robert seem more concerned, however, about who would lead them if they became Europeans [*sic*]! Thus the most distinctive aspect of the English interviews regarding European integration is the significant role played by sovereignty and national identity. In particular this extract shows the importance of public debate around the introduction of the single currency. This category covers a broad spectrum of arguments, which the extract enables us to outline. In the context

Table 4.8: Themes to do with governance and the democratic deficit, by country

	Brussels				Paris				Oxford				Total
	W	E	M	A	W	E	M	A	W	E	M	A	
Governance (-)	4/1	2/1	2/9	9/9	9/5	0/1	4/6	10/6	2/3	4/4	5/5	1/2	104
		37				41				26			
Democratic deficit (-)	3/3	3/1	3/4	6/7	3/0	1/2	2/7	12/7	3/0	3/3	4/2	3/0	82
		30				34				18			
Total		67				75				44			186

Table 4.9: Specific themes, by country

	Brussels				Paris				Oxford				Total
	W	E	M	A	W	E	M	A	W	E	M	A	
Future generations	5/0	8/0	2/2	0/0	1/0	0/1	1/0	0/3	0/1	0/1	2/0	1/0	28
		17				6				5			
Sovereignty, identity (-)	4/2	2/5	2/3	2/4	2/0	1/5	2/4	7/5	7/4	11/1	8/4	4/3	92
		24				26				42			
Enlargement (-)	2/2	1/1	1/5	2/2	4/3	3/2	1/4	3/1	1/0	1/0	1/1	1/2	44
		16				21				7			

of sovereignty, the British participants express their opposition to any form of unification or supranational government. They clearly don't appreciate getting orders from Europe or Brussels, as Jeremy points out in Extract 4.25.

Extract 4.25: Set 2, Oxford, employees

Jeremy: I think it's the case that we don't like to be told (*Lily and Stephanie agree*) like that we prefer to have free choice as to what we do where we buy our cars.

Lily: We don't want it to be imposed.

Jeremy: Therefore we don't like to be told well politically you'll think this or politically you'll think that.

In this respect, we have already seen that the British participants are different from the other groups in their criticism of over-regulation and the tendency of the EU to impose shared standards. In the context of identity, the comments refer to the loss of national identity culture and 'British' way of life. When they raise the subject of identity, the British participants emphasise the existing differences between British culture and the cultures of other European countries. Pat, a participant in a group of employees in Oxford (Set 1), questions the possibility of one day imposing a *lingua franca* on European countries, just as the euro was imposed on them:

But then they did it for the euro, didn't they? And all the countries have the euro, didn't they? All the countries are doing it. So somebody made that decision that, you know, we're all going to have the euro and all the countries went. I know we haven't but somebody might suddenly make the decision, you know, let's all [...] could be English, could be French, let's all speak French (laughs). I'd be very quiet then because I'm not very good at French.

Behind this light-heartedness, one can see the fear of loss of national identity that is clearly present, linked here to the question of currency and language. The discourse on sovereignty and loss of national identity, themes that are particularly pertinent in the English groups, causes the English participants to consider Europe as something that is alien to themselves and which, ultimately, concerns them very little. Chapter Five will come back to this alienation in more detail.

Finally, the argument according to which enlargement happened too quickly and went too far is particularly characteristic of the French corpus and, to a lesser extent, the Belgian one. The most significant difference relating to enlargement is to do with the weaker presence of this argument within the English groups. The alienation from Europe that we just mentioned is undoubtedly part of the cause. To the extent that they consider themselves to be outside European integration (in which many participants think their country is actually not involved), the borders of the European Union are logically of little importance to British participants.

This final section has enabled me to demonstrate the persistence of national frames of perception and evaluation of the European integration process for the three national cases studied here.

Conclusion

This chapter had a twofold objective. On one hand, the analysis conducted through the systematic coding of the comments within the 24 focus groups aimed to provide the means for a detailed description of the content of the discussion and, by doing so, to set the stage. On the other, and above all, it aimed to provide an understanding of how the different frames of perception are related to each other and how they were evaluated by the participants.

First, systematic analysis of the corpus caused me to nuance the amount of the discussions that actually dealt specifically with the European Union in a broad sense. Talking of European integration turned out to be a complicated exercise, particularly for lower socio-economic groups. In this regard, national differences already emerged: broadly speaking, Belgian participants talked a lot and a lot about European integration; British participants spoke relatively little but when they did so they did as asked and talked about European integration; and the French participants talked a lot but ultimately didn't talk much about European integration. The coded themes were designed to reflect the categories identified by Diez Medrano in *Framing Europe*. The removal of certain codes and the emergence of new ones between these two studies demonstrate the relevance of the analytic framework developed by that author, from the notion of national frames.

The systematic review of the four major frames of perception outlined by Diez Medrano was used as a structure for the presentation of the content of these interviews. This systematic analysis also enabled me to demonstrate the relevance of these frames of perception and evaluation in understanding the discourses of (de-)legitimisation of the integration process that are still heard today. Anchoring this coding in the wake of Diez Medrano's work also enabled us to identify a series of important evolutions. In particular, it became clear that the perceptions of participants are more negative towards the single market now than they were a decade ago. Thus in 2006, well before the financial and economic crisis, the benefits of the single market were already being tempered by discourse on legitimation among citizens. Although these criticisms are certainly more biting today, there is nothing to suggest that the frame of perception emphasising the benefits to businesses has disappeared. The results of the diachronic analysis suggest that positive and negative evaluations rather coexist in the (de-)legitimation discourse of Europeans. Faced with these crises, one may also wonder whether critique of the discord between countries was reinforced during the course of budgetary quarrels. However, one can also hypothesise that the crisis has reinforced the perception that 'states are too small'. Although the evaluations and their positive or negative intensity ought to have changed, it is also true that these are frames of perception and evaluation that remain relevant for understanding the attitudes of European citizens.

Finally, the last section of this chapter enabled us to observe the different national framings in the three cases studied. In terms of the British case, one observed – in the wake of Diez Medrano and Belot – the importance of themes to do with sovereignty and national identity as well as a tendency to evaluate European integration in a positive light in connection with the achievements of the single market. British participants also set themselves apart from their Belgian or French counterparts in their criticism of the single market, primarily in terms of immigration. The groups in Brussels or in France on the other hand, criticised the market for the harmful effects of intra-European competition on the labour market and on offshoring. In the Parisian groups, criticism in terms of inflation following the adoption of the single currency was particularly common and explains, in part, their lower level of enthusiasm for the removal of borders in Europe. On this last point, the Belgian participants proved to be the most positive, highlighting the increased ease of mobility and improved understanding between peoples that result from opening borders as benefits of this process. Finally the Belgian groups also presented an idealistic national framing, marked by support for the European integration process and the wellbeing of future generations.

Overall, the results presented in this chapter have demonstrated that the research protocol functioned well and did indeed enable me to study ordinary citizens' frames of perception and evaluation of the European integration process – including those of the lowest socio-economic groups. Indeed, although the latter appear to have the most difficulty talking about Europe, the comments of these workers and employees are extremely valuable in understanding the different discourses of (de-)legitimation. The dynamics of the discussion group also revealed their full potential. In any given country or socio-economic category, it is possible to observe elements from which the participants manage to appropriate the European theme, by attaching it to what interests and engages them directly. Inspired by the advances made by Diez Medrano (2003), systematic analysis of the coding of these collective interviews leads me to confirm that different groups have different structures of perception and therefore differing evaluations of European integration. I concluded, as does Diez Medrano, that because it remains the principal agent of political socialisation, the nation-state plays a primordial role in the formation of the individual's frames of perception – which are in fact *national frames* (Diez Medrano 2003). Understanding how ordinary citizens cognitively construct – and thus evaluate – European integration therefore remains essential.

Now that the data has been presented and validated, we can focus on the analysis of the category of ordinary citizens that is at the heart of this book: those who are indifferent and undecided.

Chapter Five

Neither Eurosceptic nor Europhile: The Median European

> There is a mixture of motives for taking this middle-of-the-road position. Some are ambivalent, seeing Europe as having a mixture of advantages and disadvantages. Others are indifferent; as long as the EU appears irrelevant to their lives they have no opinion (Rose 2013: 49–50).

In the Introduction, I discussed the need for a reconciliation of the findings of statistical analysis of Eurobarometer data and similar surveys with the findings of recent interpretive analysis of interview and focus-group data. In Chapter Two, I highlighted the uncertainty and indifference that characterised the attitudes of European citizens in the post-Maastricht period. Following these two assessments, in this chapter I propose to analyse the particular category of citizens who, when they are surveyed by Eurobarometer, say that they evaluate their country's membership of the EU as being 'neither a good thing nor a bad thing'. On average, they represent 30 per cent of the European population and 33 out of the 133 participants in the focus groups.

Focusing on this specific category is important in more than one respect. First, qualitative work has revealed that European issues are not prominent for ordinary citizens and has emphasised the difficulty, even impossibility, for ordinary citizens to appropriate the reality of the EU into their own reality, as it were. More recently, such work has also highlighted the fact that attitudes towards Europe, often uncertain, are based on diverse evaluations and feelings of varied intensity. This leads to a rebuttal of the assertion that the European public is simply divided into two categories, one 'europhile' and the other 'eurosceptic' (Dakowska and Hubé 2011: 85–100; Van Ingelgom 2012). Of course, the data presented here can make only a contribution to criticism of this binary interpretation. Thus, the discussion transcripts suggest strongly that the interpretation of Eurobarometer data is often rather hasty.

According to the Eurobarometer survey data, from the time when the group interviews were convened in spring 2006, 28 per cent of European citizens (EU15) considered that their country's membership of the EU was 'neither a good nor a bad thing', while 55 per cent considered it was 'a good thing' and 13 per cent considered it 'a bad thing'. Researchers who analyse the Eurobarometer data have often labelled those who answer 'a good thing' europhile and labelled those who answer 'a bad thing' eurosceptic. At the same time, they have tended to ignore the 'neither-nors'. In the standard Eurobarometer survey conducted in spring 2006, the percentage of 'neither-nors' is 25 per cent for the Belgians, 32 per cent for the French and 28 for the British (European Commission 2007). Moreover, there is a striking increase in the percentage of respondents in this category between 1990 and 2011. The percentages increase from 19 to 23 in Belgium, from 25 to 33 per cent in France and from 24 to 37 in Britain, while the European average went from 21 per cent to 31 per cent (Mannheim Eurobarometer Trend File, 1973–2002; European Commission 2011).

The interpretive analysis reported in this chapter shows that this response should not be ignored or discounted; it is, indeed, a specific reaction characterised by uncertainties regarding the European integration process, sometimes in the sense of ambivalence and sometimes of indifference, and based on alienation or on fatalism. I assume that I can examine the category as through a microscope (Guiraudon 2006) in order to improve the understanding of the significance, the persistence and the increase in the uncertainty and indifference of ordinary citizens towards European integration. So I wish to link my own operationalisation, for the purposes of this last part of my analysis, firmly to those of mainstream quantitative studies. As I have said, these frequently take responses to the question 'Do you think your country's membership of the EU is a good thing [...]?' as indicating an individual's support for or rejection of the integration process.

In the questionnaire completed by all the focus-group applicants, we explicitly posed this classic question. Recruitment procedures explicitly aimed to classify the participants on European questions – broadly pro and anti – so as to secure a balanced, and potentially antagonistic, discussion. But we had multiple recruitment criteria, including wanting groups to be diverse in age and ethnic heritage and homogeneous with regard to education and employment (*see* Chapter Three). So in the end we selected a number of participants whose attitudes regarding Europe were more uncertain. Of course, this is not surprising – given that they represent about 30 per cent of the population. We were also keen to recruit citizens who usually elude surveys, particularly those from the working classes, and it is notable that in these groups we had the highest recruitment of those who answered 'neither-nor' to this question. Table 5.1 presents the list of participants in this category.

Out of 133 participants, 82 participants are categorised as favourable to their country's membership (or europhile), while 18 are categorised as disapproving (or eurosceptic), according to this measure. Here I focus on the positions in the discussion of European issues of the 33 'neither-nors'. Representativeness in qualitative research is typological, not statistical, so the limited number of cases is not in itself a problem. I want to maximise understanding of the logic of these participants' positions and, as far as possible, of their motivations. So, to put their words and positions into context, I here present interpretive analysis (again produced using the software package Atlas.ti) of all 24 of the focus groups. Two-thirds of the 'neither-nor' respondents are in the most working-class categories – of the 33, 20 belong either to the category workers or employees; 16 individuals in the middle category are British, 13 are French and only four are Belgian. The Brussels corpus here is distinctive – it does not include a single 'neither-nor' respondent from among the groups of managers and activists.

Table 5.1: Participants evaluating their country's membership of the EU as 'neither good nor bad' (N = 33/133)

	Workers	Employees	Executives	Activists	Total
Brussels	Marco Farouk André	Fabien	-	-	4
Oxford	Mina Ron Mary Brenda Vicas Esther Ruth Bridget	Kylie	Alexander Derek Ian Bansuri Sanjay Rebecca	Bethany	16
Paris	Jean-Marie Cédric Zahoua Geoffrey Habiba	Magali Patrice	Michel Jean-Paul Louis	César Jules Pascal	13
Total	16	4	9	4	33

This chapter specifically aims to analyse and understand the motivations of these respondents and to attempt to explain their position. Initially, with a view to refuting a minimalist interpretation of this response category, I will show that these respondents do have cognitive frameworks that allow them to think about Europe. These frameworks are relatively homogenous among these interviewees, whatever their social class and national characteristics. Then my analysis will focus on the specific references to Europe made by them. Finally, I distinguish between three kinds of reaction: first ambivalence, then distance and alienation and, finally, fatalism. In the last section, these three kinds of reactions are scrutinised in order to assess whether they should be perceived as a tonic or a poison for European democratic legitimacy. I also ask how they can be related to the hypothesis that questions of Europe are becoming increasingly politicised in political and public discourses.

The (non-)explanation from ignorance

An obvious hypothetical explanation of this response might be that respondents are unaware, or unacquainted, and therefore are unable to react to or evaluate the fact of their country's membership, unlike their europhile and eurosceptic counterparts. This classic hypothesis is fully in line with the 'minimalist' interpretation. This implies that 'opinions' gathered from this category of respondents would be superficial, unstable and inconsistent – classifiable as 'pseudo-' or 'non-attitudes'.

This kind of interpretation has for long justified limited interest in the opinions of European citizens within European studies (Belot 2010). My empirical response to this initial explanation leads me to examine to what extent the 'neither-nor' participants actually talked about Europe in the discussions. If respondents in the 'neither-nor' category really are either indifferent to their country's membership of the EU or ambivalent about it, as opposed to stating a position that is equivalent to 'don't know', then I need to demonstrate that they do have the cognitive resources to evaluate the process of European integration. It is important that I show that their response is not attributable to greater-than-normal ignorance of European matters. We know that talking about Europe was pretty difficult for all the participants, even including the activists (*see* Chapter Four). But were the 'neither-nor' participants less able to take part in discussion, less talkative, than the others?

As Table 5.2 shows, the participants in the category 'neither-nor' do not stand out from their counterparts in the categories 'good thing' (europhile) and 'bad thing' (eurosceptic). In general, they talked almost as much about Europe as the others did, using words including the prefix Euro- (European, Europe, and so on) only slightly less. The difference is not as marked as would be expected were the hypothesis of ignorance to be supported. As we know, Europe is a topic that our respondents frequently digressed from (*see* Chapter Four). Only a fifth to one quarter of total recorded discussion is specifically about European themes. The proportion of words uttered by the 'neither-nor' respondents that are specifically about Europe is no different from their pro- and anti-Europe interlocutors (23.07 per cent against 22.05 per cent). National and social differences are, however, more striking (*see* Chapter Four). The participants in the Brussels groups talk more about Europe (25.44 per cent) than those in the Paris (19.89 per cent) and Oxford (21.26 per cent) groups. The activist groups, as would be expected, are more focused on Europe (26.80 per cent) than the groups of workers (17.65 per cent). With regard to the terms relating to Europe, the differences here are also relatively minor – a ratio of 0.0048 for the 'neither-nor' citizens compared with 0.0056 for participants in the 'good thing' and 'bad thing' categories. In sharp contrast, the ratio for the managers is 0.0071, while for the workers it is 0.0035. Notably, the Belgian average is 0.0069, compared to 0.0040 for the French corpus and 0.0064 for the British.

But are the 'neither-nor' participants less knowledgeable than the others? In order to answer this question, I have coded all explicit references to European institutions, to European policies and to its history. For example, every reference to the European Commission has been coded in this way and also every reference to the Common Agricultural Policy, every mention of a European politician, Jean Monnet for example, and every reference to a treaty, such as the Maastricht Treaty or the draft Constitution.

As Table 5.3 shows, overall the 'neither-nor' respondents are shown to be appreciably less knowledgeable in relation to the European matters, as indicated by the frequency of specific mentions of European institutions or policies. However, again, social and national differences are stronger. A difference of 3.46 references is found between the activist groups and the workers and a difference of 1.81

Table 5.2: Distribution of occurrences of the words 'Euro-', 'Europe' and 'European' plus related codes, as a percentage of total words spoken

	Total words spoken	Discussions of Europe (Words)	Discussions of Europe (%)	Euro- (Words)	Euro- (%)
Neither-nor	150998	34844	23.07	732	0.0048
Good / bad thing	672329	146723	21.82	3788	0.0056
Total	823327	181567	22.05	4520	0.0055

Table 5.3: Distribution of explicit references to Europe, its policies, history, institutions (N = 133)

	Explicit references	Number of respondents	Average
Neither-nor	77	33	2.33
Good / bad thing	387	100	3.87
Workers	72	33	2.18
Employees	80	32	2.51
Managers	117	34	3.44
Activists	191	34	5.61
Brussels	175	41	4.27
Oxford	106	43	2.46
Paris	183	49	3.73
Total	464	133	3.49

between the Belgian groups and the British. This gap is only of 1.54 between the category 'neither a good nor a bad thing' and the two other categories 'good thing' and 'bad thing'. More detailed cross-referencing, together with my interpretive analysis of the transcripts (not shown in a table), allows me to report that although the 'neither-nor' participants are noticeably less knowledgeable at the aggregate level, this effect is above all due to the British participants, whose level of knowledge is lower, with a general average of one reference per individual. In particular, within the groups of managers conducted in Oxford, one counts seven individuals in the category 'neither- nor', and these are shown to be particularly less inclined to contribute explicit references to the EU and its institutions to the discussion – with an average per individual of only 0.85. In the same vein, I have already pointed out the absence of Belgian managers and activists in the sample. This also could explain the lower frequencies of explicit references in this specific category as we have shown that both activists and Belgian participants are more inclined to mobilise explicit references when talking about Europe.

It is important here to state that explicit references to the EU, its institutions and its policies do not, in any case, mean that participants feel themselves to be knowledgeable on European questions. On the contrary, and very frequently, a feeling of ignorance is explicitly expressed by participants. These results echo the observation that I made using multinomial regression analysis, suggesting that subjective knowledge has a negative impact on opting for the 'neither-nor' category. Indeed, according to the results of the regression model, it seemed that individuals who feel more knowledgeable about the EU are less likely to adopt the uncertain attitude characterised by indifference and ambivalence. But, Europe is no less present for this group than for the other participants, even if in the end it is not very present. All these considerations, then, lead me to reject the hypothesis that the category of citizens opting for the response 'neither-nor' consists of individuals less able to talk about Europe and less knowledgeable on European themes (even if they feel less knowledgeable). In this regard, it was important that the research design and the focus-group schedule would have allowed participants to avoid talking about Europe, that is, to be uninvolved in discussion. So, this category of participants might have participated much less than the others. This is evidently not the case. The great majority of 'neither-nor' respondents, in particular those from the most privileged social categories, possessed frameworks for perception and evaluation of European integration. So it remains to explain the logic behind their uncertain reactions.

Between ambivalence and indifference

To better understand how meaning is constructed by the participants in the 'neither-nor' group, one must study their words. Following an interpretative analysis and using again the Atlas.ti software, I was able to distinguish three distinct ideal types of reaction – ambivalence, distance and fatalism – even if most of the time these are closely related.

Ambivalence

The 'neither-nor' participants canvass, rehearse and develop many and varied views with regard to European integration in the course of their discussions. Notably, they exhibit a strong fluctuation between positive and negative in their evaluations. I characterise this way of not clearly opting for either a positive or a negative evaluation as ambivalence. First, I show that the respondents from the 'neither-nor' category are characterised, in particular, by a higher level of ambivalence than the others. Then, I consider various ways in which this ambivalence is managed by them.

Table 5.4 shows the number of contributions, positive and negative in their evaluation of Europe, by the 'neither-nor', the 'good thing' and the 'bad thing' participants. As it illustrates, for the 'neither-nor' participants, the ratio of favourable to unfavourable arguments is more or less identical to that of all participants taken together (0.74 *versus* 0.73). The group of respondents who

Table 5.4: Distribution of favourable and unfavourable evaluations in participants' contributions (N = 133)

	Number of respondents	Favourable arguments	Unfavourable arguments	Ratio
Neither-nor	33	150	202	0.74
Good thing	82	293	76	3.8
Bad thing	18	88	138	0.63
Total	133	388	529	0.73

say that their country's participation is a bad thing has a ratio of favourable to unfavourable arguments of 0.63. On the face of it, this result might be surprising. It can better be understood by interpretive analysis of the transcripts.

One of the Oxford activist groups was particularly lively because of a clash between Allison, a 'membership is a good thing' participant, and James, a 'membership is a bad thing' participant. James declared himself to be close to the Conservative Party but was interpreted by the research team as close to the UK Independence Party. Allison, a pro-European party candidate in the next scheduled European elections, spoke out very clearly in favour of European integration throughout. In Extract 5.1, in response to the question 'What does it mean to be European?' Allison very clearly articulates the advantages that she sees in the EU, whereas James questions the very existence of the EU, which he perceives to be a creation in the minds of a few politicians.

Extract 5.1: Set 1, Oxford, activists

Allison: The question was 'what does it mean' personally and to other citizens. That's why I think that we are enormously privileged; we are protected as I say by law. The whole ethos that is within the European Union protects us and looks outwards as well. So I don't see that by being members of the European Union we become Aunt Sallys (*directs this at Charles*). If you look globally who else is threatening us? It gives us a strength that we wouldn't normally have had that say African people who live in India and Asia don't have that protection enshrined in laws as we do in the European Union.

James: I don't agree with anything (*gesticulates*) such as a European [...] Europe is just a collection of nation-states and a few misguided politicians are trying to persuade the rest of us that Europe is a state and it isn't.

Allison (*to James*): No I don't think anybody is trying to persuade us that it's a state.

James: I think they are.

Allison: Any more than all counties of the UK are having their identity taken away from them because we look to Westminster to be our nation-state's government.

James (*to Allison*): I think that's a totally wrong analogy.

Allison (*gesticulates towards James*): You're allowed your opinion.

James: Counties are all part of England there is no state called Europe.

Allison: I think if you went to Fife they would say that this has nothing to do with [...] Dunfermline or part of the United Kingdom and we have a [...].

James: But there is no state called Europe.

Allison (*shaking head*): I know. I never said there was one.

James: I do not feel myself to be a European. I am English and the strange thing is and strange thing is the stronger your replies become the more English I feel the less citizen of the United Kingdom.

If the unit of analysis is the discussion sequence (which for some purposes it is), this extract must be coded as both positive and negative. On that basis, James is associated with positive as well as negative and Allison with negative as well as positive, coding. If the unit of analysis is the speaker, then we have here an open, conflictual, polarised dispute with James in the negative and Allison in the positive positions. This degree of clarity and this level of antagonism are relatively unusual in the corpus. More usual is the following kind of exchange. Vicas belongs to the 'neither-nor' category.

Extract 5.2: Set 2, Oxford, workers

Vicas: They are taking the profits out and taking it back to their country while they are in a different continent. They are profiting from Europe.

Anthony: Absolutely.

Vicas: But then we are profiting as well.

Here Vicas articulates a negative evaluation of capital outflow but follows this up with a positive evaluation of citizens' benefit from economic activity and trade. I can only code Vicas, and this sequence of discussion, as both positive in his evaluation of Europe and negative. But this has a very different significance from that which applies in the cases of Allison and James in Extract 5.1. Double coding can pick up open discussion, or it can pick up ambivalence.

Table 5.4 then reflects the fact that individuals in the category 'neither-nor' tended to propose arguments both in favour of and against the process of European integration. These participants have in mind many, and often contradictory, evaluations of the European integration process. This multiplicity of arguments, as well as their complexity, leads to ambivalence and prevents them from taking a definite position on European issues.

Past, present and future

The ambivalence can be connected to considerations of time. First, from the point of view of the individual speaker, their own previous or past evaluation may give way dialectically to the opposite. Thus, seeds of doubt are sown in the mind of the arguing individual. This process was sometimes noted by the participants themselves during the discussion:

Extract 5.3: Set 2, Oxford, managers

Rebecca: Well, that's why I thought it was a good thing initially that we joined the EC but from what I read a lot of it, it seems that lots of [...] that are meant to benefit everybody. I know I'm probably being very biased here but it seems to me from what I read that a lot of the European countries twist the laws very much to suit their own favours. I'm not sure how true it is. From what I read, we tend to follow laws strictly, to the letter, very religiously whereas the others have a much more flexible interpretation on a lot of things. [...]

Rebecca: Of course in our papers we always hear you know about the Spanish fishing kind of stealing stuff in our waters and putting up an English flag and all that sort of thing. But we always hear, you tend to hear negative things don't we? Well often we do. [...]

Rebecca: I don't know. We don't know [...] Don't we all know so little about [...]? It's frightening. I mean, we are quite intelligent. [...]

Rebecca attributes a change in her position to her exposure to the British media, which, she says, promotes an almost exclusively negative picture of the integration process. In all the comments made by this participant, there is a strong sense of uncertainty about her evaluation of European integration. This is reinforced by her feeling of a lack of knowledge, which overtly upsets her.

A specific kind of ambivalence, centred on the idea of the future, is found in the Belgian corpus. In Chapter Four, I highlighted the Belgian participants' tendency to justify the process of European integration in terms of benefits for future generation. Table 5.5 details references to this theme by distinguishing the participants in the category 'neither-nor' from participants in the two other categories. It also presents a breakdown of the results by country, in order to recall how this framework of perception is characteristic of the Belgian participants.

Of 28 occurrences of the 'future generations' argument, 17 are from the Belgian discussions. Even more interestingly, of these 28, 14 relate to individuals in the 'neither-nor' category; this is true even though Belgian respondents are less present in the 'neither-nor' category (N=4). This argument, linked to the benefits that their children will derive from European integration, introduces a certain measure of ambivalence into the evaluation of the European political system. The contrast between the present and the future amounts to a contrast between a direct negative experience of the market's effects now and a national frame that articulates an ideal for future generations. On the one hand, they themselves feel the harmful effects of the opening of borders and the single market; on the other hand, they accept these, assuming that future generations will benefit.

To illustrate this reaction tinged with ambivalence, I reproduce a short extract which features Marco, one of the Brussels workers. At the time of the discussion, he was unemployed and was indeed concerned by questions of employment and, in particular, cheap labour. He denounces the harmful effects of this throughout the discussion. However, he often seems confused about his evaluation and finds it difficult to express an opinion which is clearly against Europe.

Extract 5.4: Set 1, Brussels, workers

Marco: To a certain extent I am following his project (*referring to Said's previous discussion of the United States of Europe*), the project for the future, but it's our grandchildren who will compensate for this future prospect because it's they who will reap the rewards. In any case, we're paying to some extent for the damage from the past. Rental charges have increased and then now there's the freeze. There's talk of indexation and then now there's talk of planning wage increases. So I think that the problem with the Far East commercially and with labour, there should be compensation for this. Personally I think that it is our grandchildren who will enjoy the benefits of this.

Saïd: If there are any.

For some participants, this framework conflicts with their personal interpretation of the effect of European integration in the present. Marco expresses this clearly. The wider context of the transcript shows that Marco has learned this cognitive framework, although it does not correspond to his (Marco's) personal experience of the current European reality. In some cases, these promises of a better future for future generations are reinforced by the 'ordinary' experience of European integration; in others, as is the case here for Marco, they reduce the credibility of these same promises and sow seeds of doubt. Torn between the political discourse which surrounds him and his own experience, Marco finds it really difficult to position himself in relation to European integration. On the contrary, Saïd is clearly sceptical about the benefits that future generations will derive from this.

Ideal and actual

This position in the Belgian discussions leads us to consider the ambivalence which arises from the gap between an idealised representation, of European integration as a noble idea, and the actual experience. This kind of ambivalence is frequent in the discussions, as illustrated in Extract 5.5.

Table 5.5: Distribution of the occurrences of the argument 'benefit for future generations' (N = 133)

	'Benefit for future generations'	Number of respondents	Average
Neither-nor	14	33	0.42
Good / Bad thing	14	100	0.14
Total	28	133	0.21

Extract 5.5: Set 1, Paris, workers

Zahoua: The euro, for me, it helps businesses more.

Jean-Marie: Yes, well.

Zahoua: It doesn't help us at all. Not even with quality of life. (*Shakes her head*) On the contrary, we can do less at the financial level. Already, small savers are going to spend less. It helps large businesses more.

Later on in the discussion, as the advantages linked to mobility are set out, particularly in terms of employment, Zahoua again puts this positive aspect into a more negative perspective: 'it's not as easy as that to go and work abroad' – once again emphasising the gap between the idea and the actual reality. Jean-Marie, another participant in this Paris workers' group, emphasises a further, intrinsically linked, aspect of ambivalence. On several occasions, while discussing some particular argument, most often a positive one, he immediately clarifies his comments by adding a caveat best summarised as 'in theory':

Extract 5.6: Set 1, Paris, workers

Jean-Marie: Being part of a group of markets to have a better life. At least so that all the inhabitants of the community. […]

Moderator: Being part of a group, I'm sorry, I didn't understand.

Jean-Marie: Being part of a group of countries which improves the life of every country at the same time. In theory.

Margot: Yes (*laughs*). It's made for that in any case.

Jean-Marie: That was the aim at the beginning.

Cédric: Being interested in the European market, in everything that is economic. In other words the market.

Jean-Marie: Having better solidarity as well at the level of, in the world. To work for peace in the reunited world. At least I'm talking theoretically. (*Quick look at Margot, laughs.*)

This exchange occurs after only a few minutes discussion and is already the opportunity for complicit laughs. Cédric, the third participant in the 'neither-nor' category in this Paris group, repeatedly agreed with Jean-Marie's remarks, notably by saying that 'there is in a way an enormous gap between the reality on the ground and Europe'. This gap between the 'good ideas' of Europe that the participants value and the reality on the ground is emphasised to a large extent. Zahoua's reasoning could be summarised as follows: 'Europe certainly benefits people, but not me directly'. Jean-Marie and Cédric reason that 'Europe is a good thing in theory, but in reality, it's difficult to be aware of this'. This kind of reasoning, torn between reality and experience, is largely to be found in the discourse of the 'neither-nor' participants, in particular those from the working classes.

It is interesting to note that one also finds this type of argument with ambivalent respondents from the higher-social-class and activist groups, once they take on the discourse of 'ordinary' people. This is particularly the case with Jules, a French activist from the extreme left, who also emphasises this gap between people's daily experience of Europe and the different benefits that are promoted by European integration, whether through the completion of the single market, in terms of mobility or of benefits for companies. Emmanuelle, a UMP activist who is in favour of France's membership of the EU, and who voted 'yes' in the referendum on the Constitutional Treaty, had emphasised a few minutes before that the average French citizen doubtless did not have the opportunity to travel, and Jules was keen to come back to this point:

Extract 5.7: Set 2, Paris, activists

Jules: I think that Europe, if you want it to make progress, because most people were against liberalism, that's true, but they were also against this European technocracy. So many people, on a daily basis, people who live with Europe every day that meant nothing to them. Not because they don't have the opportunity to travel, because they see on a daily basis what Europe does not give them. Because on the news, it's Bolkenstein, it's VAT. Then every day, what does that mean? (*Critical tone*) For them, not a lot, they don't notice.

Bertrand (*to Jules, smiling*): Thank you, that's what we said at the beginning: Europe is nothing, it's an illusion, really.

Jules: No, it's not an illusion because it exists.

Emmanuelle (*to Bertrand*): No, no, there is a reality.

Jules (*to Bertrand*): The economic reality, the entrepreneurs didn't expect us and there, with the Europe that is being built today, they are even happier.

In this passage, Jules presents the criticism that is present in abundance in the French left, in particular with reference to the Constitutional Treaty. This can be roughly summarised as 'yes to Europe, but not to that kind of Europe'. Here the ambivalence is explicit and politically structured and is largely to be found in the comments made by French activists belonging to the 'neither-nor' category. They think that taking a position on European integration in terms of for or against is complicated, insofar as they are 'for' the European integration plan and 'against' its realisation.

Indifference

So far, I have argued that what might look like 'uncertainty' is in many cases better interpreted as 'ambivalence'. And, in setting out these variations within the category ambivalence, I am emphasising heterogeneity in attitudes to Europe. Further, though, the participants' comments might also be attributable to a reaction of indifference. This mainly takes two forms in the discussions: indifference by distance (of which alienation is a specific variant, associated with the British groups) and indifference by fatalism.

Distances

Distance between the EU and the citizen has several dimensions. It can be understood in physical terms: 'Brussels', to which is assimilated the power of Europe, appears to be a distant city (Berezin and Díez-Medrano 2008). But the feeling of distance that is mentioned is above all symbolic and refers more widely to distance in relation to politics. In the British case, this distance is expressed by a strong feeling of otherness or alienation in relation to the process of European integration. Table 5.6 shows the distribution of the arguments which are linked to this theme.

In the discourse of the 'neither-nor' participants, there is a greater number of explicit signs of this distance. This distance is often cited and criticised but is difficult to analyse using statistical data. At the same time, the Commission is regularly concerned about 'bringing the Union closer to its citizens' (Schrag Sternberg 2013). The distance, and the indifference to which it leads, prevents the EU from enjoying the direct legitimacy which it seeks. This criticism of European institutions inevitably raises the question of the democratic governance of the EU; I discuss this further in the general conclusion. Interpretive analysis of the discussions does in fact allow me to analyse this distance and to describe it.

Louis, a Parisian executive belonging to the 'neither-nor' category, emphasises the fact that most French people would be unable to give the name of their MEP, as he or she appears to be quite distant from them. Later, he expresses his difficulty in linking with this Europe, precisely because of its distant and complex nature. Later still, he asks where the love story between the French citizen and Europe is.

Extract 5.8: Set 2, Paris, managers

Louis: No, but in fact, deep down, between each of us and France there is a kind of love story or a story of dislike: or I don't know what. Deep down we ask where is the love story between the French citizen (*he stresses the word French*) and Europe. Frankly, currently, this Europe, we want to love it but we don't really know.

Francois (*looking at Louis*): It's difficult.

Stanislas (*to Louis*): What form does it have? (*Sceptical*) Does it have forms?

Francois: It's difficult to look at this.

Louis expresses his inability to love a Europe which has a vague outline, sometimes described as a 'very remote thingamajig' sometimes as 'ectoplasm'. Here one can see how the distance which separates the citizen from European integration, implicitly compared to the smaller distance from the nation, involves an inability to love: indifference is at the heart of Louis's lack of position. The distance produces indifference and a lack of interest in European issues, reinforced by the complex nature of the construction of Europe.

This clearly emphasises the role played by the relative distance between Europe and the citizen, especially in comparison with the national level. Above all, it is clear that this is about a symbolic distance. The exercise of power in Europe is widely perceived to be the privilege of a closed world, where decisions are taken far from the citizens. The following extract illustrates the relative and symbolic nature of this distance from Europe.

Extract 5.9: Set 1, Brussels, employees

David: But OK, if there had been a referendum in Belgium: that would have been, well, I don't know (*shrugs his shoulders*) there would have been a result, that's all (*shrugs his shoulders*) (*laughter*). Yes or no (*jokingly*).

Victor: Yes, there's a result, yes (*still jokingly*) (*makes as if to throw away some papers*).

Faissal: There you go, you want it or no, you don't want it.

Moderator: That would have changed things.

Faissal: Perhaps yes, I don't know. I don't know.

Fabien: I don't know. I prefer referenda on things that happen nearer to us.

The distance perceived by Fabien is not geographical or physical. As an inhabitant of Brussels, he is in close contact with the reality of European institutions every day. Furthermore, he has very largely assimilated European terminology and

Table 5.6: Distribution of occurrences of arguments related to distance (N = 133)

	Argument related to distance	Number of respondents	Average
Neither nor	10	33	0.30
Good / Bad thing	12	100	0.12
Total	22	133	0.17

shows that he is able to argue both in favour of and against the ongoing process. But distance is always discernible in his words. What is happening in Europe is not happening 'near him'. Thus, there is indeed always a symbolic distance between the ordinary citizen and the EU.

Doubtless, the distance felt by Fabien can be more widely understood in relation to a general sense of distance from politics, which remains the privilege of a closed world. Exclusion from politics affects a substantial proportion of citizens at the national level, functioning all the more fully at the European level as Europe becomes political. If the characteristics of the EU make it into a distant, 'unidentified' object, its politicisation does not necessarily go together with any rapprochement. European institutions can become political objects, like others – from which a significant part of the population are excluded and exclude themselves.

In the groups held in Oxford, the question of distance assumes a different character. It combines a relatively greater ignorance of the process of integration, already highlighted, with a strong feeling of alienation. As Table 5.7 illustrates, this is particularly the case in the comments made by the 'neither-nor' participants.

In general, my interpretive analysis tells me that the British 'neither-nor' respondents feel themselves to be outside Europe. It is notable that the score per person for the Oxford respondents (0.49) is very close to that per person for the 'neither-nor' group. Overall, the 'neither-nor' participants mention British distinctiveness 0.51 times per person, whereas the europhile and eurosceptic participants together mention it 0.24 times per person. The latter is much the same rate as one finds in the Belgian (0.19) and French groups (0.25) in general, who do mention that 'the English [*sic*] are not like the others.'

Foreignness implies that the British participants perceive the European system as very different from the British one, without this difference necessarily being evaluated negatively. Distance and alienation are here intrinsically linked to the question of sovereignty, the importance of which I highlighted in Chapter Four. Europe is foreign and different and, consequently, it should not take decisions for Great Britain. This feeling of distance and alienation, based on the acknowledgement of differences between them and those on the continent, is apparent in the conversation of Sanjay and Rebecca, participants in one of the Oxford managers groups, when they address the question what being European means.

Extract 5.10: Set 2, Oxford, managers

Rebecca: Of course we are farther away from it. Much easier to sort of go with the flow between France and Belgium and you're just across a border you're in and out. Whereas we still, I know it's so much easier now to get across and fly across to other […], we're still a little bit insular, isolated from […].

Sanjay: Yeah.

Rebecca: You know still tends to be geographically a bit more them and us than other countries.

William: I think so.

Sanjay: There is still a lot of resistance.

Moderator: Sorry what did you say?

Sanjay: I mean from the geographical point of view we're still an island (*murmurs of agreement*).

William: It's the island that's the important bit.

Rebecca: Yes it's like my friends in Lille they spend an afternoon in Belgium. They spend an afternoon somewhere else. They hop between borders and they buy their washing powder over the border there. They buy something else over the border there and they're just […] (*interrupting herself*) they go and pick around.

William: But when you're there, don't you find it exciting to say let's go and have lunch in Italy. We'll come back via Belgium.

Rebecca: No I'm saying they've got an advantage on us in that way in that you know they […] (*interrupting herself*) there's more flowing between them.

This suggests clearly the extent to which the abolition of political borders does not have the same impact in Britain as it does for citizens who live on the continent. The physical and symbolic barrier of the Channel is still very much in effect. The process of European integration does not remove this border, still considered to be natural. The insular nature of Britain and the UK is therefore key in understanding the sense of distance in the British groups. Further, the feeling of alienation described by Sanjay and Rebecca, in particular, is also related to distance with respect to identity. The differences between the British and continental cultures are emphasised. Indifference therefore appears to be the result in this case of this feeling of otherness, based on the perception of a marked distance between Britain and the continent. This distance, physical as well as relating to identity, leads these British participants to develop a feeling of alienation from the construction of

Table 5.7: Distribution of occurrences of arguments related to British otherness and alienation (N = 133)

	Argument related to otherness and alienation	Number of respondents	Average
Neither nor	17	33	0.51
Good / bad thing	24	100	0.24
Total	41	133	0.31

Europe; evaluating Britain's membership no longer makes much sense because Britain is perceived to be only barely a part of such construction.

This framework of perception relating to European integration, based on the feeling of distance and alienation, is significant if one wants to understand those respondents who prefer not to take a position in relation to the EU. The distance which separates the citizen from Europe increases his/her feeling of individual powerlessness. In particular, the strong feeling of alienation that is clear in the British case allows, once again, the putting into a new kind of context any appearance of uniformity between citizens' attitudes to European integration, or any common underpinning to their voicing an opinion. Once again, I assert the importance of the national variable, already highlighted in Chapter Four – in particular for this specific 'neither-nor' category of citizens.

Fatalism

The second variety of indifference is anchored in a feeling derived from fatalism. Among the comments gathered from the 'neither-nor' participants, expression of the feeling 'it's a foregone conclusion' is prominent. Europe is already a fact, there, for some, and it will be, sooner or later, for the others. No retreat seems possible. The inevitability of the process seems undeniable. To take a position concerning the integration process assumes not only that the European issues are known and that the European question is of interest in the eyes of 'ordinary' citizens but also that these citizens believe that decisions should and could be taken – in other words, that things could still change (White 2011). Many of the participants do have a propensity to try to understand European issues and to evaluate them positively or negatively. However, the 'neither-nor' participants are, in contrast, characterised by a profound feeling of fatalism. For them, evaluating European integration negatively or positively is pointless, since Europe exists, no matter what. The process of European integration and its inevitability leads them to disengage. Table 5.8 presents the distribution of arguments marked by a fatalistic logic, showing very clearly how the fatalist argument is particularly characteristic of the 'neither-nor' category (0.72 versus 0.09). These participants account for 24 out of 33 occurrences of this argument.

The underlying feeling of an inability to have an influence on European decisions has several dimensions. First, the finger is pointed at the lack of information. Some participants in the groups denounce the lack of information and develop the idea that things are being done behind their backs:

Extract 5.11: Set 1, Paris, managers.

Michel: Not enough information.

Stanislas: Too much information.

Michel (*to Stanislas*): No, not enough information. Not enough, I insist.

Stanislas: I would say both.

Michel: Because when, for example, I look at information from another country, I notice that when there is an European project, they are informed about it. We aren't. They tell us at the last minute to make us swallow it.

Francois (*Looking in front of him, as if he was thinking*): Hm hm.

Louis: Oh that's true it is.

Stanislas: Yes, it's true.

Michel: It's deliberate. It's deliberate so that we don't react.

This idea of deliberate evasion of citizens' power is also found in the British groups. Kylie emphasises this aspect, while Emily addresses the subject of British citizens' general lack of understanding regarding the process of European integration and the deliberate fostering of this by authorities.

Extract 5.12: Set 2, Oxford, employees

Emily: Yeah but it's got a different [...] It has a different meaning really doesn't it? Than the way we're expected to understand that we are European. I don't think that we do understand in this country (*Kylie agrees*), generally speaking, I don't think we've been informed sufficiently to know what's involved.

Kylie: I feel personally it's a bit deliberate. Actually I think they're deliberately not telling us quite what's going on. I think in about twenty years' time we'll probably [...] they're probably kind of half hoping that we will class ourselves as European (*Stephanie agrees*).

The end of this extract underlines the fatalistic aspect of this position: 'they' hope that in 20 years' time citizens will feel themselves to be European. This aspect is highlighted by Mary, a participant in a British workers' group, when she says, concerning the adoption of the euro, that 'it's going to happen anyway, I think'. Mary has said very little in the discussion, but when she does speak it

Table 5.8: Distribution of the occurrences of arguments related to fatalism (N = 133)

	Argument related to fatalism	Number of respondents	Average
Neither nor	24	33	0.72
Good / bad thing	9	100	0.09
Total	33	133	0.25

is to emphasise this inevitability. In Extract 5.13, it's the turn of Bridget, who participated in a workers' group, to stress that it is only a question of time.

Extract 5.13: Set 2, Oxford, workers

Bridget: But this is it perhaps because it's quite new and we're not everyone is quite adjusting quite as they should be and it's just something that's will eventually build up and adjust and it's probably just going to take a while and probably more: probably all the countries feel as we feel you know it's probably we're all feeling a bit like this and: eventually it will come right and if you think about the market it would be absolutely fabulous if we could all pull together.

Anthony: Mmm absolutely yeah.

Ruth: Yeah I think so yeah.

Esther: Much better.

We see that the possibility of feeling European one day is envisaged by the 'neither-nor' participants, since Europe will happen, no matter what. The influence of a longer or shorter time-frame is here essential (Belot and Van Ingelgom 2012). Citizens are well aware of the process and seem to consider that the elites have the necessary means to 'impose' this European reality on them. Europe is there or will be there, whether this is a good or a bad thing. In the words of the 'neither-nor' participants, we can perceive a certain kind of disaffection towards politics which largely transcends the European framework. Louis, a participant in one of the Paris managers' groups, who had already emphasised the distance he felt regarding the EU, continues by denouncing the pointlessness of the French referendum.

Extract 5.14: Set 1, Paris, managers

Louis: So much so that at the present time, you really have the impression that France said no, well, I don't know any more how many 54 per cent of French people said no, but you really have the impression that they don't give a damn about the opinion of those who said no. If we read the press, we notice that little by little many European countries would be happy to do without France's opinion, France's decision. OK, France said no, we don't care. We'll continue to go forward [...].

Louis: If I remember correctly, Denmark voted no. They made them vote again a year after: yes. Where's the respect for the popular voice?

Jean-Paul: If they are asked the same thing, yes. In France, they wouldn't have asked the same thing.

Louis: It's rigged. It's rigged. You can't vote again a year after (*pulls a face*) otherwise [...].

Jean-Paul: It's true.

Louis: (*smiling towards Jean-Paul*): In that case, they would re-run all the elections every year.

On several occasions, Louis criticises the lack of citizens' influence over the process of European integration, pursuing this line to the point where he denounces a deception. In the second extract, he meets with Jean-Paul's agreement – also a participant who has evaluated his country's membership as 'neither-nor'. The impression of impotence derived from fatalism is palpable. It is essential to emphasise this insofar as the efforts undertaken by the EU to get closer to its citizens, here through introducing a referendum, produce the opposite effect with a category of citizens who denounce the machinations of politics – seen as a tendency of the EU 'not taking no for an answer' (Rose 2013: 88–90). Louis denounces both citizens' impotence but also more widely the loss of the autonomy of political power to the power of economic interests. The supremacy of the economy is widely criticised by our 'neither-nor' participants, as Extract 5.15 shows.

Extract 5.15: Set 1, Oxford, managers

Alexander: Do you think we've been forced to be European?

Derek: Yeah I think in a sense I am a bit suspicious. For example as they talk about there being a referendum at some point in the future and I always feel as if Tony Blair the government is trying to manipulate opinion and wait for the right time to get the right decision. Whereas if we had a genuine democracy, we could have an opinion at least an opinion on a referendum now to ask about different attitudes on Europe whether it's the euro or European court and all these different actors: and have a referendum now and shape policy according to that to reflect what people actually want. Rather than trying to wait until the government feels the time is right to get the decision that they want. I mean why not ask us now and then shape policy? I think that is I mean the fact that maybe the government is more interested in what big business wants in the future in Europe rather than what people want.

Derek's feeling of being manipulated by politicians is clear in this extract. But his words are part of a more radical discourse condemning the supremacy of economics over politics. On the whole, this denunciation is the sign of a certain fatalism, insofar as the participants in the category studied here only note this reality. They do not imagine that it can be any other way, both because they do not think they have access to elected representatives and/or because political representatives are perceived to be impotent, or worse, submissive, or even corrupted, by economic power. Thus, they doubt the possibility of changing the order of things and, besides, they think that Europe does not really offer an alternative; consequently, taking a position will not change any of this.

This tacit, although very critical, acceptance is particularly discernible in the fact that many of these citizens realise that one day, in the medium- or long-term, they could become European. One finds this to a large extent in the data, whatever may be the socio-economic category of the individual. Kylie, for example, remarks that politicians doubtless hoped that in about 20 years citizens would feel European; Sanjay emphasised that the fact of being European would be in conflict with his British identity, without explicitly rejecting the fact that one day he might feel European. Europe will happen, no matter what, with them or without them.

When ambivalence meets indifference

The ambivalence and the indifference that are illustrated in this chapter should not be considered to be inherent, or necessary, underpinnings of the expressed views of those survey respondents who say that their country's membership of the EU is 'neither good nor bad'. On the other hand, they are certainly not surprising. They are however important in order to qualify the change in the permissive consensus and more broadly to apprehend the democratic deficit both at the national and the European level.

First of all, I argue that this analysis suggests that ambivalence and indifference, fatalism and the variability in distance between citizens and the EU must be considered by any analyst who wishes to understand citizenship and integration. This category of responses to the Eurobarometer question should be considered independently of the others, should not be attributed straightforwardly to lack of knowledge and cannot be assimilated to lack of support. Second, I wish to emphasise the tangle and overlapping of ambivalence and indifference that characterises the 'neither-nor' response. Ambivalence and indifference regarding integration can be combined and confounded in one respondent. Here Extract 5.16 illustrates by itself this imbrication and reveals how, for Bansuri, ambivalence meets indifference.

Extract 5.16: Set 1, Oxford, managers

Bansuri: To me, it's like an ideology. Really, I still don't think in practice, it's really there. But it's a good idea.

Sundai: But I think it is. It's the only relevance depending on where you are on the social level. Whether you're affected by the system which encompasses all the countries of Europe or it does not affect you at all. So it depends on the level where you are. At a certain level you can't have weight talking about Europe. At a certain level, you can have weight talking about Europe. It all depends where you are.

Bansuri: I agree, yeah.

Sundai: Whether it should be under Europe or under Britain.

Bansuri: Because some people have taken advantage of it, they've gone to Europe. They've taken advantage of the possibility to travel and work abroad. Yet it doesn't affect me at all. It's not even my world. It's outside the world that I sort of live in or operate in. But yes, I've heard that other people have taken advantage of it if you like and people coming here because of it.

Derek: But you said a moment ago you thought Europe was a good idea, what do you mean by that? (*Bansuri, Alexander and Ian smile.*)

Bansuri: It's an ideal isn't it? All these countries working together towards a sort of same objective and yet they're not working together you know. Their sort of group is there. The framework is there but within that group of countries everyone is pursuing their own thing.

Here, Bansuri's ambivalence is so obvious that it is highlighted by Derek, who is also uncertain about his evaluation of Britain's involvement in European integration. Bansuri's ambivalence originates in the gap she perceives between the idea of Europe, which she evaluates positively, and the reality, which at best does not affect her. This emphasises a central aspect of ambivalence – the contrast between representation and direct experience that is clearly discernible in Bansuri's words and which was also apparent with other members of the 'neither-nor' category. In the same way, the feeling of distance in relation to the European reality is also apparent. When she mentions the help for mobility and the benefits of the single market, particularly for businesses, Bansuri says almost automatically that this only affects her very slightly, that all that was irrelevant to her world (which consists of links between the Asian subcontinent and Britain). In such words, one finds signs of the distance between the EU and the lived, diurnal world. Later, in the discussion of the question of the distribution of power in Europe, Bansuri explicitly expresses this idea of distance when she says: 'maybe that's because the European bargain is too far out there. Because there are things at home that you can do.' Clearly, here, ambivalence meets indifference (or the other way round).

None of the reactions described in this chapter is incompatible with the thesis of increased visibility of European issues in the post-Maastricht era or with the essence of the post-functionalist model (Hooghe and Marks 2008). However, they invite us to reconsider the impact of the process of European integration on the reactions of ordinary citizens. Indeed, making the EU more visible is also to complicate the issue, as European integration is a flexible reality. Informing oneself involves taking cognisance of existing arguments, which are both positive and negative. The growing politicisation of European issues has led to, or strengthened, ambivalence about the process of European integration, whether that process is implicit and administrative or explicit and politically structured. My analysis indicates the need to consider the hypothesis that a greater visibility of European debates and issues, as well as a more direct experience of the EU, may itself lead to ambivalence, itself be a source of unpredictability and uncertainty. We should also consider that politicisation, defined this time as political normalisation of European integration, may transform support into indifference, rather than into informed or qualified opposition. In my reading, there are two distinct forms of indifference: distance and fatalism. Here, politicising European integration leads ordinary citizens to more generally assimilate this 'into politics'. Finally, the consequences for the democratic game are not the same, depending on whether one talks of ambivalence or of indifference. Ambivalence leads to a degree of unpredictability to which European elites find difficulty in adapting, particularly those who are anxious to bring citizens closer to their EU in a democratic framework. Indifference produces apathetic behaviour. It is clear that the tangle of reactions of ambivalence and indifference renews the classic questions of the EU's democratic deficit. At best, this tangle strengthens apathy and produces extremely low electoral participation. At worst, ambivalent citizens go to the ballot boxes and indifferent ones become politicised selectively, leading to instability and unpredictability in European political life.

Chapter Six

Conclusion: Integrating Uncertainties

[...] the Community may, in any case, be too closely identified with existing structures and established values to be accepted as the legitimate vehicle for effective social changes (Lindberg and Scheingold 1970: 257).

Beyond the conventional story

The concept of legitimacy has attracted increasing attention over the past two decades in the context of reflections on democracy, governance and the 'crisis' of legitimacy at the European level. In this context, the social legitimacy of European integration is defined as 'a broad societal (empirically determined) acceptance of the system' (Weiler 1991: 416). Yet views on the democratic deficit of the EU and its search for legitimacy have changed dramatically in recent years. As a result, understanding what people think about European integration and why they have developed such opinions is crucial. In a context of perceived political and economic crisis, the focus of Europeanists – along with journalists, experts and politicians – has been on opposition to the EU among both political actors and citizens (Leconte 2012; Serricchio, Tsakatika and Quaglia 2012; Wessels 2007). Today there is extensive recognition that euroscepticism is a more significant phenomenon in the post-Maastricht period than it was in the earlier decades of the European integration process (Vasilopoulou 2013).

In explaining this scepticism, most Europeanists tell a conventional story that goes something like this. Once upon a time, on the European continent, there was a permissive consensus (Lindberg and Scheingold 1970); a consensus that meant European integration began amidst the general indifference of ordinary citizens. The permissive consensus referred to an enchanted land where citizens of the member-states were either generally supportive of their governments' actions to promote further European integration or not interested in or affected by it at all. This sentiment was said to have characterised the first decades of European integration and to have ended in the 1990s, with the difficulties surrounding the ratification of the Maastricht Treaty. From that moment, the EU had to face a constraining dissensus (Hooghe and Marks 2008), which came to disrupt this enchanted land. This sleeping giant of dissensus was rapidly named 'euroscepticism' by scholars and journalists. The EU was increasingly subject to public contention over European matters; citizens moved away from the European project and polarisation of their attitudes towards European integration increased. In other words, a cleavage between europhiles and eurosceptics emerged (Fligstein 2008).

The European public was becoming increasingly sceptical of European integration and decisions could no longer be taken without popular consent. In the wake of these developments, the politicisation of the European political order was more and more at the heart of many academic debates (Bartolini 2005; De Wilde 2011; De Wilde and Zürn 2012; Hix and Bartolini 2006).

By the end of the 1990s, however, European studies had experienced a qualitative turn that told a very different tale, to those academics and commentators who were willing to listen. Contrary to the established understanding of the breakdown in the permissive consensus and the growing polarisation of opinion (often reduced to rising euroscepticism), qualitative studies converge in demonstrating the low salience of European integration for ordinary citizens (Duchesne 2010; Duchesne, Frazer, Haegel and Van Ingelgom 2013; Gaxie, Hubé and Rowell 2011; Meinhof 2004; White 2011, to name a few). The discrepancy observed between mainstream quantitative analyses and qualitative studies led to the approach taken in this book: analysing the indifference and indecision of ordinary citizens using both quantitative and qualitative data and methods in a mixed-methods perspective. Comprehension of the social legitimacy of European integration as a complex political reality requires the concerted efforts of different disciplines and a combination of different types of data and methods. The task of this book was thus twofold. On one hand it sought to improve understanding of the lack of salience of European issues for a growing part of the public and on the other to address the puzzle of the discrepancy between these two research traditions.

The aforementioned qualitative studies and the convergence of their results with those presented in this book prompt us to reconsider the widely accepted premises of the conventional story. I therefore suggest that the evolution of citizens' reactions to the European integration process cannot be reduced to the alleged end of the permissive consensus and subsequent rise of euroscepticism in the post-Maastricht period. Through its mixed-methods perspective, this book demonstrates that an interpretation based on the binary of permissive consensus and euroscepticism is empirically incomplete (if not erroneous) in many different ways.

In emphasising the dynamics behind the evolution of research on citizens' attitudes towards the EU, the first chapter of this volume suggests that the alleged breakdown in the permissive consensus amongst citizens needs to be put into perspective. The evolution of research on public opinion has been driven by political and institutional developments, theoretical trends in EU studies and the available survey data (Ray 2006). The role assigned to European citizens has changed over the course of integration and they are now assumed to hold opinions on European issues that are both politicised and polarised. My first step in re-evaluating the evolution of citizens' attitudes, therefore, was to distance this analysis and its results from the normative models that characterise the different periods of European integration (*see* Chapter One). In order to do this empirically, I needed to adopt a long-term analytic perspective. Therefore, in Chapter Two, I demonstrated that the levels of mean, variance and kurtosis were not significantly different in the 1990s and in the 1970s. This means that, in the 1970s, the period during which the permissive-consensus model was dominant, the situation was not significantly different from that observed in the post-Maastricht period, which supposedly signalled the end of this model in terms of citizens' attitudes. The kurtosis measures, which describe the evolution of the 'pointiness' of the distribution, are particularly important in this observation (Di Maggio, Evans and Bryson 1996; Down and Wilson 2008). In the post-Maastricht period, none of the eight countries studied in this chapter presented kurtosis levels below -1.3, a value that would suggest a certain trend towards polarisation of public opinion. On the contrary, the events of Maastricht led to a flattening of most of the national distributions and a reinforcement of the median category, which is characterised by indifference and ambivalence. Moreover, dividing the period into three (1973–81; 1982–1991; 1992–[...]) enables us to better account for the evolution that can be observed over the long term.

My demonstration is based on the importance of this median 'neither-nor' category, its stability and even its increase in size over time. It is therefore not sufficient to simply analyse support for or resistance to integration; the intensity of this (non-)support must also be taken into account. Although it is impossible to deny the impact of Maastricht on the European political system, both on an institutional and a political level, these results show that it seems to have slowed the enthusiasm for integration rather than 'broken' the permissive consensus. This echoes results obtained in similar research (Down and Wilson 2008; Eichenberg and Dalton 2007).

In order to further characterise these uncertain and indifferent reactions towards European integration, I used an exploratory quantitative analysis to focus more specifically on the middle-of-the-road attitudes of a large proportion of ordinary citizens (*see* Chapter Two). This approach uses regression analysis with the most recent Eurobarometer survey including both questions of my index (2004). This analysis demonstrates that these attitudes of indifference *and* ambivalence cannot be equated to the critical assessments of European integration that characterise Eurosceptic citizens. Indeed, citizens who are ambivalent and indifferent are more supportive of their national governments and have greater trust in the EU. At the same time, they are also more proud of being European than their eurosceptic counterparts, but they declare they know less about the EU. They also distinguish themselves from the more supportive citizens, particularly on measures of politicisation and cognitive mobilisation.

Moreover, the current situation is also tainted by this uncertainty. Chapter Two analyses the impact of the economic crisis to show that, even in this context, citizens are becoming increasingly uncertain about the integration process rather than turning their backs to the EU *en masse*. This analysis uses the neither-nor category as a proxy for indifference and ambivalence and in so doing demonstrates that the basic shift in public attitudes towards European integration is, in fact, towards indifference *and* ambivalence and not yet (or not only) towards rejection. As a result, it is no longer possible to summarise the current situation simply in terms of the thesis of the breakdown in the permissive consensus in European public opinion (in the countries where this consensus existed), nor to conclude that there is a polarisation of opinion in any of the eight countries studied in Chapter

Two (yet). Indeed, the percentage of the 'neither-nor' category rose steadily from 17 per cent in March 1991 to 31 per cent in 2011, whereas the 'bad thing' category rose from 7 per cent to 18 per cent over the same period. In Belgium, France and Great Britain – the three countries also analysed using focus groups – between 1991 and 2011 (the last Eurobarometer available), the 'neither-nor' category went respectively from 22 per cent, 22 per cent and 19 per cent to 21 per cent, 33 per cent and 37 per cent.

These results were further explored through the qualitative analysis of 24 focus groups conducted in Brussels, Paris and Oxford. The detailed qualitative exploration of the 'neither-nor' category shed new light on the indifference and indecision of ordinary people to the integration process as a logical and substantial reaction rather than as a leftover from the acceptance *versus* rejection dichotomy. Indeed, my qualitative analysis of the 'neither-nor' category began by demonstrating that the citizens who choose this category do have information and knowledge about the EU – perhaps even too much information, as some participants declared. However, they are characterised by a feeling of fatalism, distance and ambivalence towards the European integration process. The politicisation of the EU has made citizens, especially those in the lower classes, more uncertain about the consequences of European integration. While they do not oppose this process, they are increasingly unsure about its economic consequences, find it an opaque process and see themselves as powerless to stop it. Fatalistic indifference is reflected in the weakening of the belief that the European system offers an opportunity for the improvement of the conditions of its citizens. This feeling covers at least two realities: the conviction that it is impossible to have an impact on the decisions of European leaders and/or the belief that even leaders are powerless to resolve citizens' problems, particularly in a globalised world. Indifference and ambivalence are generated by several, often intersecting, processes: the increasing complexity of the European Union, due to increased access to information, and the feeling of distance or alienation related to the addition of a level of power. It is also due to a clear degree of fatalism as a consequence of the elite-driven integration process or frequent discrepancies between norms (to be European is perceived as a normative injunction in most places) and social experiences (citizens do not experience Europe in the same ways and some of them lack any conscious experience of it at all). This analysis suggests that ambivalence and indifference, fatalism and the variability in distance between citizens and the EU must all be taken into account in understanding citizenship and integration.

Building on these results, it is clearly important to bridge the gap between qualitative and quantitative research traditions, both theoretically and empirically.

Bridging the gaps

Although the discrepancy between quantitative and qualitative results has been commented on by Europeanist scholars, little effort has been made to account for it empirically and theoretically. The first step was made in our last co-authored book *Overlooking Europe* (Duchesne *et al.* 2013). Indeed, this volume and the project on which it is based, *Citizens Talking About Europe,* were built on decades of careful scrutiny of citizens' attitudes towards European integration. National and social comparisons were at the heart of the project and therefore of its results (Duchesne 2013; Duchesne *et al.* 2010; Haegel 2013). Building on the results of *Overlooking Europe,* the current book moves further towards building a bridge between quantitative and qualitative works on citizens' attitudes and reactions towards the European integration process.

Empirically, *Integrating Indifference* sought to build this bridge by adopting a mixed-methods research design. The empirical demonstration is organised in three sections. The first part builds on previous quantitative work (Down and Wilson 2008) and mobilises a complementary longitudinal analysis based on a support index that includes an indifferent and undecided category (Eurobarometer data, 1970–2004). These results thus reflect the low salience of European integration for ordinary citizens observed in qualitative European studies. Survey data was re-analysed in order to provide another reading of the evolution of citizens' reactions. The bridge was also built on careful scrutiny of attitudes in order to develop the comparative qualitative design for the focus groups. Finally, the qualitative analysis explores a specific response to survey questions in order to make sense of this middle-of-the-road category. Consequently, the results presented in this book use a mixed-methods approach to contribute to the study of the processes of acceptance and/or resistance to the current phase of European integration. They all contribute to the demonstration that Europeans have to a certain extent become more indifferent and more ambivalent that they used to be.

On the theoretical level, these analyses invite us to question the acceptance of change in the political order by investigating not only the degree of support citizens have for the European political system and the type of support they express, but also the intensity of this support. I do not question the contrast between the pre- and post-Maastricht periods in terms of the parallel growth of the competence of the EU and the publicity around European issues. But what I do seek to refute is the argument that European integration has become a salient issue for a majority of Europeans. As argued elsewhere, ordinary citizens most often simply overlook Europe (Duchesne *et al.* 2013). Knowing, experiencing and seeing European integration does not mean that the EU is important in everyday lives. The salience of an issue cannot be equated with its presence alone. Moreover, both passive and active forms of acceptance are relevant to the legitimacy of a political order.

None of the reactions described in this volume are incompatible with the thesis of increased visibility of European issues in the post-Maastricht era, nor with the essence of the post-functionalist model (Hooghe and Marks 2008). However, they invite us to reconsider the impact of the European integration process on the reactions of ordinary citizens in at least two ways.

Firstly, as European citizens have gained more information on and experiences of the positive and negative aspects of integration, they have become more ambivalent about the European project. This also leads us to question the view that political competition and politicisation of the European issue will lead to information that can change citizens' perceptions and preferences (Hix and

Bartolini 2006). Indeed, I have observed that making the EU more visible also means complicating the issue, because European integration is a flexible reality. Informing oneself involves becoming aware of existing arguments, which are both positive and negative. Increased politicisation of European issues has led to increased ambivalence about integration. It is not unusual for those who support increased politicisation from a normative perspective to believe that integration is linked to democratisation and that, if citizens were more knowledgeable and better informed, they would take a position for or against EU policy according to their future interest. My analyses indicate, however, that greater visibility of European issues and more direct experience of the EU may, in fact, lead to ambivalence and itself be a source of unpredictability and uncertainty among European citizens.

Contrary to the ambivalence recently studied by Catherine E. de Vries and Florian Stoeckel, attitudes marked by ambivalence in this book are not necessarily associated with less certainty (de Vries 2013; Stoeckel 2013). The index constructed in the Chapter Two is extremely demanding. The robustness and stability of the middle-of-the-road category demonstrates that it is not a non-attitude. Instead this attitude is rational, pragmatic and stable and can be understood as a result of the integration process if it is placed in the broader picture of social transformations and the context of globalisation. For a long time, citizens of the EU founding member-states have accumulated experience and instigated debate about the positive and negative consequences of integration in political or economic terms. However, they have also been socialised in different national contexts that have been more or less willing to promote the EU (Diez Medrano 2003). As a result, ideal images of European integration have had to find a way to coexist with more or less negative experiences of the EU, leading to ambivalence that seems all-but irrational and/or unstable. However, the recognition of this ambivalence by citizens themselves has resulted in its own dose of what James D. Wright qualified as *assent* or *pragmatic acquiescence*.

Secondly, we also need to consider that politicisation (defined this time as a political normalisation of European integration) may transform support into indifference, rather than into informed or qualified opposition. The current literature underlines increased public debate over European matters in election and referendum campaigns, as well as in party and media discourse (de Vries 2007; Hobolt 2009; Hobolt and Brouard 2011; Kriesi *et al.* 2008; van der Eijk and Franklin 2004). Without calling this fact into question, this leads me to re-examine the consequences that this increased debate on European matters may have on ordinary citizens' beliefs. In this instance, politicising European integration tends to lead ordinary citizens to equate this process with 'normal politics'. In my reading, there may be two distinct reactions to this normalisation: indifference by distance and indifference by fatalism.

Indifference by distance is based on European integration being increasingly considered 'normal politics', which leads citizens to use proxies based on national politics when reacting to European integration (Anderson 1998). These reactions are characterised by a certain remoteness from politics. Stefano Bartolini's argument is convincing when he says that politicisation (I would be tempted to add:

and the daily experience of European integration) may give rise to expectations that cannot be satisfied in reality and which, in the long term, may deepen the gap between the EU and its citizens (Hix and Bartolini 2006: 53). Moreover, this gap – like the one that exists at the national level – results in a significant number of citizens abandoning politics – abandoning a politicised EU rather than opposing it. By becoming 'normal politics', the EU may 'be too closely identified with existing structures and established values to be accepted as the legitimate vehicle for effective social changes' (Lindberg and Scheingold 1970: 257).

There is a second reaction to this normalisation of European politics: fatalism. European citizens are increasingly unsure about the economic consequences of European integration and globalisation but, more importantly, they find both of these processes opaque and see themselves as powerless to stop them. This feeling of fatalism is fed by at least two rationales: the conviction that is impossible to have an impact on the decisions of European leaders (citizens often don't even know who they are) and the belief that even these leaders are powerless to resolve citizens' problems, particularly in a globalised world. Here globalisation can be seen as a source of a- or de- politicisation of European politics, as has been demonstrated at the national level (Hay 2007: 123–52). Moreover, the first conviction is most likely fuelled by the 'not taking no for an answer' pattern that characterises the way referendums are used in the EU (Rose 2013: 88–90). Participants in the focus groups, in particular the French, were clearly not fooled by this strategy. According to some of them, the fact that the Constitutional Treaty was rejected in two founding states changed nothing. In this respect, the adoption of a recycled depoliticised treaty by the European Council early in 2007 confirmed their belief (Rose 2013: 89).

The conviction that it is impossible to influence EU political leaders is intrinsically linked to the sense that Brussels is too 'distant from the world they live in', to quote Bansuri, one of the Oxonian participants. There is thus a material and/or symbolic distance that separates respondents from EU realities, as my analysis shows. This feeling of geographic and/or social distance from Brussels (even for Belgian participants) manifests itself in the interviewees' difficulty in assigning specific responsibilities to the EU in terms of public action (Aldrin 2011; Rose 2013). Generally speaking, the negative impressions of the participants in the CITAE project are linked to the remoteness, complexity and opaqueness of a process perceived as difficult to understand. Even though they have experienced the EU and have demonstrated (even if only a little) explicit knowledge about the EU and its functioning, indifferent and ambivalent citizens almost always feel insufficiently qualified to have an opinion about it and they therefore withdraw from engagement with EU politics.

To conclude, I do not deny that on the theoretical and empirical level there has been a

general rise of politicization from the 1980s onward, when there was a remarkable increase in political authority – especially following the Single European Act – and when the political opportunity structure was more favourable – especially in the form of increased media receptiveness and a more dense occurrence of crises and treaty negotiations (De Wilde and Zürn 2012: 145).

However this general rise of macro-level politicisation did only not lead to an increase in eurosceptic opinions. It also led to an increase in the indifference and indecision of ordinary citizens. The analysis presented in this book leads us to reconsider the view that the increased visibility of European issues – in the sense of a greater presence of positive and negative arguments in public debate – leads to a polarisation of opinions (De Wilde 2011). As a result, these analyses raise questions as to the implicit causal relationship, constructed by most studies, between the evidence of political conflict on one hand (the reinforcement of so-called eurosceptic parties or the failure of the referendums, for example) and the polarisation of citizens' attitudes on the other (De Wilde 2011; De Wilde and Zürn 2012). This link is often implied from political resistance or active mobilisation, without any empirical evidence of a genuine polarisation of attitudes. There are several reasons for this biased perception of an increasing polarisation. First, it is important to remember that the politicisation observed during the various referendums and their negative outcomes often has more to do with unfavourable international conjuncture or an internally fragile political and economic situation than it does with citizens taking a stand against European integration. Second, the apparent increase in media mobilisation on European issues, along with oft-repeated discourse on the rise in euroscepticism, also probably contributes to the impression of an increase in citizens' polarisation. Moreover, one should not assimilate sporadic incidents of politicisation with the more cumulative processes that could indeed lead to a general politicisation (Duchesne and Frognier 2002). Finally, I have demonstrated that, on a methodological level, the choice of time periods and measurement instruments as constraints on the data also have a role to play in European scholars' relative blindness to this evolution.

This book emphasises how greater politicisation could also lead to greater ambivalence and indifference, in other words to greater uncertainty.[1] It is, therefore, not clear that the popular mood towards the EU reflects the level of dissensus amongst elites. The politicisation of European matters by elites, media and political parties does not necessarily lead to the polarisation of citizens' attitudes (De Wilde 2011). It may also lead to more ambivalent and indifferent attitudes, as underlined in this book. Consequently, indifferent and ambivalent attitudes must be perceived as demonstrative manifestations of a politicisation of the European integration process, in the same way as is the polarisation of elite attitudes. Indifferent and ambivalent attitudes result partly from the politicisation process. This book treats these citizens as rational beings, responding realistically to the (European) political world as they experience it. I argue for the fundamental

---

1. Uncertainty has to be understood here as an attitude. Thus I am not referring to uncertainty about what their attitudes *are*.

political competence of this group. These citizens should be considered as distinct from their europhile and eurosceptic counterparts; their attitudes should not be simply attributed to a lack of knowledge and cannot be assimilated to lack of support. A failure to take this into account would lead to the false conclusion that the European public has become more polarised over integration; that they either favour or oppose European integration (De Wilde 2011).

This book calls for a revision of the current research on citizens' attitudes towards European integration and, consequently, on social legitimacy.

Indifference, ambivalence and democracy

Understanding the nature, scope and content of indifference and indecision has far-reaching implications for the analysis of the process of European integration and the state of democracy in Europe. The ambivalence and indifference that are illustrated in this book should not be considered to be inherent or necessary foundations of the view that membership of the EU is neither good nor bad. I use this category as a microscope to analyse a phenomenon that is as evident as it is difficult to grasp empirically: indifference and ambivalence towards the EU and more broadly towards politics in general.

The results presented in this volume are most likely unsurprising for scholars outside European studies interested in (de-)politicisation or alienation (Dalton 2004; Hay 2007, to name a few). I do not want to overstate the uniqueness of what I am saying, nor exaggerate the contrast with what has long been said outside European studies. Indeed, if we go back to the work of James D. Wright (1976), we can distinguish between three ideal-types of citizens. First, the *consenters*, who intentionally adopt the rules of social and political life, consent in an active way because they are interested in political life and have some knowledge of it and even feel competent to participate, regardless of their political preferences. Second, the *dissenters*, who are conscious of the rules of social and political life but refuse them and who are, like the consenters, interested in political life. Finally, the *assenters,* whose approval is without any commitment, participation and/or interest in political activities; to some extent they can be seen as indifferent to politics. Consenters and dissenters have been widely studied, in the form of europhiles and eurosceptics, but the assenters or 'euro-indifferents' have been neglected by European studies so far. Wright's contrasting argument offers a middle ground between consent and dissent – something the author called *assent* or *pragmatic acquiescence* (Wright 1976). What I have argued here is that the attitudes of many Europeans today can be more accurately described as based on assent rather than consent or dissent.

The findings of this book have important consequences for our democracies and the European democracy in particular. Indifference, defined as the lack of interest in 'political life' (and, in this case in particular, in European integration), is not necessarily or inherently a negative attitude towards the legitimacy of a political order, as long as it shows passive acceptance of the political system. The importance of belief must not be underestimated in this, however diffuse or unconscious it may be. The excessive influence of dissidents or the presence of too many apathetic citizens, that is, assenters, may pose a threat to the serenity of pluralist democracies however.

It seems clear that indecision and ambivalence do not have the same consequences for the democratic order because, in a situation of sporadic politicisation by elites, this sentiment generally leads to unpredictability in ordinary citizens' behaviour – for example, during a referendum campaign (Franklin, Marsch and McLaren 1994). Understanding middle-ground attitudes towards European integration is therefore key to understanding the success of anti-EU parties and the dynamics of EU-related referendums. Here I strongly agree with Liesbet Hooghe and Gary Marks, when they stress that European integration has been slowed not because people have changed their minds but because elites have become increasingly divided on the issue (Hooghe and Marks 2008: 13). If the game has changed, it is, above all, because it has become more complex and less readable for ordinary citizens. Far from being illogical or unstructured, their indecision and indifference can be read as a consequence of the growing politicisation of European issues.

European democrats – myself among them – will probably be disappointed by the empirical results of this book and some may perhaps even be sceptical. However for anyone who cares about the state of our democracies and, more importantly, about citizens, it is time to stop listening to our own fairy tale and begin listening more carefully to ordinary citizens. Of course when listening to citizens, European scholars will probably feel uneasy at some of the evidence of popular beliefs. Scholars who accept that legitimacy is the phenomenon that people are willing to accept domination on normative grounds, regardless of the specific beliefs on which acceptance is based, will not be disturbed by this book. Those who focus on mobilisation and emphasise that eroding trust does not necessarily imply civic apathy will also pass by this book unconcerned and continue to ignore these passive citizens. Scholars who admit that fatalism and distance can lead to alienation at the individual level will be more concerned by the evolution demonstrated here. They will be particularly concerned if they share, as I do, the point of view that the so-called democratic deficit of the EU is only one symptom among others of an internal transformation in the history of democracy.

The consequences of this uncertain reaction to the democratic game are not the same depending on whether one talks of ambivalence or of indifference (Yoo 2010). Ambivalence leads to a degree of unpredictability to which European elites find it difficult to adapt, particularly those who are anxious to bring citizens closer to the EU in a democratic framework. Indifference produces apathetic behaviour and, potentially, blocks good reception of political information offered by political actors or the media. It is clear that the tangle of reactions of ambivalence and indifference renews the classic questions of the EU's democratic deficit. At worst, this tangle strengthens apathy and produces extremely low electoral participation. At best, ambivalent citizens go to the ballot boxes and the indifferent ones become selectively politicised, leading to instability and unpredictability in European political life.

As democrats and European citizens, scholars are most likely concerned about witnessing this growth in indifference. The more pessimistic among them will probably agree with Antonio Gramsci, writing in 1917:

Indifference is the deadweight of history. The indifference operates with great power on history. The indifference operates passively, but it operates. It is fate, which cannot be counted on. It twists programs and ruins the best-conceived plans. It is the raw material that ruins intelligence (Gramsci 2012: 52).

Those who are more optimistic will instead agree with Richard Rose, who argues, in the conclusion of his last book, that:

Indifference or hesitancy about the EU is not a sign of principled opposition to further integration, but of an inclination to make pragmatic judgment on a proposal (Rose 2013: 155).

Whatever the point of view adopted, agreeing with this last declaration means, above all, taking Europeans seriously when they make a pragmatic judgment. They have judged European democracy and the European economy harshly and they were right to do so. Not taking 'no' for an answer and pushing forward the integration process have lead citizens to believe that European integration will go on regardless of what they do or who they vote for. Moreover, despite the four national referendums that were held on the European Constitution, 73 per cent of Europeans were not asked to give their direct consent to this important EU evolution and the size of the excluded majority reached 99 per cent for the Lisbon Treaty (Rose 2013: 93). In light of these figures, it is clear that the belief that citizens don't have a say in European integration is simply based on pragmatic observation.

Commentators, politicians and European scholars breathlessly repeat that it is not possible to continue European integration without further consent from the people. However, EU leaders repackaged almost all the substantive content of the draft Constitution, shorn of the symbols of statehood, into the Lisbon Treaty (Rose 2013: 40). The second time around, governments in France and the Netherlands did not take the risk of consulting their citizens via referendums; and when Irish voters rejected the Lisbon Treaty, a second referendum was called and the Treaty came into effect in 2009. Given this record, it is difficult to argue that decisions can no longer be made without popular consent.

If we go back to the primary definition of the permissive consensus given by Valdimer Orlando Key, then 'the existence of a permissive opinion distribution may mean that if the indicated action is taken dissent will not be widespread' (1961: 32). The case of the Constitutional Treaty, followed by the Lisbon Treaty, makes it possible to cynically argue that the indicated action was taken. However it came at a price. The Community was primarily a creature of the elites (Lindberg and Scheingold 1970: 41) and for many Europeans this is still the case. Indeed, some European citizens believe that European politics is quite removed from the world they live in. Europe is a polity but they don't see themselves as part of it. Lots of European citizens strongly believe that they do not have any way of influencing the course of European integration. Others don't believe that politicians, either national or European, are able to influence it. The assenting part of the population are 'spectators to somebody else's game' as James C. Wright put it (1976). He writes:

> The chief distinguishing trait of assenters is that they go along with the system, not because they are 'deeply attached to the regime as such', but because the system is pretty much beside the point of their lives and felt concerns (Wright 1976: 268).

Most of the reactions towards European integration discussed in this volume seem to fit this description perfectly. From this point of view, studying the middle-of-the-road category of citizens has contributed to the understanding of the ways this new European political order is appropriated by its citizens. It raises questions as to a form of tacit acceptance that, in many ways, echoes the permissive-consensus model, which hasn't completely disappeared in the post-Maastricht era (although it has been transformed), as this book has demonstrated. This tacit consent of the people, the mirror of elite consensus, has been replaced by a passive acceptance, tainted with indifference and above all indecision in the face of increasing elite dissent. As we have seen throughout this book, citizens' reactions towards European integration are characterised by a fatalism regarding the declining belief that European integration offers any opportunity for defence against the deterioration of citizens' living conditions. Most citizens are indifferent towards the EU because they don't see it as the political level responsible for the problems that concern them, whether they are local, European, or global (Duchesne *et al.* 2013; White 2011). The EU lacks salience in the minds of Europeans: 'of the five most salient issues in most west European democracies – health care provision, education, law and order, pension and social security policy, and taxation – none is primarily an EU competence' (Moravcsik 2002: 15). To this extent, the EU is indeed 'outside the world' most citizens live in.

I have argued that indifference and indecision represent a significant phenomenon that has to be taken into account when analysing empirical legitimacy. This book offers an alternative diagnosis of trends in citizens' support for European integration over the last forty years and explores the meaning of middle-of-the-road, uncommitted answers to survey questions related to support for the EU and European integration. It offers an empirical contribution to the literature on public opinion towards the EU, suggesting novel sources of (de-) legitimation of a political construction widely seen as being in a kind of crisis over its 'democratic deficit'. It shows that the evolution of citizens' relations to the European integration process cannot be reduced to an alleged ending of the permissive consensus and subsequent rise in Euroscepticism.

Integrating Indifference focuses on the middle-of-the-road attitudes of ordinary citizens towards the European integration process, characterised by indifference *and* indecision. Taking an innovative approach and simultaneously complementing previous quantitative and qualitative literature, this book opens new perspectives on the analysis of citizens' reactions towards European integration. These reactions do not reflect either a positive or a negative dominant evaluation of the EU but instead refer to specific articulations of cognitive frameworks. I emphasise the tangle and overlapping of ambivalence and indifference. Ambivalence and indifference regarding integration can be combined and are generally found together in a given respondent. This overlap has been demonstrated both by mobilising quantitative survey data and qualitative analysis. The index constructed in Chapter Two enclosed a median category that was at the same time characterised by ambivalence ('EU country's membership being neither good nor bad') and indifference ('feeling indifferent if the EU was scrapped'). This category has grown over time and cannot be assimilated either to europhilia or to euroscepticism. Furthermore, the qualitative exploration of the 'neither-nor' category confirms the overlap of the logic of indifference and ambivalence. The findings of this book suggest that the critical distinction between ambivalence and indifference is not as straightforward as suggested by recent studies on ambivalence (Stoeckel 2013).[2] This link should clearly be further analysed and characterised both empirically and conceptually as these two reactions are not independent and do not have the same democratic consequences.

Further work on indifference and ambivalence should focus on performing comparative analyses to identify and explain different patterns of these uncertainties both at the national and European levels. Having said this, I am not implying here that the domestic and global levels can be readily distinguished from the European level by European citizens. On the contrary, we have argued elsewhere that citizens in Britain, France and Francophone Belgium are 'overlooking' Europe, ignoring it in favour of globalisation, economic flows and crises of political corruption (Duchesne *et al.* 2013). This book has also reaffirmed that citizens employ proxies rooted in beliefs about domestic politics when reacting to European integration process (Anderson 1998). Here the appropriate criteria used for assessing the legitimacy of the EU are anchored in national beliefs about politics. Moreover, the logic of fatalism that leads to indifference has reminded us of the need to consider the global sources of de-politicisation that are in play, when considering both domestic de-politicisation and indifferent reactions towards the EU (Hay 2007). Putting forward the argument made in the introduction, the results of this book bring out the permanent and inseparable overlap between different levels – local, regional, national, supranational and international – which it is essential to keep in mind for any study in European integration. This means that the European citizen does not exist independently of the national citizen. These uncertain

---

2.   Note that Florian Stoeckel does not define indifference and ambivalence in the same way I do in this book. He defines indifference in a very narrow way, close to the 'don't know' category, enclosing the less knowledgeable citizen. Some of the discrepancies observed between our results come from this conceptual distinction.

reactions should be analysed for themselves but also because they can be used as a microscope to examine how our democracies are evolving. Thus, uncertainties do not simply raise the question of the extension of democracy to the European level. Rather, they impact on the future of the very life of modern democracy. The indifference and indecision of ordinary citizens should therefore be further analysed and understood, given that, without any doubt, these uncertainties represent an ongoing challenge for the EU and, even more importantly, for its member-states. In this respect, this book could have been entitled *Integrating Uncertainties*.

To conclude, integrating these indifferent and uncertain citizens should be our primary concern as political analysts. As Colin Hay writes in his book, *Why We Hate Politics*:

> Political analysts surely have some responsibility towards their subject matter – particularly, one might reasonably surmise, when it comes to diagnosing and seeking solutions to clearly articulated political pathologies. The contemporary condition of disengagement and disenchantment with politics itself is as clear an instance as one could conceivably imagine of such situation. Yet it is a topic which has received less attention than this significance might lead one to expect (Hay 2007: 4).

These reactions of indifference and uncertainty to European integration are consistent with existing national democratic realities. As political scientists we therefore have a responsibility to seek to understand them on their own terms and to give them the scientific attention they deserve.

Appendices

Appendix One: Index of support for European integration

Table A1.1: Index of support towards European integration (1973–2002, EU8)

Dissolution question	Membership question			
	Good thing	Neither-nor	Bad thing	Total
Great regrets	44.3% (N=143689)	3.4% (N=10937)	0.7% (N=2275)	48.4% (N=156901)
Indifference	18.3% (N=59428)	17.4% (N=56367)	4.0% (N=12816)	39.7% (N=128611)
Relieved	0.9% (N=2983)	3.4% (N=10030)	8.0% (N=25803)	12.0% (N=38816)
Total	63.5% (N=206100)	23.8% (N=77334)	12.6% (N=40894)	100% (N=323328)

Source: Mannheim Eurobarometer Trend File (1973–2002)

Table A1.2: Index of support, percentages by year (1973–2002, EU8)

Index of support	1973	1975	1977	1981	1982	1983	1984	1985	1986	1987	1988	1989	1990	1991	1992	1993	1994	1995	1998	2001	2002
Strong opposition %	10.0	7.5	10.1	10.7	11.6	8.3	7.6	7.9	7.2	6.3	6.9	5.5	5.2	4.8	8.4	8.5	8.4	9.4	9.1	11.5	8.9
Moderate opposition %	5.8	4.3	7.3	8.3	7.7	7.6	7.1	7.2	5.9	6.6	6.1	5.9	5.9	5.8	7.9	8.2	7.4	7.7	9.5	8.9	8.4
Neutral position %	17.8	17.9	17.4	24.5	20.6	18.8	20.9	18.9	18.1	17.2	19.1	17.3	16.3	15.1	17.3	19.5	19.1	18.4	20.8	25.8	24.7
Moderate support %	20.6	19.6	19.4	22.3	18.3	22.8	23.3	23.2	22.9	23.5	23.1	23.1	21.7	22.5	20.0	21.0	20.6	20.6	20.3	21.8	20.3
Strong support %	45.8	50.7	45.8	34.2	41.8	42.4	41.1	42.7	45.9	46.4	44.8	48.3	50.9	51.8	46.4	42.8	44.4	43.9	40.4	31.9	37.8

Source: Mannheim Eurobarometer Trend File (1973–2002)

Table A1.3: Values of mean (1973–2002, EU8)

Mean	1973	1975	1977	1981	1982	1983	1984	1985	1986	1987	1988	1989	1990	1991	1992	1993	1994	1995	1998	2001	2002
Belgium	1,082	1.239	1.166	0.774	0.867	1.183	0.943	1.014	1.158	1.117	1.129	1.085	1.139	1.174	0.949	0.903	0.865	0.897	0.639	0.774	0.796
Denmark	0,129	0.19	0.007	-0.019	0.003	0.193	-0.013	0.004	0.449	0.189	0.237	0.214	0.443	0.687	0.734	0.644	0.419	0.503	0.525	0.388	0.707
France	1,128	1.168	0.959	0.736	0.936	0.919	1.034	1.169	1.216	1.271	1.186	1.149	1.097	1.075	0.838	0.758	0.859	0.719	0.716	0.54	0.5
Germany	1,351	1.19	1.18	0.864	0.974	1.162	1.135	0.981	1.166	1.022	0.946	1.035	1.174	1.219	0.869	0.839	0.901	0.915	0.697	0.693	0.873
Great Britain	-0,308	0.43	-0.074	-0.45	-0.333	-0.068	-0.039	-0.015	0.061	0.227	0.205	0.519	0.501	0.616	0.331	0.272	0.249	0.158	0.066	-0.067	0.088
Ireland	0,624	0.951	0.738	0.468	0.481	0.419	0.395	0.633	0.811	0.998	1.07	1.271	1.293	1.296	1.211	1.234	1.407	1.389	1.396	1.302	1.323
Italy	1,247	1.244	1.179	1.129	1.169	1.192	1.174	1.242	1.251	1.315	1.317	1.382	1.461	1.454	1.339	1.268	1.336	1.382	1.293	0.884	1.243
Netherlands	1,226	1.386	1.351	1.197	1.312	1.381	1.296	1.336	1.413	1.402	1.329	1.383	1.405	1.432	1.342	1.28	1.202	1.164	1.114	0.824	1.05
UE8	0,864	1.016	0.835	0.609	0.708	0.834	0.832	0.856	0.946	0.971	0.928	1.028	1.071	1.108	0.88	0.814	0.852	0.818	0.733	0.536	0.696

Source: Mannheim Eurobarometer Trend File (1973–2002)

Table A1.4: Values of variances (1973–2002, EU8)

Variance	1973	1975	1977	1981	1982	1983	1984	1985	1986	1987	1988	1989	1990	1991	1992	1993	1994	1995	1998	2001	2002
Belgium	1.059	0.951	1.105	0.929	1.118	0.845	0.984	0.830	0.778	0.902	0.932	0.896	0.919	0.873	1.177	1.187	1.145	1.166	1.372	1.253	1.033
Denmark	2.823	2.706	2.731	2.153	2.556	2.261	2.316	2.421	2.472	2.526	2.604	2.430	2.319	2.165	2.135	2.196	2.363	2.255	2.225	2.190	1.976
France	0.980	1.037	1.351	1.181	1.266	1.260	1.086	1.055	1.023	0.975	1.111	1.144	1.153	1.243	1.693	1.769	1.595	1.690	1.642	1.563	1.674
Germany	1.012	1.139	1.239	1.296	1.521	1.260	1.159	1.349	1.247	1.368	1.425	1.467	1.267	1.263	1.794	1.647	1.661	1.674	1.828	1.621	1.500
Great Britain	2.441	2.623	2.492	2.194	2.488	2.179	2.214	2.197	2.146	2.089	2.027	1.840	1.910	1.772	2.008	1.888	2.054	2.114	1.940	2.076	1.939
Ireland	1.904	1.805	2.193	1.903	2.058	1.906	2.000	1.969	1.719	1.505	1.431	1.122	1.130	1.043	1.196	1.108	1.840	0.897	0.784	0.923	0.862
Italy	0.774	0.892	1.101	0.976	0.976	0.905	0.806	0.827	0.774	0.735	0.737	0.732	0.743	0.758	1.007	1.095	0.937	0.962	0.977	1.310	0.948
Netherland	0.926	0.868	0.989	0.987	0.991	0.861	0.805	0.924	0.725	0.732	0.847	0.770	0.785	0.656	0.879	0.926	0.960	1.030	1.250	1.431	1.144
UE8	1.750	1.536	1.805	1.731	1.894	1.638	1.560	1.596	1.516	1.467	1.499	1.386	1.371	1.320	1.688	1.681	1.669	1.746	1.740	1.759	1.668

Source: Mannheim Eurobarometer Trend File (1973–2002)

Table A1.5: Values of kurtosis (1973–2002, EU8)

Kurtosis	1973	1975	1977	1981	1982	1983	1984	1985	1986	1987	1988	1989	1990	1991	1992	1993	1994	1995	1998	2001	2002
Belgium	0.509	0.434	0.865	-0.123	-0.416	0.990	-0.115	0.150	-0.325	0.334	0.301	0.511	0.811	0.631	0.033	-0.052	-0.083	0.258	-0.446	-0.277	-0.227
Denmark	-1.666	-1.577	-1.628	-1.307	-1.536	-1.370	-1.413	-1.475	-1.344	-1.509	-1.536	-1.457	-1.236	-0.891	-0.790	-0.965	-1.306	-1.193	-1.148	-1.223	-0.700
France	0.253	0.507	-0.165	-0.398	-0.328	-0.108	-0.164	0.713	0.874	1.363	0.853	0.599	0.169	0.351	-0.542	-0.655	-0.393	-0.609	-0.567	-0.689	-0.862
Germany	0.846	0.341	0.445	-0.555	-0.395	0.357	-0.251	-0.431	0.050	-0.225	-0.293	-0.052	0.391	0.757	-0.521	-0.524	-0.425	-0.401	-0.978	-0.637	-0.510
Great Britain	-1.443	-1.394	-1.522	-1.212	-1.433	-1.343	-1.388	-1.372	-1.320	-1.267	-1.205	-0.886	-0.921	-0.728	-1.141	-1.099	-1.205	-1.284	-1.179	-1.271	-1.166
Ireland	-0.797	-0.104	-0.849	-1.058	-1.102	-1.116	-1.176	-0.916	-0.465	0.017	0.504	1.372	1.851	1.872	1.070	1.279	2.721	2.874	2.420	2.171	2.403
Italy	0.646	1.173	1.008	0.575	0.709	1.347	0.498	1.113	1.173	1.189	1.174	1.817	2.132	2.403	1.741	1.409	1.480	2.199	0.996	-0.077	0.567
Netherland	1.015	1.900	2.183	1.309	1.905	2.806	1.762	2.638	2.387	2.758	1.700	2.749	2.922	3.724	2.697	2.129	1.585	1.400	0.756	-0.149	0.732
UE8	-0.292	0.231	-0.462	-0.714	-0.734	-0.352	-0.304	-0.271	0.019	0.058	-0.037	0.255	0.350	0.547	-0.356	-0.472	-0.369	-0.466	-0.675	-0.810	-0.647

Source: Mannheim Eurobarometer Trend File (1973–2002)

Appendix Two: Description of variables

Variables	Survey question used (Standard EB 64.0)	Coding
Sex		1 = male 0 = female
Age	'How old are you'	Two dummy variables for younger people (15–24 years old) and older people (55 years old and over) (reference category: all others)
Occupation	'What is your current occupation'	Four dummy variables for managers, white collars, workers and inactive (reference category: all others)
Education	'How old were you when you stopped full-time education'	Recoded into two dummy variables: 'Education: low' denotes respondents who were 16 or younger; 'Education: high' refers to respondents who were 20 or older (reference category: all others)
Political scale	'In political matters people talk about 'the left' and 'the right'. How would you place your views on this scale?'	Two dummy variables for 'left' (1–4) and 'right' (7–10) (reference category: all others)
Satisfaction with the life they lead	'On the whole, are you very satisfied, fairly satisfied, not very satisfied or not at all satisfied with the life you lead?'	1 = very/fairly satisfied 0 = all others
Financial situation	'What are you expectations for the next 12 months: will the next 12 months be better, worse or the same, when it comes to the financial situation of your household?'	Two dummy variables for 'better' and 'worse' (reference category: all others)
Trust in national government	'For each of the following institutions, please tell me if you tend to trust it or tend not to trust it? – The [nationality] government'	1 = tend to trust 0 = all others

Variables	Survey question used (Standard EB 64.0)	Coding
Trust in the EU	'For each of the following institutions, please tell me if you tend to trust it or tend not to trust it? – The European Union'	1 = tend to trust 0 = all others
Knowledge about the EU (Scale 6–10)	'Using this scale, how much do you feel you know about the European Union, its policies, its institutions?'	Scale from 1 (know nothing at all) to 10 (know a great deal) recoded as follow: 1 = 6 to 10 0 = all others
Understand how EU works	'I understand how the European Union works'	1 = tend to agree 0 = all others
Leadership opinion index		Two dummy variables for 'low' and 'high' (reference category: all others)
Proud to be national	'Would you say that you are very proud, fairly proud, not very proud, not at all proud to be (nationality)?'	1 = very/fairly proud 0 = all others
Proud to be European	'Would you say that you are very proud, fairly proud, not very proud, not at all proud to be European?'	1 = very/fairly proud 0 = all others
Loss of national identity	'What does the EU mean to you personally?'	1 = respondents choosing the item 'Loss of our cultural identity' 0 = all others

Appendix Three: Example of advertisement for participants (Oxford)

DEPARTMENT OF POLITICS AND INTERNATIONAL RELATIONS
University of Oxford

DEPARTMENT OF
POLITICS
AND
INTERNATIONAL
RELATIONS

Participants required
for a research project

Citizens Talking
Pay: £40

We are looking for volunteers to take part in a
group discussion of social issues.
Sessions will be held between now and 8 April
(exact dates and times to be confirmed).

You must be over 18, of British citizenship.
Sorry – no students.

Location: Manor Road Building (near High Street,
Queen's Lane bus stop)

No previous knowledge required.
Anonymity of participants is guaranteed.

Duration of the session: approx. 3 hours, incl. breaks and refreshments.
Payment in cash at the end of the session.

If you are interested, please contact Firstname Lastname:
By email: firstname.lastname@abcdefg.hi.jk
By phone: 0123456789 (if unavailable, please leave a message)
By text message: Text the word 'Study' followed by your phone number or
email address to 0123456789

Appendix Four: Questionnaires (Oxford)

Initial telephone questionnaire for all candidates

Good morning/afternoon

You've applied to participate in our group discussions. Are there any questions you would like to ask me about it? (*Record all questions asked*)

Before we invite you to participate, we'd like to ask you a few questions about your work and your life, and to get your opinions about some matters. Do you have ten minutes now? Is it OK with you for us to do this?

If yes, date and start time:.....................................

If not, when can I call you back? ....

In this research, we are guaranteeing participants' anonymity. People can be called by nicknames throughout the process. Would you like to choose a name to call yourself?
Chosen pseudonym:

....

We are now going to ask some questions, which will enable us to decide whether you should be invited to join one of the groups:

Are you:

Male	
Female	

What is your exact age? ....|__|__| years

Are you:

- married	
- widowed	
- divorced	
- separated	
- single	
- co-habiting	

At what age did you leave full-time education?...................|__|__| years

Are you now:

- in full-time employment (at least 35 hours a week)	
- in part-time employment (between 15 and 35 hours a week)	
- employed for less than 15 hours per week	
- working for a family member	
- unemployed	
- in full-time education or training	
- retired	
- home-maker	
- disabled	
- other	

If you are employed (or have been employed) what is your profession or job (or, what was the last profession or job you worked at)?

Thank the respondent for giving the most detailed and accurate description of their work, and for answering further questions about it:

Are you or have you been:

- self-employed, or employer of others	
- in a salaried post in a private company	
- in a salaried post in the public sector	

When you were 15 years old, what job did your father do?

Record as much detail as possible; please don't use abbreviations

When you were 15 years old, what did your mother do?

Record as much detail as possible; please don't use abbreviations

In politics, people talk about left and right. Where would you put yourself, on a scale which goes from 1 to 10, where 1 is the most to the left, and 10 the most to the right?

Left	1	2	3	4	5	6	7	8	9	10	Right

Don't know	
Won't answer	

Did you vote in the General Election of May 2005?

Yes	
No	

If yes, **how did you vote?**

Conservative	
Liberal Democrat	
Labour	
Green	
SNP/Plaid Cymru	
SDLP	
UKIP	
BNP	
Other: _____	
Don't know	
Wont' say	

If you were able to vote in a referendum regarding the Treaty establishing a Constitution for Europe, would you:

Vote	
Not vote	

If you would vote **would you vote:**

Yes	
No	
Don't know	
Won't answer	

Thank you very much. We are going to look at the responses, and we will contact you to let you know whether you have been selected. Please, can you let me have your contact details?

Last name ....

First name ....

Address ....

Telephone ....

Mobile ....

Email ....

Just before we finish, can I check your availability on some possible dates? Can you tell me whether you would be able to come, and if you can make a day, what time would suit you?

Date	NO	Yes, which time?
Thu March 23		
Fri March 24		
Sat March 25		
Tues March 28		
Wed March 29		
Thu March 30		
Fri March 31		
Mon April 3		
Tues April 4		
Thu April 6		
Fri April 7		

Thank you very much. You will be hearing from us shortly.

End time ....

Post-interview notes:

1. Total time taken for interview:

2. Estimate of competence (ease of comprehension of the questions):

    Very easy /__1__/__2__/__3__/__4__/__5__/ very difficult

3. Cooperation:

    Very cooperative /__1__/__2__/__3__/__4__/__5__/not at all cooperative

4. Sympathetic and friendly attitude:

    Very sympathetic/__1__/__2__/__3__/__4__/__5__/ hostile

5. Confidence:

   Very confident /__1__/__2__/__3__/__4__/__5__/ lack of confidence

6. Tendency to domination during the interview:

   Interviewee dominant /__1__/__2__/__3__/__4__/__5__/ interviewer dominant

7. Number of calls necessary to complete the questionnaire:

Questionnaire for selected participants (to be filled by telephone or face to face before the beginning of the session)

   Good morning/afternoon/evening.

In advance of the discussion session you have agreed to participate in, we want to ask you, and the other participants, some questions that will be helpful when we analyse the way the discussion goes. This is going to take about 15 minutes. Thank you very much for the time.

Contact no:

Research name:

Are you:

Male	
Female	

What is your exact age? |___|___| years

Are you:

- married	
- widowed	
- divorced	
- separated	
- single	
- co-habiting	

At what age did you leave full-time education? |___|___| years

Are you now:

- in full-time employment (at least 35 hours a week)	
- in part-time employment (between 15 and 35 hours a week)	
- employed for less than 15 hours per week	
- working for a family member	
- unemployed	
- in full-time education or training	
- retired	
- home maker	
- disabled	
- other	

If you are employed (or have been employed) what is your profession or job (or, what was the last profession or job you worked at)?

Thank the respondent for giving the most detailed and accurate description of their work, and for answering further questions about it:

Are you or have you been:

- self-employed, or employer of others	
- in a salaried post in a private company	
- in a salaried post in the public sector	

When you were 15 years old, what job did your father do?

Record as much detail as possible; please don't use abbreviations

When you were 15 years old, what did your mother do?

Record as much detail as possible; please don't use abbreviations

Are you are a home-owner? *If yes* **Do you have just one or more than one properties? Own home? Second home? A property that is rented?**

How many children under the age of 18 do you have? (Include children of your partner, and/or adopted or fostered children).

None	
One	
More than one	

|___|___| children

Could you tell me your religion, if you have one?

- Catholic	
- Jewish	
- Muslim	
- Orthodox	
- Protestant/Church of England	
- Other: which?	
- None	
- Don't know/not answered	

If you have a religion, **would you say you are:**

Practising	
Non-practising	

In our society, there are some groups who are more or less at the top of the society, and others who are nearer the bottom. If ten is at the top and one at the bottom, where would you say you are?

Top	1
	2
	3
	4
	5
	6
	7
	8
	9
Bottom	10

Can you tell me to which party or political organisation you feel the closest to, or anyway, the least distant from?

- Extreme left	
- Communist	
- Socialist	
- Green/Environmentalist	
- Conservative	
- Nationalist	
- Extreme right	
- Other: _____	
- None	
- No answer/don't know	

In politics, people talk about left and right. Where would you put yourself, on a scale which goes from 1 to 10, where 1 is the most to the left, and 10 the most to the right?

Left	1	2	3	4	5	6	7	8	9	10	Right

Don't know	
Won't answer	

Did you vote in the General Election of May 2005?

Yes	
No	

If *yes,* **how did you vote?**

Conservative	
Liberal Democrat	
Labour	
Green	
UKIP	
Other: _____	

When you are with friends, do you discuss political issues, frequently, sometimes, or never?

Frequently	
Sometimes	
Never	

When you have an opinion about something that you feel very strongly about, do you typically try to convince your friends, colleagues or family to adopt your opinion?

Frequently	
Sometimes	
Rarely	
Never	

How do you keep up with news and current affairs?

Newspapers and magazines:

Frequently	
Sometimes	
Rarely	
Never	

Can you tell me the titles of newspapers and magazines that you read regularly?

Television:

Frequently	
Sometimes	
Rarely	
Never	

Can you tell me what TV channels you usually watch?

Radio:

Frequently	
Sometimes	
Rarely	
Never	

Can you tell me which radio stations you usually listen to?

Internet:

Frequently	
Sometimes	
Rarely	
Never	

Can you tell me which sites you usually visit?

In general, do you think that Britain's membership of the European Union is a good thing, or a bad thing?

A good thing	
A bad thing	

Do you think of yourself mostly as:

English	
Welsh	
Scottish	
Irish/Northern Irish	
British	

In the future, do you think you will feel yourself to be English/Scottish/Welsh/British only, English/Scottish/Welsh/British and European, European and English/Scottish/Welsh/British, or European only?

British only	
… and European	
European and …	
European only	

Would you say that you are very proud, proud, not very proud, or not proud at all to be British?

Very proud	
Quite proud	
Not very proud	
Not at all proud	

Would you say that you are very proud, proud, not very proud, or not proud at all, to be European?

Very proud	
Quite proud	
Not very proud	
Not at all proud	

For each of the following issues, do you think decisions should be made by the British government, or do you think they should be made together by the members of the European Union?

	British Government	European Union	Don't Know
Defence			
Environment			
Employment and unemployment			
Agriculture, fishing and food			
Education			
Culture			
Immigration			

Which of the following two opinions do you most agree: 'the welfare state makes our society more just' or 'the welfare state reduces the desire to work'?

The welfare state makes our society more just	
The welfare state reduces the desire to work	

Do you believe that homosexual couples should be allowed to adopt children?

Should be allowed	
Should not be allowed	

In general, what do you think about people who live in Britain but who are not citizens of the European Union: are there too many of them? Or are there too few?

Too many	
Not too many	
Too few	

Thank you very much for responding to our questions.

Appendix Five: Participants (pseudonyms), by group, with principal characteristics

Pseudonym	Sex	Age	Education	Profession	Left Right	Vote	Referendum	EU Membership	Identity	Origin
PARIS										
PAR Workers Set 1										
Albert	M	42	Brevet/BEPC	Naturopath (unemployed)	5	NV	NV	G	World	White
Ghislaine	F	26	Brevet/BEPC	Care assistant	4	L. Jospin	NV	G	NE	Afro-Caribbean
Geoffrey	M	33	CAP ou BEP	Print worker	5	NV	N	NGNB	NE	White
Lionel	M	42	Brevet/BEPC	Security officer	DK	O. Besancenot	N	G	EN	White
Yasmina	F	35	Brevet/BEPC	Home-maker	DK	NV	NV	B	NE	Maghreb
Habiba	F	41	Bac general	Home-maker (and secretarial work for family business)	4	L. Jospin	No	NGNB	Other	Maghreb
PAR Workers Set 2										
Jean-Marie	M	53	Brevet/BEPC	Auto mechanic (unemployed)	DK	C. Lepage	No	NGNB	NE	White
Cédric	M	38	Bac général	Charge nurse	DK	L. Jospin	Nul	NGNB	NE	White
Jeannette	F	25	Brevet/BEPC	Care worker in training (numerous jobs)	6	NV	NV	G	Other	Africa
Zahoua	F	45	Brevet/BEPC	Medical secretary (unemployed)	1	NV	NV	NGNB	N	Maghreb
Margot	F	40	CAP ou BEP	Lorry driver	DK	C. Lepage	NA	B	N	White
Gérald	M	37	CAP ou BEP	Heating engineer	DN	NV	NV	G	N	Other European

Pseudonym	Sex	Age	Education	Profession	Left Right	Vote	Referendum	EU Membership	Identity	Origin
PAR Employees Set 1										
Laetitia	F	23	Bac +2	Sales engineer	6	J. Chirac	NV	B	N	White
Magali	F	28	Bac +2	Receptionist/telemarketing	DK	J. Chirac	NA	NGNB	NE	White
Victor	M	30	Bac +2	Higher technician, logistics	2	N. Mamère	N	G	E	White
Patrice	M	33	Bac tech/pro.	Butler	DK	NV	NV	NGNB	NE	White
Hadia	F	36	Bac +3 à +5	Project leader, advertisement (unemployed)	3	NV	NV	G	NE	Maghreb
Clelia	F	24	Bac+2	Receptionist/illustrator	5,5	NA	NV	?	?	White
PAR Employees Set 2										
Pablo	M	43	Bac tech/pro.	Secretarial work (unemployed)	7	J. Chirac	No	G	N	Other European
Samira	F	26	Bac +2	Restaurant manager	5	L. Jospin	No	B	N	Maghreb
Aline	F	41	Bac +2	Sales engineer (unemployed)	6	J. Chirac	NV	B	E	White
Martin	M	46	Bac+2	Graphic designer (unemployed)	3	L. Jospin	-Y	G	NE	White
PAR Managers Set 1										
Francis	M	30	Bac +3 à +5	IT professional	7	J. Chirac	Y	G	EN	White
Inès	F	39	Bac +2	Fashion designer	7	J. Chirac	N	G	NE	White

Pseudonym	Sex	Age	Education	Profession	Left Right	Vote	Referendum	EU Membership	Identity	Origin
Fabienne	F	26	Doctorat	Doctoral student	3	M.-G. Buffet	N	B	World	White
Gabriel	M	59	Bac +3 à +5	Printing advisor	3	L. Jospin	Y	G	NE	White
Toufik	M	24	Bac +3 à +5	Engineer	4	NV	NV	G	NE	Maghreb
Serge	M	42	Bac +3 à +5	Chartered accountant	5	L. Jospin	N	B	EN	White
Céline	F	31	Bac +3 à +5	Translator	4	NV	N	G	NE	White
PAR Managers Set 2										
François	M	42	Bac +3 à +5	Computer/logistics manager	9	J. Chirac	Y	G	NE	White
Michel	M	46	Bac +3 à +5	Management controller	6	J. Chirac	N	NGNB	EN	White
Patrick	M	38	Bac +3 à +5	Tax law specialist, civil servant	DK	J. Chirac	Y	G	EN	White
Jean-Paul	M	60	Doctorat	Math professor, university	6	NV	Y	NGNB	NE	White
Louis	M	49	Bac +3 à +5	Teacher/photographer (ex-marine officer)	3	L. Jospin	N	NGNB	E	White
Stanislas	M	50	Bac +3 à +5	Information officer (medical)	5	J. Chirac	Nul	G	NE	White
PAR Activists Set 1										
César	M	35	Bac +3 à +5	Lawyer (unemployed)	6	J. Chirac	Y	NGNB	Other	Afro-Caribbean
Karl	M	21	Bac +3 à +5	Student (engineer)	8	NV	N	G	NE	White
Cheik	M	40	Bac tech/pro	Municipal agent	6	J. Chirac	NV	G	NE	Maghreb

Pseudonym	Sex	Age	Education	Profession	Left Right	Vote	Referendum	EU Membership	Identity	Origin
Pierre-Antoine	M	23	Bac +3 à +5	Communications manager (party)	4	F. Bayrou	Y	G	NE	White
Déborah	F	30	Doctorat	Doctoral student	5	L. Jospin	Y	G	EN	White
Guy	M	59	Bac +3 à +5	Coach personal development / finance expert	2	N. Mamère	N	G	N	White
Dimitri	M	48	Bac +3 à +5	Principal private secretary (arrondissement mayor)	3	L. Jospin	Y	G	NE	White
PAR Activists Set 2										
Norbert	M	65	Bac +2	Journalist (retired)	10	J.-M. Le Pen	N	B	NE	White
Jules	M	46	Brevet/BEPC	Photographer	3	R. Hue	N	NGNB	World	White
Adrien	M	32	Bac +3 à +5	Editor/temporary teacher	2	N. Mamère	N	G	NE	White
Bertrand	M	47	Bac +3 à +5	Communications adviser	5	J.-M. Le Pen	N	B	N	White
Pascal	M	41	Bac +3 à +5	Engineer (researcher)	2	R. Hue	N	NGNB	NE	White
Emmanuelle	F	29	Bac +3 à +5	NGO manager	8	J. Chirac	O	G	NE	White
BRUSSELS										
BXL Workers Set 1										
Justine	F	38	Humanités sup gén	Accountant (unemployed)	10	NV	DK	G	NE	Africa
Rose	F	27	In training (adverstisement)	Receptionist	5	Cdh	DK	G	NE	White

Pseudonym	Sex	Age	Education	Profession	Left Right	Vote	Referendum	EU Membership	Identity	Origin
Sidi	M	27	Humanités inf	Working man	4	Ecolo	DK	G	E	Maghreb
Marco	M	43	Humanités inf	Temporary worker	6	NV	DK	NGNB	NE	White
Saïd	M	24	Humanités sup gén	Youth activity worker (unemployed)	NA	PS	Y	G	N	Maghreb
Ali	M	32	Graduat	Care worker	2	PS	N	G	NE	Maghreb
BXL Workers Set 2										
Christophe	M	24	Humanités sup pro/techn.	Working man (unemployed)	5	MR	N	G	NE	White
Farouk	M	28	Humanités sup pro/techn..	Security guard	4	PS	N	NGNB	NE	Maghreb
André	M	35	Humanités sup gén	Woodworker (black market)	5	NV	N	NGNB	World	Other European
Dona	F	56	Humanités sup pro/techn.	Caretaker	7	MR	DK	G	NE	Other European
Ming	F	24	Graduat	Waitress	3	PS	N	G	EN	Asia
BXL Employés 1										
Faissal	M	27	Licences/Master	Temp/unemployed graphic designer	5	Ecolo	Y	G	EN	Maghreb
David	M	24	Humanités supérieures prof./techn.	Sergeant	4	PS	Y	G	EN	White
Victor	M	28	Humanités sup. générales	Office worker	NA	Other	DK	G	N	White

Pseudonym	Sex	Age	Education	Profession	Left Right	Vote	Referendum	EU Membership	Identity	Origin
Fabien	M	26	Licences/Master	IT adviser	7	MR	Y	NGNB	EN	White
BXL Employees Set 2										
Michèle	F	26	Humanités sup. générales	Temp food industry	7	MR	NV	G	NE	White
Jonathan	M	29	Humanités sup. générales	Computer technician	6	DK	Y	G	E	White
Tina	F	32	Humanités sup. générales	Sales assistant (unemployed)	5	PS/MR	Y	G	World	Maghreb
Maria	F	40	Humanités sup. générales	Office worker (television)	3	NV	Y	G	NE	Other European
Pierre	M	54	Humanités sup. générales	Foreman	3	Cdh	N	B	N	NA
BXL Managers Set 1										
Alban	M	28	Licences/Master	Engineer nuclear industry	8	MR	DK	G	N	White
Roger	M	59	NA	Executive electronics	4	PS	Y	G	EN	White
JF	M	29	Licences/Master	NGO manager	3	Ecolo	Y	G	EN	White
Claire	F	51	Doctorat	General practitioner	7	Cdh	DK	G	EN	White
Franck	M	40	Humanités inférieures	Restaurant and shop manager	7	Ecolo	DK	G	NE	White
Valérie	F	45	Licences/Master	Journalist and researcher	6	Cdh	Y	G	NE	White
BXL Managers Set 2										
Aurélien	M	28	Licences/Master	Parliamentary attaché	8	MR	Y	G	NE	White
Stéphane	M	30	Licences/Master	Parliamentary attaché	7	MR	Y	G	NE	Asia

Pseudonym	Sex	Age	Education	Profession	Left Right	Vote	Referendum	EU Membership	Identity	Origin
Clément	M	33	Candidatures	General practitioner	6	Cdh	Y	G	NE	White
Maxime	M	25	Licences/Master	Teacher	2	Ecolo	N	G	World	Maghreb
Simon	M	30	Licences/Master	Relations officer (party)	2	PS	N	G	NE	White
Romain	M	20	Humanités supérieures génénales	Student	1	PS	Y	G	NE	White
BXL Activists Set 2										
Gérard	M	26	Licences/Master	Shopkeeper	5	MR	Y	G	NE	White
Brandon	M	27	Licences/Master	Musician	2	PS	N	G	EN	Other European
Ludovic	M	25	Graduat	Secretary	NA	PTB-UA	N	G	World	NA
Viviane	F	29	Doctorat	Elected representative	3	Ecolo	N	G	Other	Asia
Charles-Henri	M	26	Licences/Master	Legal adviser	5	Cdh	Y	G	NE	White
OXFORD										
OXF Workers Set 1										
Mina	F	48	A-Level, AS-Level	Private care assistant	7	Labour	DK	NGNB	World	Black Asian
Robert	M	32	GCSE or O'Level	Tankdriver (disabled)	7	NV	Y	G	NE	White
Ron	M	31	VCE, AVCE, NVQ L3	Technician (car industry)	5,5	Labour	DK	NGNB	N	Black Asian

Pseudonym	Sex	Age	Education	Profession	Left Right	Vote	Referendum	EU Membership	Identity	Origin
Mary	F	54	GCSE or OLevel	School cleaner	7	Ind.	Y	NGNB	N	White
Brenda	F	37	GCSE or OLevel	Post person and receptionist	DK	NV	N	NGNB	N	White
OXF Workers Set 2										
Vicas	M	29	VCE, AVCE, NVQ L3	Forklift driver	DK	NA	DK	NGNB	N	Black Asian
Esther	F	32	GCSE or OLevel	Kitchen assist, catering, cleaning (unemployed)	3,5	NV	DK	NGNB	N	White
Ruth	F	48	GCSE or OLevel	Care assistant, office worker (unemployed)	8	Cons.	DK	NGNB	N	White
Bridget	F	52	GCSE or OLevel	Receptionist (unemployed)	9,5	NV	DK	NGNB	N	White
Anthony	M	53	GCSE or OLevel	Working man (early retired)	5,5	LibDem	DK	G	NE	White
OXF Employees Set 1										
Nina	F	31	Foundation d°, NVQ L4	Care support worker	3	Labour	Y	G	EN	White
Pat	F	37	A-Level, AS-Level	Admin/secretarial work	4,5	Labour	DK	G	N	Black
Mel	F	51	A-Level, AS-Level	Receptionist (part time)	5,5	DK	DK	G	NE	White
Kenneth	M	51	A-Level, AS-Level	Office support worker	5,5	LibDem	Y	G	NE	White

Pseudonym	Sex	Age	Education	Profession	Left Right	Vote	Referendum	EU Membership	Identity	Origin
Mike	M	45	A-Level, AS-Level	Office manager	6	NV	N	B	NE	White
Kamal	M	24	BA, BSc, degree	Team leader in catering business	5	Ind	N	G	N	Black Asian
OXF Employees Set 2										
Stephanie	F	33	VCE, AVCE, NVQ level 3 …	IT trainer	5	Cons	N	G	N	White
Kylie	F	33	BA, BSc, degree	Office worker (unemployed)	2	Ind	DK	NGNB	N	White
Lily	F	37	BA, BSc, degree	Homemaker (former HR manager)	5	Labour	Y	G	NE	White
George	M	22	BA, BSc, degree	Temp, office worker	3	LibDem	Y	G	EN	White
Emily	F	82	VCE, AVCE, NVQ L3 …	Clerical work (retired)	1	Labour	DK	G	NE	White
Jeremy	M	67	Foundation d°, NVQ L4	Director in engineering sector (retired)	5,5	LibDem	DK	G	N	White
OXF Managers Set 1										
Sundai	M	36	BA, BSc degree	Store manager	7	Labour	Y	G	NE	Black
Alexander	M	39	A-Level, AS-Level	Bank manager	8	Cons	N	NGNB	N	White
Derek	M	37	PhD or Dphil	Lecturer and researcher	3	Cons	DK	NGNB	NE	White
Ian	M	38	BA, BSc degree	Salesman	7	Cons	N	NGNB	N	White

Pseudonym	Sex	Age	Education	Profession	Left Right	Vote	Referendum	EU Membership	Identity	Origin
Bansuri	F	42	VCE, AVCE, NVQ L3	Personal development trainer	5,5	NV	N	NGNB	N	Black Asian
OXF Managers Set 2										
Sanjay	M	24	BA, BSc, degree	Accountant	6	LibDem	DK	NGNB	N	Black Asian
Joe	M	27	BA, BSc, degree	Fundraising	3	Labour	DK	G	N	White
Alya	F	23	BA, BSc, degree	Office manager	3,5	NV	Nul	G	N	NA
William	M	67	Master degrees	IT consultant (retired)	3	Labour	Y	G	NE	White
Rebecca	F	52	BA, BSc, degree	School teacher (unemployed)	6,5	LibDem	DK	NGNB	N	White
Rachel	F	28	BA, BSc, degree	Human resources manager	5	NV	Y	G	EN	White
OXF Activists Set 1										
Bethany	F	79	Foundation d'NVQ L4	Councillor	5	Labour	Y	NGNB	NE	White
Allison	F	57	Primary school	Housewife and volunteer	4	LibDem	Y	G	NE	White
Charles	M	71	A-Level, AS-Level	District councillor (ex IT consultant and finance advisor)	6	Cons	Y	B	N	White
Annabel	F	26	BA, BSc, degree	Campaign manager	3,5	Labour	Y	NA	NA	White
James	M	61	Master degrees	Company director	8	Cons	N	B	Other	White
Lewis	M	70	PhD or Dphil	County councillor (ex health advocacy)	1	Green	N	DK	World	White

Pseudonym	Sex	Age	Education	Profession	Left Right	Vote	Referendum	EU Membership	Identity	Origin
OXF Activists Set 2										
Kevin	M	20	A-Level, AS-Level	Student	3	Labour	Y	G	NE	White
Ben	M	19	A-Level, AS-Level	Student	5,5	Cons	N	B	N	White
Tim	M	23	BA, BSc, degree	Production editor	4	LibDem	Y	G	NE	White
Nick	M	21	A-Level, AS-Level	Student	6	Cons	N	G	NE	White

Key:

Pseudonym: name chosen by participant, or allocated by researcher in later anonymisation process

Education: categories correspond to national qualifications

Profession: as declared by participant

Left/right: Politically, people speak of left and right. On a scale of 1–10, where 1 is extreme left and 10 is extreme right, where would you put yourself? DK: don't know. NA: no answer

Vote: did you vote at the last general elections? (List of candidates or parties provided) NV: no vote.

Referendum: For the French: Did you vote in the referendum of ratification of the Treaty establishing a constitution for Europe on the 29th of May 2005? Yes, no, did not vote, refuse to answer. For the others: If you had to vote in a referendum would you vote…

EU Membership: In general, do you think that (your country's) membership of the European Union is a good thing, or a bad thing? G: good thing; B: bad thing. NDNB: neither good nor bad. DK: don't know. NA: no answer

Identity: In the near future, do you think you will feel yourself to be (nationality) only, (nationality) and European, European and (nationality), or European only? N: National only; NE: national and European; EN: European and national; E: European only; World: citizens of the world (spontaneous).

Origin: for the French and Belgian, researchers' evaluation. For the British, question asked.

Bibliography.

Abélès, M. (1997) 'De l'Europe politique en particulier et de l'anthropologie en général', *Cultures et conflits* 28: 33–58.

Aldrin, P. (2010) 'L'invention de l'opinion publique européenne: Genèse intellectuelle et politique de l'Eurobaromètre', *Politix* 89(1): 79–101.

—— (2011) 'Les Eurobaromètres entre science et politique. Retour sur la fabrique officielle de l'opinion européenne', in D. Gaxie, N. Hubé, M. de Lassale and J. Rowell (eds), *L'Europe des Européens. Enquête comparative sur les perceptions de l'Europe*, Paris: Economica.

Anderson, C. J. (1998) 'When in doubt, use proxies: attitudes toward domestic politics and support for European integration', *Comparative Political Studies* 31(5): 569–601.

Anderson, C. J. and Kaltenhaler, K. (1996) 'The dynamics of public opinion toward European integration, 1973–1993', *The Journal of International Relations* 2(2): 175–199.

Anderson, C. J. and Reichert, S. (1995) 'Economic benefits and support for membership in the EU: a cross-national analysis', *Journal of Public Policy* 15(3): 231–249.

Atikcan, E. O. (2010) *Framing the European Union: Explaining the 2005 Constitutional Referenda Results* (Doctoral Thesis), McGill University, Montreal.

Balibar, E. (2001) *Nous citoyens d'Europe ? Les frontières, l'Etat, le peuple*, Paris: La Découverte.

Banks, J. A. (1979) 'Sociological theories, methods and research techniques: a personal viewpoint', *Sociological Review*, 27(3): 75-84.

Barbour, R. (2007) *Doing Focus Group*, Londres: Sage Publication.

Bartolini, S. (2005) *Restructuring Europe: Centre formation, system building and political restructuring between the nation-state and the European Union*, Oxford: Oxford University Press.

Beetham, D. (1991) *The Legitimation of Power*, Basingstoke: Palgrave Macmillan Ltd.

Beetham, D. and Lord, C. (1998) *Legitimacy and the European Union*, London/ New York: Longman.

Bellamy, R. and Castiglione, D. (2003) 'Legitimizing the Euro-"polity" and its "regime": the normative turn in EU studies', *European Journal of Political Theory* 2(1): 7–34.

Belot, C. (2000) *L'Europe en citoyenneté. Jeunes Français et Britanniques dans le processus de légitimation de l'Union européenne* (Thèse doctorale de science politique), University of Grenoble.

—— (2002) 'Les logiques sociologiques de soutien au processus d'intégration européenne : éléments d'interprétation', *Revue internationale de politique comparée* 9(1): 11–29.

— (2005) 'Les attitudes des citoyens à l'égard de l'intégration européenne', in E. Nadal, M. Marty and C. Thiriot (eds), *Faire de la politique comparée. Les terrains du comparatisme*, Paris: Editions Karthala.

— (2010) 'Le tournant identitaire des études consacrées aux attitudes à l'égard de l'Europe. Genèse, apports, limites', *Politique européenne* 30(1): 17–44.

Belot, C. and Cautrès, B. (2006) 'Variabilités du soutien des citoyens de l'Europe des Quinze à l'Union européenne', in C. Belot and B. Cautrès (eds), *La vie démocratique de l'Union européenne*, Paris: La documentation française.

— (2008) 'Opinion publique', in J. Lacroix, P. Magnette and S. Saurugger (eds), *Science politique de l'Union européenne*, Paris: Economica.

Belot, C. and Van Ingelgom, V. (2012) '*Introducing temporality as a predicting factor for citizens' attitudes towards European integration. A mixed-method perspective*', Paper presented at the Sixth Pan–European Conference on EU Politics, University of Tampere, Finland. .

Berezin, M. and Díez–Medrano, J. (2008) 'Distance matters: place, political legitimacy and popular support for European integration', *Comparative European Politics* 6(1): 1–32.

Blondel, J., Sinnott, R. and Svensson, P. (1998) *People and Parliament in the European Union: Participation, democracy and legitimacy*, Oxford: Clarendon Press.

Boussaguet, L. and Dehousse, R. (2008). A Europe of Lay People: A Critical Assessment of the First EU Citizens' Conferences, in E. Vos (ed.), *European Risk Governance: Its Science, Its Inclusiveness and Its Effectiveness* (Vol. 6), Mannheim: University of Mannheim.

Brigenar, A. P. and Jolly, S. K. (2005) 'Location, location, location: National contextual factors and public support for European integration', *European Union Politics* 6(2): 155–180.

Brouard, S., Wilkerson, J., Baumgartner, F.R., Timmermans, A., Bevan, S., Breeman, G., Breunig, C., Chaques, L., Green–Pederson, C., Jennings, W., John, P., Jones, B. D. and Lowery D. (2009) 'Comparer les productions législatives : enjeux et méthodes', *Revue internationale de politique comparée* 16(3): 381–404.

Bruter, M. (2004) 'Civic and cultural components of European identity: a pilot model of measurement of citizens' levels of European identity', in R. K. Hermann, T. Risse and M. Brewer (eds), *Transnational Identities: Becoming European in the EU*, Oxford: Rowman & Littlefield Publishers.

— (2005) *Citizens of Europe? The Emergence of a Mass European Identity*, New York: Palgrave Macmillan.

Carey, S. (2002) 'Undivided loyalties: is national identity an obstacle to European integration?', *European Union Politics* 3(4): 387–413.

Cautrès, B. and Grunberg, G. (2007) 'Position sociale, identité nationale et attitudes à l'égard de l'Europe. La construction européenne souffre–t–elle d'un biais élitiste ?', in O. Costa and P. Magnette (eds), *Une Europe des élites ? Réflexions sur la fracture démocratique de l'Union Européenne*, Bruxelles: Editions de l'Université de Bruxelles.

Cinnirella, M. (1997) 'Towards a European identity? Interactions between the national and European social identities manifested by university students in Britain and Italy', *British Journal of Social Psychology* 36(1): 19–31.

Coenen-Huther, J. (2003) 'Le type idéal comme instrument de la recherche sociologique', *Revue française de sociologie*, 44(3): 531-547.

Cohen, A. and Vauchez, A. (eds) (2007) *La Constitution européenne. Elites, mobilisations, votes*, Bruxelles: Presses de l'Université libre de Bruxelles.

— (2011) Standard Eurobarometer 76.

Conover, P. J., Searing, D. D. and Crewe, I. M. (2002) 'The Deliberative Potential of Political Discussion ', *British Journal of Political Science*, 32: 21–62.

Converse, P. (1964) 'The nature of belief systems in mass publics', in A. Apter (ed.), *Ideology and Discontent*, New York: Free Press.

Council, European (1996) *Presidency Conclusions*, Turin: European Council.

Crawford, M. (1995) *Talking Difference: On Gender and Language*, London: Sage Publications.

Crespy, A. and Verschueren, N. (2009) 'From Euroscepticism to resistance to European integration: an interdisciplinary perspective', *Perspectives on European Politics and Society* 10(3): 377–393.

Creswell, J. W. (2003) *Research Design Qualitative, Quantitative and Mixed Methods Approaches*, London: Sage.

Dakowska, D. and Hubé, N. (2011) 'Le monde européen ne se divise pas en deux catégories. Ambivalences des attitudes et diversités des arguments à l'égard de l'Europe', in D. Gaxie, N. Hubé, M. de Lassale and J. Rowell (eds), *L'Europe des Européens. Enquête comparative sur les perceptions de l'Europe*, Paris: Economica.

Dalton, R. J. (2004) *Democratic Challenges, Democratic Choices: The erosion of political support in advanced industrial democracies*, Oxford: Oxford University Press.

de Vries, C. E. (2007) 'Sleeping giant: fact or fairytale? How European integration affects vote choice in national elections', *European Union Politics* 8(3): 363–85.

— (2013) 'Ambivalent Europeans? Public support for European integration in East and West', *Government and Opposition* 48(03): 434–461.

de Vries, C. E. and Steenbergen, M. E. (2013) 'Variable opinions: the predictability of support for unification in mass European publics', *Journal of Political Marketing* 12(1): 121–141.

De Wilde, P. (2011) 'No polity for old politics? A framework for analyzing the politicization of European integration', *Journal of European Integration* 33(5): 559–575.

De Wilde, P. and Zürn, M. (2012) 'Can the politicization of European integration be reversed?', *Journal of Common Market Studies* 50(S1): 137–153.

Dehousse, R. (1995) *Institutional Reform in the European Community: Are there alternatives to majoritarian avenue?* Florence: EUI CADMUS EUI Research Repository.

— (2006) 'The Unmaking of a Constitution: Lessons from the European Referenda ', *Constellations*, 13(2): 151–164.

Delors, J., Independent, 26 Juillet 1993.

Déloye, Y. (2008) 'En guise de conclusion: ce que résister veut dire ou les paradoxes d'une construction européenne face aux contingences historiques et aux logiques politiques nationales', *Revue internationale de politique comparée* 15(4): 678–679.

Desrosières, A. and Thévenot, L. (1996) *Les catégories socioprofessionnelles*, Paris: La Découverte.

Deutsch, K. (1953) *Nationalism and Social Communication: An inquiry into the foundations of nationality*, New York: Technology Press of Massachussetts Institute of Technology and Wiley.

di Maggio, P., Evans, J. and Bryson, B. (1996) 'Have America's social attitudes become more polarized?', *American Journal of Sociology* 102(3): 690–755.

Diez Medrano, J. (2003) *Framing Europe: Attitudes to European integration in Germany, Spain and the United Kingdom*, Princeton/Oxford: Princeton University Press.

Diez Medrano, J. and Gutierrez, P. (2001) 'Nested identities: national and European identities in Spain', *Ethnic and Racial Studies*, 24(5): 753–778.

Down, I. and Wilson, C. J. (2008) 'From "permissive consensus" to "constraining dissensus": a polarizing union?', *Acta Politica* 43(1): 26–49.

Druckman, J. N. (2001) 'The implications of framing effects for citizen competence', *Political Behavior*, 23(3): 225–256.

Duchesne, S. (2006) 'Des nations à l'Europe, "l'Europe au–delà des nations" mais aussi "l'Europe contre les nations". Pour une approche dynamique et complexe de l'identification à l'Europe', *Annales d'études européennes* 8: 137–52.

— (2010) 'L'identité européenne, entre science politique et science fiction. Introduction', *Politique européenne*, 30(1): 7–16.

— (2013), 'Social gap: the double meaning of "overlooking"', in S. Duchesne, E. Frazer, F. Haegel and V. Van Ingelgom (eds), *Citizens' Reactions to European Integration Compared: Overlooking Europe*, New York: Palgrave MacMillan, pp.65–95.

Duchesne, S. and Frognier, A.-P. (1995) 'Is there a European identity?', in O. Niedermayer and R. Sinnott (eds), *Public Opinion and International Governance*, Oxford: Oxford University Press.

— (2002) 'Sur les dynamiques sociologiques et politiques de l'identification à l'Europe', *Revue française de science politique* 52(4): 355–74.

— (2008) 'National and European identifications: a dual relationship', *Comparative European Politics* 6: 143–168.

Duchesne, S. and Haegel, F. (2004a) *L'enquête et ses méthodes. L'entretien collectif*, Paris: Nathan Université.

— (2004b) 'La politisation des discussions au croisement des logiques de spécialisation et de conflictualisation: Contribution à un rapprochement des analyses en termes de "policy" et "politics"', *Revue française de science politique*, 54(6): 877–909.

— (2009) What political discussion means and how the French and the (French Speaking) Belgians deal with it, in K. Ikeda, L. Morales and M. Wolf (eds.), *The Role of Political Discussion in Modern Democracies in a Comparative Perspective,* London: Routledge, pp. 44–61.

Duchesne, S., Frazer, E., Haegel, F. and Van Ingelgom, V. (eds) (2013) *Citizens' Reactions to European Integration Compared: Overlooking Europe,* New York: Palgrave Macmillan.

Duchesne, S., Haegel, F., Frazer, E., Van Ingelgom, V., Garcia, G. and Frognier, A.-P. (2010) 'Europe between integration and globalisation: social differences and national frames in the analysis of focus groups conducted in France, francophone Belgium and the United Kingdom', *Politique européenne* 30(1): 67–106.

Easton, D. (1965) *A Systems Analysis of Political Life,* Chicago: The University of Chicago Press.

— (1975) 'A re-assessment of the concept of political support', *British Journal of Political Science* 5(4): 435–57.

Ehin, P. (2008) 'Competing models of EU legitimacy: the test of popular expectations', JCMS: *Journal of Common Market Studies* 46(3): 619–40.

Eichenberg, R. C. and Dalton, R. J. (1993) 'Europeans and the European Community: the dynamics of public support for European integration', *International Organization* 47(4): 507–34.

— (2007) 'Post-Maastricht blues: the welfare state and transformation of citizen support for European integration, 1973–2002', *Acta Politica* 42: 128–152.

Elman, C., Kapiszewski, D. and Vinuela, L. (2010) 'Qualitative Data Archiving: Rewards and Challenges', PS: *Political Science & Politics*, 42: 23–27.

European Commission (2001) *European Governance, A White Paper,* Luxembourg: European Commission.

— (2001a) European Governance, A White Paper, Luxembourg: Office for Official Publications of the European Communities.

— (2001b) How Europeans see themselves. Looking through the Mirror with Public Opinion Surveys, Brussels: European Commission Press and Communication Service.

— (2007) Standard Eurobarometer 64.

Favell, A. (2008) *Eurostars and Eurocities: Free Movement and mobility in an integrating Europe,* Oxford: Blackwell.

Favell, A. and Guiraudon, V. (2009) 'The sociology of the European Union: an agenda', *European Union Politics* 10(4): 550–576.

— (2011) *Sociology of the European Union,* New York: Palgrave Macmillan.

Ferry, J.-M. (2000) *La question de l'Etat européen,* Paris: Gallimard.

Fligstein, N. (2008) *Euroclash: The EU, European identity and the future of Europe,* Oxford: Oxford University Press.

Føllesdal, A. and Hix, S. (2006) 'Why there is a democratic deficit in the EU: a response to Majone and Moravcsik', *Journal of Common Market Studies* 44(3): 533–62.

Franck, C. and Boldrini, S. (2006) 'Union européenne : Dynamiques d'union politique, de légitimation et d'identité dans le contexte constitutionnel', *Annales d'études européennes* 8.

Franklin, M., Marsch, M. and McLaren, L. (1994) 'Uncorking the bottle: popular opposition to European unification in the wake of Maastricht', *Journal of Common Market Studies* 32(4): 455–72.

Frazer, E. and Van Ingelgom, V. (2013). Representation and Legitimation. In S. Duchesne, E. Frazer, F. Haegel and V. Van Ingelgom (eds.), *Citizens' Reactions to European Integration Compared: Overlooking Europe*, Basingstoke: Palgrave MacMillan, pp. 124–159.

Frognier, A. -P. (2000) 'Identité et participation électorale: pour une approche européenne des élections européennes', in G. Grunberg, P. Perrineau and C. Ysmal (eds), *Le vote des Quinze. Les élections européennes du 13 juin 1999*, Paris: Presses de Science Po.

Frognier, A.-P. and Van Ingelgom, V. (2007) 'La légitimité, le soutien politique et le comportement électoral', in A.-P. Frognier, L. Dewinter and P. Baudewyns (eds), *Elections : le reflux ? Comportements et attitudes lors des élections en Belgique,* Bruxelles: De Boeck.

Fuchs, D. (2011) 'Cultural diversity, European identity and legitimacy of the EU: a theoretical framework', in D. Fuchs and H.-D. Klingemann (eds), *Cultural Diversity, European Identity and the Legitimacy of the EU*, Cheltenham & Northampton: Edward Elgar.

Gabel, M. (1998) 'Public support for European integration: an empirical test of five theories', *Journal of Politics*, 60(2): 333–354.

Gabel, M. and Palmer, H. (1995) 'Understanding variation in public support for European integration', *European Journal of Political Research* 27: 3–19.

Gamson, W. (1992) *Talking Politics*, Cambridge: Cambridge University Press.

Garcia, G. and Van Ingelgom, V. (2010) 'Étudier les rapports des citoyens à l'Europe à partir d'entretiens collectifs : Une illustration des problèmes de la comparaison internationale en méthodologie qualitative', *Revue internationale de politique comparée* 17(1): 131–167.

Gaxie, D., Hubé, N., de Lassale, M. and Rowell, J. (eds) (2011) *L'Europe des Européens. Enquête comparative sur les perceptions de l'Europe*, Paris: Economica.

Gaxie, D., Hubé, N. and Rowell, J. (eds) (2011) *Perceptions of Europe: A comparative sociology of European attitudes*, Colchester: ECPR Press.

Georgakakis, D. and de Lasalle, M. (eds) (2007) *La nouvelle gouvernance européenne. Genèses et usages politiques d'un livre blanc,* Paris: PUS.

Glaser, B. G. and Strauss, A. L. (1967) *The Discovery of Grounded Theory: Strategies for qualitative research*, Chicago: Adline Publishing Company.

Göncz, B. (2013) 'A persistent east–west divide? The effect of the crisis on people's perception of the European Union', in A. Ágh and L. Vas (eds),

European Futures: The perspectives of the new member states in the new Europe, Budapest: Budapest College of Communication and Business.

Gramsci, A. (2012), *Pourquoi je hais l'indifférence*, Paris: Editions Payot et rivages, p. 52 also available online in English at http://eagainst.com/articles/antonio-gramsci-i-hate-the-indifferent/ (accessed 7 January 2014), among other websites. .

Guiraudon, V. (2006) 'The EU through European's eyes: political sociology and EU studies', *EUSA Review* 19(1): 1–7.

Haas, E. B. (1958) *The Uniting of Europe: Political, social and economic forces, 1950–1957*, Stanford, CA: Stanford California Press.

Habermas, J. (2000) *Après l'Etat–nation. Une nouvelle constellation politique*, Paris: Fayard.

Haegel, F. (2013) 'National frames: reactions to a multi-level world', in S. Duchesne, E. Frazer, F. Haegel and V. Van Ingelgom (eds), *Citizens' Reactions to European Integration Compared: Overlooking Europe*, Basingstoke: Palgrave MacMillan.

Haegel, F. and Garcia, G. (2011) 'Les enquêtés disent-ils toujours la même chose?', *Revue française de science politique*, 61(3): 483.

Hallstein, W. (1972) *Europe in the Making*, London: Allen & Unwin.

Harmsen, R. (2007) Is British Euroscepticism still unique ? National exceptionalism in comparative perspective. In J. Lacroix and R. Coman (eds.), *Les résistances à l'Europe. Cultures nationales, idéologies et stratégies d'acteurs,* Bruxelles: Ed. de l'Université de Bruxelles, pp. 69–92.

Hay, C. (2007) *Why We Hate Politics*, Cambridge: Polity.

Hix, S. and Bartolini, S. (2006) 'La politisation de l'Union européenne: remède ou poison?', in *Notre Europe. Etudes et recherches*, Policy paper n°19 available online at http://www.notre–europe.eu/media/policypaper19–fr.pdf (accessed 7 January 2014).

Hobolt, S. B. (2009) *Europe in Question: Referendums on European Integration*, Oxford: Oxford University Press.

Hobolt, S. B. and Brouard, S. (2011) 'Contesting the European Union? Why the Dutch and the French rejected the European Constitution', *Political Research Quarterly* 64(2): 309–22.

Hooghe, L. (2007) 'What drives euroscepticism? Party–public cuing, ideology and strategic opportunity', *European Union Politics* 8(1): 5–12.

Hooghe, L. and Marks, G. (2004) 'Does identity or economic rationality drive public opinion on European integration?', *Political Science and Politics* 37(3): 415–420.

— (2005) 'Calculation, community and cues: public opinion on European integration', *European Union Politics* 6(4): 419–443.

— (2008) 'A post functionalist theory of European integration: from permissive consensus to constraining dissensus', *British Journal of Political Science* 39: 1–23.

Hooghe, L., Marks, G. and Wilson, C. J. (2004) 'Does left/right structure party positions on European integration?', in G. Marks and M. Steenbergen (eds), *European Integration and Political Conflict*, Cambridge: Cambridge University Press.

Horeth, M. (1999) 'No Way out for the beast? the unsolved legitimacy problem of european governance', *Journal of European Public Policy*, 6(2): 249–268.

Hurrelmann, A. (2008) 'Constructing multilevel legitimacy in the European union: a study of British and German media discourse', *Comparative European Politics* 6: 190–211.

Hurrelmann, A. and Schneider, S. (2013) *Is North American Regionalism Less Politicized than European Integration?* Evidence from Focus Groups. Paper presented at the The Legitimacy of Regional Integration in Europe and the Americas: Empirical and Comparative Perspectives, LMU Munich.

Imig, D. and Tarrow, S. (eds) (2001) *Contentious Europeans: Protest politics in an emerging polity*, New York: Rowman & Littlefield.

Inglehart, R. F. (1967a) 'An end of European integration?', *American Political Science Review* 61: 91–105.

— (1967b) *The Socialization of Europeans*, University of Michigan.

— (1970a) 'Cognitive mobilization and European identity', *Comparative Politics* 3(1): 45–70.

— (1970b) 'The new Europeans: inward or outward–looking', *International Organization* 24(4): 129–39.

— (1971) 'Changing value priorities and European integration', *Journal of Common Market Studies* 10: 1–36.

— (1977a) 'Long term trends in mass support for European unification', *Government and Opposition* 12(2): 150–177.

— (1977b) *The Silent Revolution: Changing values and political styles among western publics*, Princeton: Princeton University Press.

Inglehart, R. F., Rabier, J. R. and Reif, K. (1987) 'The evolution of public attitudes toward European Integration', *Journal of European Integration*, 10(2–3): 135–155.

Janssen, J. (1991) 'Postmaterialism, cognitive mobilization and public support for european integration', *British Journal of Political Science* 21(4): 443–68.

Johnson, R. B., Onwuegbuzie, A. J. and Turner, L. A. (2007) 'Towards a definition of mixed methods research', *Journal of Mixed Methods Research* 1(2): 112–33.

Joseph, J. G., Emmons, C. A., Kessler, R. C., Wortman, C. B., O'Brien, K. and Alii, A. (1984) 'Coping with the threat of AIDS: an approach to psychosocial assessment ', *American Psychology*, 39: 1297–1302.

Jupp, V. (2006) 'Reflexivity', in V. Jupp (ed.), *The SAGE Dictionary of Social Research Methods*, London: SAGE Publications Ltd, pp. 258–60 and available online at http://srmo-sagepub-com.acces-distant.sciences-po. fr/view/the-sage-dictionary-of-social-research-methods/SAGE.xml (accessed 6 January 2014).

Karp, J. A., Banducci, S. A. and Bowler, S. (2003) 'To know it is to love it? Satisfaction with democracy in the European Union', *Comparative Political Studies* 36(3): 271–92.

Kelle, U. (2005) '*"Emergence vs. Forcing" of Empirical Data? A Crucial Problem of "Grounded Theory" Reconsidered*', Forum: Qualitative Social Research, 6(2).

Key, V. O. (1961) *Public Opinion and American Democracy*, New York: Alfred A. Knopf, Inc.

Kieffer, A., Oberti, M. and Preteceille, E. (2002) 'Enjeux et usages des catégories socioprofessionnelles en Europe', *Sociétés Contemporaines*, 45–46: 5–15.

Kies, R. and Nanz, P. (2013) *Is Europe Listening to Us? Successes and failures of eu citizen consultations*, Ashgate/Roehampton University.

Kitzinger, S. (2003) 'The influence of the nation–state on individual support for the European Union', *European Union Politics* 4(2): 219–41.

Kriesi, H., Grande, E., Lachat, R., Dolezal, M., Bomschier, S. and Frey, T. (2008) *West European Politics in the Age of Globalization*, Cambridge, UK and New York: Cambridge University Press.

Kuhn, T. (2011) 'Individual transnationalism, globalisation and euroscepticism: an empirical test of Deutsch's transactionalist theory', *European Journal of Political Research* 50(6): 811–37.

Lacroix, J. (2004) *L'Europe en procès*, Paris: Cerf.

— (2007) Une Europe sans corps ni tête. La pensée française après le 29 mai. In J. Lacroix and R. Coman (eds.), *Les résistances à l'Europe. Cultures nationales, idéologies et stratégies d'acteurs*, Bruxelles: Ed. de l'Université de Bruxelles, pp. 155–166.

Lacroix, J. and Magnette, P. (2008) 'Théorie politique', in C. Belot, P. Magnette and S. Saurugger (eds), *Science politique de l'Union européenne*, Paris: Economica.

Lagroye, J., François, B. and Sawicki, F. (2006) *Sociologie politique*, Paris: Presses de Sciences Po et Dalloz.

Leca, J. (2009) '"The empire strikes back": an uncanny view of the European Union. Part I – Do we need a theory of European integration?', *Government and Opposition* 44(3): 285–340.

Leconte, C. (2010) *Understanding Euroscepticism*, Basingstoke: Palgrave MacMillan.

— (2012) 'Eurosceptics in the rotating Presidency's chair: too much ado about nothing?', *Journal of European Integration* 34(2): 133–49.

Lindberg, L. and Scheingold, S. (1970) *Europe's Would–Be Polity*, Englewood Cliffs, NJ: Prentice–Hall.

Lord, C. and Magnette, P. (2004) 'E pluribus unum? Creative disagreement about legitimacy in the EU', *Journal of Common Market Studies* 42(1): 183–202.

Magnette, P. (2006) 'Politiser l'UE? Oui, mais comment?', *Notre Europe. Etudes et recherches*, available online at http://www.notre–europe.eu/media/ReactionsMAgnette–fr_01.pdf (accessed 7 January 2014).

Majone, G. (1998) 'Europe's "democratic deficit": the question of standards', *European Law Journal* 4(1): 5–28.

Manent, P. (2006) *La raison des nations. Réflexions sur la démocratie en Europe*, Paris: Gallimard.

McLaren, L. (2002) 'Opposition to European integration and fear of lost of national identity: debunking a basic assumption regarding hostility to the integration project', *European Journal of Political Research* 43(6): 895–911.

— (2007) 'Explaining mass-level euroscepticism: identity, interests and institutional distrust', *Acta Politica* 42: 233–51.

Meinhof, U. (2004) 'Europe viewed from below: Agents, victims and the threat of the other', in R. Herrmann, T. Risse–Kappen and M. Brewer (eds), *Transnational Identities: Becoming European in the EU*, Oxford: Rowman & Littlefield Publishers.

Miller, D. (1995) *On Nationality*, Oxford: Oxford University Press.

Monnet, C. (1998) 'La répartition des tâches entre les femmes et les hommes dans le travail de conversation', *Nouvelles questions féministes,* 19(1): 9–34.

Moravcsik, A. (2002) 'In defence of the "democratic deficit": reassessing legitimacy in the European Union', *Journal of Common Market Studies* 40(4): 603–24.

— (2004) 'Is there a "democratic deficit" in world politics? A framework for analysis', *Government and Opposition* 39(2): 336–63.

Morgan, D. L. (1993) *Focus groups and Surveys,* Paper presented at the Annual Meeting of American Sociological Association, Pittsburg.

— (1996) 'Focus Groups', *Annual Review of Sociology*, 22: 129–152.

— (1997) *Focus Groups as Qualitative Research*, London: Sage Publication.

Neunreither, K. (1994) 'The democratic deficit in the European Union: towards closer cooperation between the European Parliament and the national parliaments', *Government and Opposition* 29(3): 299–314.

Nicolaïdis, K. and Howse, R. (2001) *The Federal Vision*, Oxford: Oxford University Press.

Niedermayer, O. (1995) 'Trends and contrasts', in O. Niedermayer and R. Sinnott (eds), *Public Opinion and Internationalized Governance,* Oxford: Oxford University Press.

Niedermayer, O. and Sinnott, R. (1995) *Public Opinion and Internationalized Governance*, Oxford: Oxford University Press.

Noelle-Neumann, E. (1984) *The Spiral of Silence: Public opinion, our social skin,* Chicago: Chicago University Press.

Obradovic, D. (1996) 'Policy legitimacy and the European Union', *Journal of Common Market Studies* 34(2): 191–221.

Olsen, J. P. (2003) 'What is a legitimate role for Euro–citizens?', *Comparative European Politics* 1: 91–110.

Pilet, J.-B. and Van Haute, E. (2007) Les réticences à l'Europe dans un pays europhile. Le cas de la Belgique in J. Lacroix and R. Coman (eds.), *Les résistances à l'Europe. Cultures nationales, idéologies et stratégies d'acteurs*, Bruxelles: Ed. de l'Université de Bruxelles, pp. 211–227.

Prodi, R., Foreword European Commission: European Governance, A White paper, Luxembourg: Office for Official Publications of the European Communities, 2001.

Quermonne, J. -L. (2001) *L'Europe en quête de légitimité*, Paris: Presses de Sciences Po.

— (2006), 'Faut-il politiser l'Union selon l'axe gauche-droite?' *Notre Europe Etudes et recherches.*

Rabier, J. R. (1966) *L'opinion publique et l'Europe*, Bruxelles: Institut de Sociologie.

Ray, L. (2006) 'Public opinion, socialization and political communication', in K. E. Jorgensen, M. A. Pollack and B. Rosamond (eds), *Handbook of European Union Politics*, London: Sage.

Risse, T. (2003) 'The Euro between national and European identity', *Journal of European Public Policy* 10(4): 487–505.

Risse–Kappen, T. (1996) 'Exploring the nature of the beast: international relations theory and comparative analysis meet in the European Union', *Journal of Common Market Studies* 34(1): 53–80.

Rosamond, B. (2000) *Theories of European Integration*, Basingstoke: Palgrave MacMillan.

— (2008) 'Open political science, methodological nationalism and European Union studies', *Government and Opposition* 43(4): 599–612.

Rose, R. (2013) *Representing Europeans: A pragmatic approach*, Oxford: Oxford University Press.

Rothschild, J. (1977) 'Observations on political legitimacy in contemporary Europe', *Political Science Quarterly* 92: 487–501.

Rozenberg, O. (2007) La faute à Rousseau? Les conditions d'activation de quatre idéologies critiques de la construction européenne en France. In C. Ramona and L. Justine, (eds.), *Résister à l'Europe: figures des oppositions au modèle européen*, Bruxelles: Ed. de l'Université de Bruxelles, pp. 129–153.

Sauger, N., Brouard, S. and Grossman, E. (2007) *Les Français contre l'Europe? Les sens du référendum du 29 mai 2005*, Paris: Presses de Sciences Po.

Saurugger, S. (2008) 'Une sociologie de l'intégration européenne?', *Politique européenne* 2(25): 5–22.

Saurugger, S. and Mérand, F. (2010) 'Does european integration theory need sociology?', *Comparative European Politics* 8(1): 1–18.

Scharpf, F. (2000) *Gouverner l'Europe*, Paris: Presse de Sciences Po.

— (2007) 'Reflections on multilevel legitimacy', *MPIfG Working Paper*, 7(3), Köln: Max Planck Institute for the Study of Societies.

Schild, J. (2001) 'National versus European identities? French and German in the European multi–level system', *Journal of Common Market Studies* 39(2): 331–51.

Schmidt, V. A. (2008) 'Délibération publique et discours de légitimation en France et en Grande-Bretagne face à l'intégration européenne', *Revue internationale de politique comparÈe*, 15: 555–571.

Schmitter, P. (1996) 'Examining the present Euro-polity with the help of past theories', in G. Marks, F. Scharpf, P. Schmitter and W. Streeck (eds.), *Governance in the European Union:* Thousand Oaks, Calif.: Sage.

— (2008) 'On the way to a post-functionalist theory of EU integration', *British Journal of Political Science* 39: 211–15.

Schrag Sternberg, C. (2013) *The Struggle for EU Legitimacy: Public contestation, 1950–2005*, Basingstoke: Palgrave MacMillan.

Serricchio, F., Tsakatika, M. and Quaglia, L. (2012) 'Euroscepticism and the global financial crisis', *Journal of Common Market Studies* 51(1): 51–64.

Smith, A. (1995) *L'Europe politique au miroir du local: les fonds structurels et les zones rurales en France, en Espagne et au Royaume–Uni*, Paris: L'Harmattan.

— (1999) '"L'espace public européen": une vue (trop) aérienne', *Critique internationale* 1(2): 169–80.

Spiering, M. (2004) British Euroscepticism, in R. Harmsen and M. Spiering (eds.), *Euroscepticism: Party Politics, National Identity and European Integration,* Amsterdam: Rodopi B.V, pp. 127–150.

Steenbergen, M., Edwards, E. and de Vries, C. (2007) 'Who's cuing whom? Mass–elite linkages and the future of European integration', *European Union Politics* 8(1): 13–35.

Stoeckel, F. (2013) 'Ambivalent or indifferent? Reconsidering the structure of EU public opinion', *European Union Politics* 14(1): 23–45.

Taggart, P. (1998) 'A touchstone of dissent: euroscepticism in contemporary western European party systems', *European Journal of Political Research* 33(3): 363–88.

Taggart, P. and Szczerbiak, A. (2012) 'Coming in from the cold? Euroscepticism, government participation and party positions on Europe', *Journal of Common Market Studies* 51(1): 17–37.

van der Eijk, C. and Franklin, M. N. (2004) 'Potential for contestation on European matters at national elections in Europe', in G. Marks and M. Steenbergen (eds), *European Integration and Political Conflict,* Cambridge: Cambridge University Press.

Van Ingelgom, V. (2010) *Intégrer l'indifférence : une approche comparative, qualitative et quantitative, de la légitimité de l'intégration européenne* (Thèse de doctorat en Science politique), Institut d'études Politiques de Paris, Université catholique de Louvain.

— (2011) Les perceptions citoyennes de l'intégration européenne à travers l'expression de focus groups, in C. Cheneviere and G. Duchenne (eds.), *Les modes d'expression de la citoyenneté européenne*, Louvain-La-Neuve: Presses Universitaire de Louvain, pp. 108–125.

— (2012) 'Mesurer l'indifférence. Intégration européenne et attitudes des citoyens', *Sociologie* 1(3): 1–20.

Vasilopoulou, S. (2013) 'Continuity and change in the study of euroscepticism: plus ça change?', *Journal of Common Market Studies* 51(1): 153–68.

Wallace, H. (1993) 'Deepening and widening: problems of legitimacy in the EC', in S. Garcia (ed.), *European Identity on the Search for Legitimacy*, London: Pinter.

Weatherford, M. S. (1992) 'Measuring political legitimacy', *American Political Science Review* 86(1): 149–66.

Weber, M. (1968) *Economy and Society*, New York: Bedminster Press.

Weiler, J. (1991) 'Problems of legitimacy in post 1992 Europe', *Aussenwirtschaft* 46: 411–37.

— (1998) *The Constitution of Europe*, Cambridge: Cambridge University Press.

Weiler, J. H., Haltern, U. R. and Mayer, F. C. (1995) 'European democracy and its critique', *West European Politics* 18(3): 4–39.

Wessels, B. (2007) 'Discontent and European identity: three types of Euroscepticism', *Acta Politica* 42: 287–306.

White, J. (2011) *Political Allegiance After European Integration*, Basingstoke: Palgrave Macmillan.

Wight, D. (1994) 'Boys' thoughts and talks about sex in a working class locality of glasgow', *The Sociological Review*, 42: 177–199.

Wilkinson, S. (2004) 'Using focus groups'. In D. Silverman (ed.), *Qualitative Research: Theory, method and practice*, London: Sage, pp. 177–199.

Wright, J. D. (1976) *The Dissent of the Governed: Alienation and democracy in America*, New York: Academic Press.

Yoo, S.-J. (2010) Two types of neutrality: ambivalence versus indifference and political participation, *The Journal of Politics*, 72(1), 163–177.

Zaller, J. (1992) *The Nature and Origins of Mass Opinions*, Cambridge: Cambridge University Press.

Index

Afghanistan war, views of 130, 131
Amsterdam Treaty (1997) 39, 46

Belgium
  ALCESTE analysis and 120
    EU knowledge and 118, 120
  CITAE study and 88, 89, 96, 100,
    106, 108, 115, 117, 118, 122,
    124, 127, 139, 140, 148
    EU mobility and 133–4, 142,
      144–5, 149, 160
    globalisation and unity argument
      128–9, 130
    legitimacy issues and 137
    'neither-nor' participants in 152,
      153, 159–60, 178
    Constitutional Treaty and 88–9, 91,
      100, 138
    integration support analysis 56, 70,
      71, 91, 187
      attitude polarisation in 61, 64, 67
  Maastricht Treaty, ratification of 3
Bolkenstein directive 126, 127, 162

citizen conferences 83
citizens, ideal-types of 183
Citizens Talking About Europe
  (CITAE project) 1–2, 8, 12, 81, 82,
  87–106, 179
  (de-)legitimation frames in 109,
    113, 115, 121–38, 148–9
    border elimination and 132–4, 135,
      138, 139–40, 142, 143, 144–5
    CAQDAS programme, use of
      112
    governance and democracy
      135–8, 144, *147*
    national frames and 110, 138–9,
      144–8

    shared perception/evaluation and
      109–110, 132, 144, 148, 149
    single market evaluations 122–8,
      129–30, 132, 138, 139, 149
    small states and globalisation
      128–9, 130, 132, 138, 178, 181
    'Unity is Strength' argument and
      128–30, 131
  EU support findings 89–91, 144–50,
    178, 181
    EU discussion level 117–18, 120,
      121
    national comparisons 118, 139,
      142, 144–8
    participants knowledge and 117,
      116, 123
    social group differences and 118,
      121
focus groups, use in 87, 89, 92, 106,
  108–9, 117
  Eurosceptic participants in 100
  gender and ethnicity in 100–2,
    106
  interpretive analysis of 152
  polarisation, creation of 99–100,
    101, 102
  selection process and 92, 97,
    100–2, 106
multiple correspondence analysis
  94–6
participant categories and lists 152
  'neither-nor' numbers 152, *153*
politicisation process and 108
study design 87–9, 97–9, 102–5,
  148–9, 152, 179
  coding protocol and 111, 112–15,
    148, 150
  comparative qualitative method-
    ology, use of 106

discussion scenario *104*
grounded-theory approach and
  113
as politicisation test 98–9, 102–3
recruitment constraints 97–8, 152
see also focus group methodology
citizenship, European 10, 17, 171, 178
citizen role, changes in 43
politicisation of 43
collective interviews 81, 83, 84, 93
  CITAE project and 98, 99, 103, 108,
  114, 150
  EU themes distribution *119*
  methodological problems of 93
  research use of 85, 86, 87, 98, 106
Common Agricultural Policy (CAP)
  131
Constitutional Treaty (2005) (2005) 2,
  4, 12, 18, 37, 39, 46, 76, 81, 185
  CITAE project and 100, *101*, 115,
  138, 169–70, 181
  constraining dissensus, model of 13,
  15, 18, 19, 38–40, 44, 46, 47, 48,
  58, 91, 175
euroscepticism and 175

democratic deficit (EU) 1, 18, 26, 36,
  37, 43, 45, 137, 171, 175, 184, 186
  ambivalence/indifference, effect on
  173, 184–5
  CITAE project and 137–8, 144, *147*
  evaluation criteria and 29
  see also legitimacy (EU)
'democratic malaise' (EU) 4
Denmark
  euroscepticism in 60
  integration support analysis 54, 56,
  60, 70, 71, 89
    attitude polarisation in 60, 61,
    64, 67
  MaastrichTreaty ratification and
  17, 25
depoliticisation 121, 187
Erasmus programme 132, 143
EU enlargement 127–8, 131–2

CITAE project results and *147*, 148
governance, critique of 131–2
euro and single currency 127, 128,
133, 140–2, 147–8
Eurobarometer surveys 2, 6–7, 8,
10, 12, 23, 31, 151–2
  integration studies, use in 6–7, 13,
  31, 34, 36, 43, 88, *90*, 106, 151,
  151–2, 171
  europhile/eurosceptic interpretations of 151
  index of support use in 48, 50,
  71–2, *74*, 76, 78
  'neither-nor' percentages in
  151–2
limits of 88, 151
see also Mannheim Eurobarometer
  Trend File

European integration, attitude studies
  7, 11, 13–14, *19*, 40, 43, 45, 68–9,
  88, 105, 109–10, 151, 178–9, 182–8
  alienation and 152, 163, 178, 183,
  184
  ambivalence and 3, 12, 13, 15, 47,
  68, 151, 152, 156, 171, 173, 177,
  178, 179, 180, 181, 182, 184,
  187
  EU trust and 177
  globalisation context and 180
  indifference, distinction with 187
  issue politicisation and 173, 180
  representation/direct experience
  and 172
  see also integration, 'neither-nor'
  analysis
constraining dissensus *see* constraining dissensus, model of
indifference and 3, 13, 14, 15, 25,
  47, 68, 69–73, 105, 106, 150,
  151, 152, 156, 171, 173, 177,
  180, 181, 182, 183–8
  apathy and 184
  by distance 163–4, 171, 172,
  173, 178, 180, 181

elites and 184
Eurobarometer data and 151–2, 171
fatalism and 14–15, 152, 163, 167–71, 173, 178, 181, 184, 186, 187
use of notion and 3, 12, 15, 78, 183
see also integration, 'neither-nor' analysis
national governments, trust in and 72, 73, 177
national identity and 34–5, 82, 88, 110, 138–9, 187
permissive consensus *see* permissive consensus, theory of
polarisation of opinions and *see* polarisation
politicisation and *see* politicisation
referendums, effect on 39, 40, 41, 181, 184, 185
societal legitimacy, study of and 5–6, 183
acceptance beliefs and 6, 11, 14
national framing and 14, 138
sociological approach and 9–11, 23–4, 81
cognitive-mobilisation theory 23–4
socialisation, role in 11, 23
see also focus group methodology
theories/models of 20–3
elitism and 20–3
explicit/diffuse support and 24
functionalist perspective 22, 24
intergovernmental approach 20–1
mixed-methods perspective 7, 8, 13, 81, 106, 176, 179
quantitative/qualitative studies and 7–8, 14, 86, 88, 105–6, 109, 110, 151, 152, 176, 178–9, 187
triangulation strategy and 13, 106
see also Citizens Talking About

Europe (CITAE); europhilia; euroscepticism; integration index of support study
European Parliament 4, 26
legitimacy of 137
voting and 4, 23
absentionism and 4
europhilia 153, 154, 165, 183, 187
use of concept 151, 175
euroscepticism 1, 2, 13, 14, 18, 37–8, 39, 40–1, 47, 57, 58, 68, 69, 71–2, 107, 153, 154, 165, 175, 176, 182, 183, 186
definition/concept of 37–8, 40–1, 71, 151
indifference/undecided category and 71–2, 76, 151, 177, 183, 187
study of 7, 8, 37, 45, 176
occupation and 71
as politicisation process 46, typologies and 41
eurozone crisis (EU) 4, 12, 76
legitimacy beliefs, effect on 14, 149
discourses and (CITAE project) 110, 132, 149

focus group methodology 81, 82–6, 112, 151
CITAE study selection process 92–4, 98–9, 105–6
remuneration strategy 92–3
salience of opinions and 98–9
typification of social categories and 94
see also Citizens Talking About Europe (CITAE) project
focus group definition 83
politicisation and 98
research advantages of 83–6
common sense observation and 84
marginalised groups and 84–5
qualitative/quantitative combination and 86
survey data use and 86

see also collective interviews
frame/framing notion of 108
  research use of 108, 148
France
  CITAE study and 88, 89, 96, 100,
    106, 108, 115, 118, 120, 124,
    126–7, 139, 148
  borders/mobility and 132–3, 142,
    143, 161
  distance, feelings of 163–5, 168
  enlargement, speed of and 148
  EU governance and 136
  European unity and 131–2
  fatalistic arguments and 170
  inflation/economic issues and
    140–2, 143, 149
  information, lack of argument
    168
  legitimacy issues and 137
  national identity and 133
  'neither-nor' participants in 152,
    153, 161–2, 163–4, 168, 178
  Constitutional Treaty referendum
    37, 39, 72, 88, 91, 100, 120, 138,
    162, 163, 169–70, 185
  integration support analysis 54, 56,
    60, 70–1, 91, 187
  attitude polarisation in 60, 61,
    64, 67
  MaastrichTreaty ratification and
    17, 25

Germany
  CITAE project 115
  integration support analysis 52, 56,
    70, 71, 89
  attitude polarisation in 61, 64, 67
globalisation and the EU 128–9, 181
  European power and 128–9, 132,
    136
  integration attitudes and 138, 180,
    181, 187
Greece, eurozone crisis and 132

identity, European 1, 32–3, 128, 131,
    132, 133, 140
  ambivalence/indifference and 177
  border elimination and 132–3
  national identity and 33, 36, 73, *74*,
    133, *147*
    fear of loss of 145, 147–8
  unity and power arguments 131–2
  see also Citizens Talking About
    Europe (CITAE) project
immigration (EU), attitudes to 124–5,
    133, 139–40
  mobility/borders and 132–3, 141–2,
    143, 144–5
integration index of support study
    47–78, 82, 89, 177, 179, 180, 187,
    189
  constraining dissensus thesis and 91
  data and variables in 48
  evolution of support *51, 53*
    OLS regression analysis 52, 54,
      61
  indifferent/undecided attitudes and
    69–78, 89, *91*, 177
    euroscepticism analysis of 71–3,
      75, 78, 177
    national government trust and 72,
      73, 75
    'neither-nor' category, use of
      76–7, 78, 91
    occupation analysis *70*, 71, *74*
    variables and analysis 72–5
  permissive consensus and 51–7
    breakdown of 47–8, 54, 55, 56,
      57, 61, 67, 78
  polarisation hypothesis and 57–64,
    78
    variance and kurtosis measures,
      use of 59–61, 64–8, 78, 176–7
  politicisation, role of 75, 91
integration, 'neither-nor' attitude
    analysis 152–73, 177–8, 187
  cognitive frameworks and 153, 187
  discussion level (EU) and 154, *155,*
    156

knowledge of EU and 154–5,
156, 167, 178
lack of information argument and
168, 178
economic power and 170–1, 178
Eurobarometer data and 151–2, 171,
178, 181
future generations benefit argument
160–1
ideal/actual reality of integration
and 160–3, 172, 180
national/social differences and
154–5, 167
participants and *153*
socio-economic categories of
171, 178
reaction ideal types 153, 156
ambivalence and 153, 156–7,
171, 172, 178
distance/alienation and 153, 156,
163–5, 167, 171, 178
fatalism and 153, 156, 163,
167–71, 178
see also under Belgium; France;
United Kingdom
Iraq war, views of 130, 131
Ireland
integration support analysis 54, 56,
71, 89
attitude polarisation in 64, 67
Lisbon Treaty and 37, 185
Italy
integration support analysis 56, 70, 89
attitude polarisation in 61, 64, 67

legal positivism 21
legitimacy 4–5, 27
concept/definition of 4, 5, 9, 21–2,
42, 175
Beetham and 6
democracy and 27, 175
Easton and 6, 30–1, 41
Weber and 5–6, 9, 21, 42
Weiler and 21
formal democratic and 21

internal/external dimensions of 5
social beliefs and 5, 6
study of 4–5
legitimacy, political (EU) 3, 4, 11, 17,
25–6, 42–4, 107, 175, 187
CITAE project and 135–8
citizens' opinion studies 30–4
diffuse/specific support (Easton)
and 31, 34
inputs-based/outputs-based
support 32
citizens' role in 43, 44
direct and indirect legitimacy 26–7
discourses of (de-)legitimation and
108, 110
notion of frame and 108
distance/indifference, feelings of
and 163, 186
input legitimacy and 135
national legitimacy and 11
permissive consensus and 17, 24,
25, 37
research and 12, 17, 27–30, 42–4, 179
citizen support (Easton) and
30–1, 34, 41
models of legitimation and 12,
20, 21–2, 42, 43
normative and empirical approaches to 12, 27–8, 29, 32,
34, 42
theoretical evaluation criteria and
27–9
liberal democracy 27
Lisbon Treaty 2, 37, 76, 185

Maastricht Treaty (1992) 3–4, 15,
17–18, 25, 38, 39, 43, 46, 48, 54,
56, 76
integration attitudes, effect on 68,
78, 175, 177
ratification process and 17–18, 29,
30, 37, 52, 55, 61, 64
Mannheim Eurobarometer Trend File
48, *51, 53, 55, 57, 60, 62–3, 66, 69,
70, 78, 91, 189–92*

media, EU coverage 10, 26, 76, 107,
    184
    EU legitimation and 108
    euroscepticism and 159, 182
    mobilisation on EU issues and 107,
        182, 184
Metaplan 102

Netherlands, the
    Constitutional Treaty referendum
        37, 39, 72, 185
    integration support analysis 55, 56,
        60, 70, 71
        attitude polarisation in 60, 61, 64
Nice, Treaty of (2001) 39, 46

opinion surveys 6, 31, 85
    research difficulties and 92, 98, 110

permissive consensus, theory of 3,
    13, 15, 17, 18, 19, 20–3, 24, 25, 33
    n.21, 37, 44, 46, 47, 52, 56, 57, 68,
    171, 175, 176, 185, 186
    'shadow citizen', notion of 20, 25,
        43, 45
    Maastrict Treaty ratification and
        175, 177
    passive acceptance and 186
    see also integration index of support
        study
polarisation 46, 57, 68–9, 98, 106, 107,
    175, 176, 182–3
    europhile/eurosceptic cleavage and
        175, 183
    measurement of 47, 177
    visibility of EU issues and 182
    see also under integration index of
        support study
politicisation 4, 7, 15, 18, 38, 41–2,
    45–6, 57, 68, 107, 173, 176, 178,
    179, 180–1, 182
    ambivalence and 180, 182
    definitions/concepts and 107 n.1,
        173
    globalisation, effect on 181

information and discourse 107–8,
    179–80
media and 182
polarisation, effect on 182–3
post-functionalism 38–9, 46, 172

Single European Act (SEA) 52, 181–2
Spain, CITAE project and 115

transnationalism 132

unemployment (EU) and 121, 125
United Kingdom
    CITAE study and 88, 96, 100, 106,
        108, 118, 120, 123, 124, 125,
        142, 148
    alienation from Europe and 148,
        163, 165–7
    fatalist arguments and 168–9,
        170–1
    governance and legitimacy issues
        135, 136–7, 144, 170–1
    identity/sovereignty and 145–8,
        149, 165, 166–7, 168, 171
    immigration, evaluation and
        124–5, 139, 142
    information, lack of argument
        168
    'neither-nor' participants in
        152, 153, 157–9, 165, 166–7,
        168–9, 171–2, 178
    single market and globalisation
        129–30, 139, 149, 172
    Constitutional Treaty and 89, 100
    euroscepticism in 60, 88
    integration support analysis 52, 54,
        55, 56, 70–1, 91, 187
        attitude polarisation in 61, 64, 67

www.ingramcontent.com/pod-product-compliance
Lightning Source LLC
Chambersburg PA
CBHW072102020426
42334CB00017B/1602